# THE BOYS IN THE BUNKHOUSE

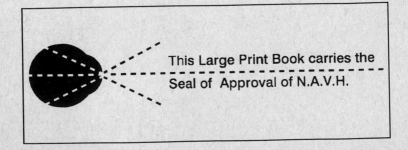

This Large Print Book carries the
Seal of Approval of N.A.V.H.

# THE BOYS IN THE BUNKHOUSE

## SERVITUDE AND SALVATION IN THE HEARTLAND

# DAN BARRY

**THORNDIKE PRESS**
*A part of Gale, Cengage Learning*

GALE
CENGAGE Learning·

Farmington Hills, Mich • San Francisco • New York • Waterville, Maine
Meriden, Conn • Mason, Ohio • Chicago

## GALE
### CENGAGE Learning®

### LIBRARY OF CONGRESS CATALOGING-IN-PUBLICATION DATA

Names: Barry, Dan, 1958– author.
Title: The boys in the bunkhouse : servitude and salvation in the heartland / Dan Barry.
Description: Waterville, Maine : Thorndike Press Large Print, [2016] | Series: Thorndike press large print popular and narrative nonfiction Originally published: New York, NY : Harper, an imprint of HarperCollins Publishers, [2016] | Includes bibliographical references.
Identifiers: LCCN 2016020186 | ISBN 9781410493095 (hardback) | ISBN 1410493091 (hardcover)
Subjects: LCSH: People with mental disabilities—Abuse of—Iowa—Atalissa. | People with mental disabilities—Employment—Iowa—Atalissa. | Atalissa (Iowa)—History. | Iowa—History. | Large print type books. | BISAC: HISTORY / Social History.
Classification: LCC HV3006.I63 B37 2016 | DDC 331.5/950977768—dc23
LC record available at https://lccn.loc.gov/2016020186

Published in 2016 by arrangement with Harper, an imprint of HarperCollins Publishers

Printed in Mexico
1 2 3 4 5 6 7 20 19 18 17 16

# TO THESE MEN

For, while the tale of how we suffer, and how we are delighted, and how we may triumph is never new, it always must be heard. There isn't any other tale to tell, it's the only light we've got in all this darkness.

— JAMES BALDWIN

# PREFACE

*Willie Levi*

First thing, get them birds out the coop.

When the truck sighs to a stop in the turkey plant's feather-flecked dock, it's time to unload. You open a crate and grab a forty-pound turkey that wasn't too happy about being caged in the first place but sure as hell doesn't want to leave it now. He knows. He ain't stupid. He can tattoo you black and blue just by beating his wings, or pop you right in the balls, so grab him by the legs, tuck him under an arm, and flip him. Then hang that bird — hang 'im! — upside down on one of them shackles moving toward the plant's mouth. Watch him get swallowed up.

Willie Levi did this hundreds, thousands of times a day, for years, for decades, turning the shit-flutter task into an artistic performance of movement and sound, like some Astaire of slaughter. He was the turkey whisperer. He talked to the birds, and they talked back, as if sharing an interspecies understanding about the fetters of fate.

"I go," he says, and makes the face of just having swallowed an egg whole. He puffs out his cheeks and summons his turkey song from somewhere deep within, a haunting aria unrelated to the gobble-gobble of child's play. Guttural and true and anxious and mournful, Willie's song carries an insight earned from having spent nearly as much time with turkeys as with humans, on scratch-dirt ranches, in henhouses and tom pens, on the loading docks, along the assembly lines of evisceration, in Texas, Iowa, Missouri, South Carolina, his clothes flaked with their guts and fingernails caked with their blood. His shelter, his food, his paltry earnings — his every joy and sorrow — were controlled by a company whose very name invokes the damn bird that dictates his life: Henry's Turkey Service.

"And they talk right back to me," he says. "I go . . . And they go . . ."

But Levi did more than talk to these panicked creatures. He eased them into an acceptance that their time had come, comforting them in their final moments like an adult child whispering to a shrunken parent in a rented hospice bed that it's all right, it's all right, you can let go.

"I pat 'em on the belly when I get 'em on the shackle," he says. "I say, 'Okay, okay, Tom, quieten down.' "

Okay, Tom, okay. Quieten down. Let go, little bird, let go.

"Get them out the coop," Levi says. "Send them to the kill room."

Time for Willie Levi is either today, or not.

Today he might remove the two plastic white spoons he keeps tucked into one of his socks pulled high and beat out a clickety-clackety rhythm. He might tell you he prefers being called Levi; just Levi. He might get depressed, and fall quiet. Or he might sing one of those hymns he came to know so well as a robed member of the Sunshine Singers, a traveling choir at the Mexia State School. He remembers all them songs, he says: "What a Friend We Have in Jesus"; "He's Got the Whole World in His Hands"; "The Old Rugged Cross."

So I'll cherish the old rugged cross
'Til my trophies at last I lay down
I will cling to the old rugged cross
And exchange it someday for a crown

Today is today, and one day closer to his favorite day of the year, his birthday, which

13

he will tell you whether it is the day before, the day after, or Christmas, his wandering left eye measuring your reaction to the news.

August 19, 1946, is the thick, muggy day that Willie Levi is born in the eastern Texas city of Orange. His father is a mill-worker, when he works. His mother is a hotel maid who knows from the moment she holds her first child that he is "mentally deficient," as a state report would later put it. If there is a "normal" to his family, to his time, he "did not act" it.

What has transpired from that blessed day until today is the time-contracted past for Levi: a jumble of many moments, any one of which could have happened a half year ago or a half century ago. But today is today, and what a friend we have in Jesus.

He grows up in a shotgun house a few hundred yards from an old burial site for slaves. People are always coming and going in that ramshackle home, a sister named Idabelle, a brother named Joseph, a cousin called Toot-Toot, a nephew called Hookie. There's Oscar, and Theresa, and Shirley Mae, and Pookie, who once ate mud, and Willie Levi cannot tell you the last time he saw any of them.

His mother, Rosalie, works at the swanky Jack Tar Orange House Hotel down by the

14

Sabine River, where white people stay when they visit this city of sawmills, shipyards, and oil. The hotel's postcards say "Prepare to be Pampered," and Rosalie does her part, making the beds, scrubbing down the bathrooms. But Ernest, his father, pretty much drinks beer for a living. Drinks so much Schlitz that one of Levi's chores is to rouse his daddy with buckets of cold water to the face.

"I ask my daddy, 'Are you mad I woke you up?' " Levi says. "And he say, 'You did the right thing waking me up, so I won't be late for work.' "

Doctors advise Levi's mother that her firstborn should be placed in an institution, but she chooses not to hear all the fancy words that come down to separating mother from child. So Levi goes to school with all the other poor black children in that part of Orange. He has a teacher named Miss Odom, and she is very nice, and she lives with her two daughters in a yellow house that he likes to visit and say "trick or treat" on Hallowe'en. But he has another teacher who once hit him with a razor strap for putting tacks on the instructor's chair, and who knows what mischief maker planted that thought in Levi's head. Before long, he is taking the short walk to the Emma H.

15

Wallace School, a looming, tan-brick building formerly known as the Orange Colored School. But in the language of officialdom, his education remains "limited."

Out of school, Levi is working at a doughnut factory, boxing them babies up. And then he's at the squat brick train station in Orange, wearing a dark suit and earning tips by helping older people with their luggage. When the conductor shouts his farewell song, Levi lustfully joins in:

"All aboar-r-r-d!"

Willie Levi is now a man-boy of nineteen. His soaked father is nowhere to be found, and his worried, overworked mother is in Rusk State Hospital for the mentally ill. An aunt named Miss Louise depends on welfare for food and she just can't take care of the boy anymore. So, one hot June morning, Levi and his sister, Idabelle, take a long bus ride with lots of station stops — they get fried chicken at one of them! Finally, they reach some far-off Texas place that boasts of being a great destination no matter how you pronounce it. But you pronounce it *Meh-HAY-ya,* almost like a greeting called out on the street.

Mexia, Levi.

They visit a campus with a sprawl of buildings, just outside town. It is a special school with the feel of a military encampment, for good reason, but the people are nice and everything is fine. Then Idabelle explains that she has to go, but he has to stay. She says she doesn't want to leave, but she has to. And he has to stay.

Levi tells Idabelle that he wants to go back to Orange. It is a plea he will make many, many times in the decades to come, as he is taken to places much farther from Orange than Mexia, places out of his home state of Texas entirely, places devoted to turkeys.

I want to go back to Orange, he says, and will keep saying. I want to go home.

But the Orange, Texas, that Levi longs for no longer exists.

That old slave-burial site, once known simply as "the colored cemetery," sits beside US highway 90, along a brown-water creek bed aloud with peepers and adorned with discarded plastic-petal flowers. Frogs squashed by hearses are baked into the cemetery's dirt road, an epitaph more than equal to those carved into the marble and stone.

Here lie former slaves and veterans of wars fought in foreign lands and on neighboring streets. Here, too, lies the distinctive blues guitarist Clarence "Gatemouth" Brown, beneath a tombstone shaped like the electric

Gibson Firebird that always loomed at his crotch. A few feet away rests Emma H. Wallace, a local black educator so beloved that the city renamed a high school in her honor while she was still its principal.

The school, which once counted Levi among its students, now stands abandoned, its windows broken, the letters at its apex suggesting an unfinished game of hangman, or a puzzle from *Wheel of Fortune:*

EM_ A _ _AL_ A__
SENIOR HIGH SCHOOL

The train station, where Levi once called all to board, is closed. The Jack Tar Orange House Hotel, where the black mother of a challenged son once pampered white guests, is gone; it was demolished as part of a riverfront redevelopment plan. And though the shotgun house that Levi grew up in still stands, it stands empty.

So Levi has no home in Orange to go to anymore. No mom, no dad, no Toot-Toot, or Shirley Mae, or Pookie, who ate mud.

His home is located in today, which is one day closer to his birthday, when his mother held him as an infant and refused to let go, keeping him as long as she could.

You'll know Levi when you see him: a

wild-haired, white-bearded black man in his late sixties who walks as if in fear of falling. He has a few strands of Mardi Gras beads draped over his burnt-orange Texas Longhorns shirt, and a pair of white plastic spoons tucked into one of his knee-high socks.

Ask him, and he'll sing a turkey song that will go right through you.

# ONE

*Atalissa, Iowa*

Late evening, in the small Iowa city of Muscatine. In a rustic hilltop house with a view of the Mississippi River through winter-stripped trees. A social worker, exhausted from another day on the front lines of the human condition, finding comfort in domestic routine. Dinner. Cleanup. Bedtime. Wake up and do it all over again.

Her husband was out working the night shift as a warehouse supervisor. Her eight-year-old stepson, exhausted from his second-grade grind, was already asleep. The family's German shepherd was spent after putting in a full day as a beloved pain in the ass. But her one-year-old daughter was protesting the tyranny of bedtime with another act of civil disobedience.

Just another night. And here was this bone-weary mother, Natalie Neel-McGlaughlin, thirty-one, tall, with unruly blond hair wrangled into a ponytail, coaxing her baby to sleep as the cedar slats of her A-frame kept the cold night at bay, when her cell phone rang.

The numbered exchange glowing with urgency signaled a work-related call. Not that unexpected, since Neel-McGlaughlin was a "social worker III" with the Iowa Department of Human Services, and tonight was her turn to field after-hours calls for the Muscatine County office. Although eight years in the profession hadn't exactly hardened her, she'd lost the ability to be surprised by what people do to one another. Some of her cases sprung from carelessness: the accidental rollover in bed that smothers a baby. Others were rooted in something more unnerving: the children who show up at a Davenport hospital, sickened by the poison fed to them by their mother.

What now?

The disconnected phrases tumbling from her cell phone all but dared her to determine the context and solve the word puzzle.

*A couple dozen disabled men. All from Texas. Living in an old boarded-up schoolhouse out in Atalissa. For decades. Eviscerating turkeys in a meat-processing plant. For decades. Financially exploited. For decades.*

What she thought was: Can't be. This is frigging 2009! What she said was: Could

24

you please repeat that?

*Men with physical and mental disabilities, living in an old schoolhouse, eviscerating turkeys for very little money, for decades. Exploited.*

She thanked the caller, because that is what you do, and telephoned her supervisor, who agreed that the bizarre tip warranted follow-up. She then arranged for a couple of law enforcement officials to follow her in the morning to this place called Atalissa, known to her only by a green exit sign along Interstate 80.

The morning followed its flow.

Natalie Neel-McGlaughlin chose an outfit to balance the need to look professional, given her law enforcement escort, with practicality, given her destination. Khaki pants and a denim jacket would do. She closed the bedroom door so as not to disturb her sleeping husband, just back from work. Got her dark-haired stepson fed and down to the bus stop. Strapped her curly-blond baby into the back of the burgundy Geo Prizm, a rolling office-cum-playpen, cluttered with smashed Cheerios and stubbed Marlboro Menthol Lights, child toys and work papers. There were twelve years and 160,000 miles on it, but she preferred her Prizm to the state-issue sedans. She'd rather not show up at someone's house in a car bearing the Iowa Department of Human Services emblem on its side. The difficulties of life are daunting enough without announcing them to the neighbors.

Heading into Muscatine, a small city hard against the Mississippi, Natalie entrusted her daughter to a day-care worker who was like family, then stopped to collect the supervisor who was intrigued by these allegations from Atalissa. For a short while, they drove beside the river, a trembling dreamscape able to redirect your thoughts from everyday nonsense to existential matters of time, life, and, yes, death.

Neel-McGlaughlin had never been in the Mississippi's stirring waters, even though she lived only a half mile from its banks. She preferred to experience its seductive beauty from afar — say, from the terra firma of her wraparound porch. Every year, it seemed, someone fell sway to the great river's mesmeric pull, only to vanish into its murky flow.

She turned north, the river now at her back.

The social worker guided her compact car through the mild and sunny February morning and headed north on Iowa highway 38, the residential areas of Muscatine giving way to quiescent fields the color of hay. She had skipped breakfast again, although she hoped to grab a Diet Dr Pepper at some point. Her Marlboro Menthol Lights would have to do. She never smoked in the house, and never in the car when the kids were with her. And yes, yes, she planned to quit someday. Just not today. Too much going on.

Neel-McGlaughlin had come to social work with more insight into the dynamics of troubled families — and the government's role in child protection — than most of her colleagues. While her father worked for the telephone company in southeast Iowa, her mother mostly remained in their rural, isolated home. Things would be fine for a while, and then her mother would stop taking her medication, disappear, and wind up at Mount Pleasant. That's how you'd say it in Iowa: Mount Pleasant. Shorthand for the state's oldest psychiatric facility.

Her parents divorced when she was seven, and her dad prevailed in the difficult custody battle for her and her younger brother. But their father believed that corporal punishment fostered good behavior, and now, as a stressed single parent working full-time, he sometimes fell back on that strategy. Red marks on your arms and legs signaled to everyone in school and on the street that a price had been paid for some perceived act of misbehavior.

Before long, Iowa's social services department, regarded by her relatives as an evil agency hell-bent on breaking up families, became involved. One summer, the authorities sent young Natalie and her brother to live with an aunt and uncle. To his great credit, though, their father underwent therapy, managed his frustrations, and became better at handling the many challenges of single parenting. He is not the same angry person he once was. And his baby granddaughter loves her grandpa.

Given this background, the profession of social work seemed to choose Neel-McGlaughlin, rather than the other way around. By the age of twenty-two, she was a college-educated social worker for the Iowa Department of Human Services, the same agency that had come to her door when she was a child.

A veteran now, she had seen Iowans at their most vulnerable — on the Meskwaki Indian settlement of Tama County, in the crack-riddled Davenport hovels of Scott County, in the remote outposts of Wapello

County, where you might find someone living in a falling-down farmhouse with a score of cats, dogs, and chickens. She often tried to counter the resistance she met by signaling that just because someone works for a state agency, it doesn't mean she's had no complications in her own family. That nobody's life is perfect. That she's been there too.

But the caller had spoken of men with physical and mental challenges, an area in which she was less experienced. She knew that intellectual disability meant having significant limitations in reasoning, learning, and problem solving, as well as in adaptive behavior — in the navigation of everyday life. She knew, too, that it occurs before the age of eighteen, before the full formation of the brain, and that its causes were many: genetics, problems during pregnancy, fetal alcohol syndrome, certain childhood diseases, a blow to the head, malnutrition . . .

Beyond that, she was like most people. She didn't know much.

Neel-McGlaughlin and her supervisor pulled over at the Tipton exit along Interstate 80, outside the old Cove restaurant, closed now, but once known for its oatmeal pie topped with vanilla ice cream. Waiting for the social workers were a Muscatine County deputy sheriff in a marked sedan and a pair of agents from the Iowa Bureau of Criminal Investigation, in black SUVs.

The incongruous caravan of three cop cars and one wine-colored Prizm turned west on US Route 6. It traveled just four miles before coming upon a hokey but earnest sign:

WELCOME TO ATALISSA
POP. 271 & 2 GRUMPS

They turned right on Atalissa Road, drove up a rare hill, and pulled into a gravel-dirt driveway. It led to a turn-of-the-century schoolhouse painted an improbable turquoise, in garish contrast with the surrounding acres of fallow brown. One of those old-fashioned two-person swings sat on the sloping front lawn, close to a skeletal weeping willow.

The two-story building's windows and front door were boarded up, and several smaller buildings, including a Quonset hut, were attached haphazardly in the back. After hunting about, the visitors found a side entrance into what had been the school's gymnasium — and stepped into a kind of fun-less funhouse. Its walls were painted the colors of Lego toys — blue, red, yellow — and adorned here and there with three-foot-tall playing cards: a joker, an old maid. Snowmelt dripped from the compromised ceiling into strategically placed trash bins, and an odor that Neel-McGlaughlin knew only too well from her work — that blend of piss and filth and wet — owned the air. The smell of neglect that all but slapped you in the face.

*Hello? Anybody here?*

The seeping squalor did not shock her, at least not at first. She had seen worse. The sight of a moldy, urine-stained mattress leaning upright against a wall, for example, caused her not to recoil in horror, but rather to consider how best to remove the eyesore: Oh, we probably don't want *that* hanging around.

She was more unnerved by the building's mazelike layout, which seemed to follow the design of one of those creepy M. C. Escher illustrations. You go down to go up, and up to go down, through this building to that building and back again, passing the infantilizing gymnasium, the sticky-floored kitchen, the dining room with the gash in its ceiling. Some of the bedrooms carved from old classrooms were tidy, the knick-knacks and personal effects arranged just so; others were too repulsive to imagine spending an hour in, much less an entire night.

The longer Neel-McGlaughlin stayed, the greater her disorientation. The many space heaters plugged into overloaded electrical sockets. The malodorous bathroom, with open stalls signaling the forfeiture of privacy. The cockroaches! The place was a two-story roach motel.

A man appeared, mustache drooping, brown hair long and parted in the middle. Identifying himself as the supervisor, Randy Neubauer, he began talking in midconversation, as if the visitors already understood the context of the jarring surroundings. About bosses back in Texas who were financially exploiting these boys with intellectual disability — most of whom were working at the moment, at the turkey plant just up the road. About broken promises of a retirement home for the boys in Texas. About how the bosses weren't sending up enough money to maintain the building, which is why, for example, you're seeing water dripping from holes in the ceilings.

Neel-McGlaughlin could not quite process what she was hearing and seeing. But soon other social workers and investigators arrived to help, following a cell phone call that her supervisor had made to higher-ups in Human Services. The more eyes and ears the better, because this just wasn't making any sense.

She and another social worker soon noticed a small man blending into the background, a balding wisp in his late fifties who gave an apologetic smile along with his name: Pete Graffagnino. He lived in the schoolhouse as one of the "boys," as Neubauer was calling them, but he cooked and cleaned instead of working in the plant.

Graffagnino offered only vague answers to their perfunctory questions about the living arrangements, and he did not seem to have a grasp on a few basics, including how much he earned. But when Neel-McGlaughlin's colleague left the room, this man motioned for her to come closer, and began to speak whisper-soft into her ear.

*Can I tell you something just between you and me?*

*Of course,* she said.

*I just want to go somewhere where I'm happy. And I'm not happy here. They're mean to us.*

*How are they mean?*

*They holler and cuss at me all the time.*

*Have they ever hit you?*

Graffagnino looked down.

*No, not me. I do what I'm supposed to. I keep my nose to the ground, and just take care of myself.*

Neel-McGlaughlin would later call the encounter her what-the-fuck moment. This was not just a case of financial exploitation; not just one of a few men living in shabby circumstances. Something else was happening here. Not me, Pete Graffagnino had said. Not me, but . . .

Okay, she thought. We've got more.

The social worker watched as a couple of vans pulled up to the schoolhouse to disgorge a score of men, many with hair graying, faces lined, their bodies bent and stiff from another day's work. The boys.

Some shied from the visitors and headed straight for the fetid showers. Others, more curious and welcoming, offered filthy hands with blood-limned fingernails. A few of these hands were not curved so much as forked from "pulling crop," which Neel-McGlaughlin later learned was the yanking of feed-filled craws from the freshly dead turkeys that swung on shackles along the plant's assembly line.

The men gathered around her, talking over one another as they vied to introduce themselves. So many men, and none more eager to connect than the short black guy in his early sixties with a straying eye and a pronounced limp. He said he was Willie Levi, from Orange, Texas. He could play the spoons, he said, and his birthday, August 19, was coming up.

As she tried to keep track of all the names, Neel-McGlaughlin took note of the poor hygiene, the missing or rotting teeth. No clinical term of social work quite captured the situation before her as well as the colloquialism running through her mind: one hot mess.

Here were Levi and Gene and Raymond and Keith and Kenny and Carl Wayne and Paul and John and Jeff and Brady and Bill and Henry and Snoopy and Cowboy and John Orange and Frank and Preston and James and the Penner brothers, Robert and Billy. And Pete, of course, smiling as if already sorry for what awaited.

Twenty-one men with intellectual disability, all Texans, living hard in a run-down Pee-Wee's Playhouse in Nowhere, Iowa. How the hell, she wondered, did this hot mess happen?

■ ■ ■ ■

# Two

■ ■ ■ ■

*Kenneth Henry in Goldthwaite, Texas*

The oven of a central Texas summer bakes the town of Goldthwaite to its parched and wild roots. In the courthouse square, a Confederate soldier stands at attention from atop a century-old memorial, but there is little to guard against. Nothing moves in the midafternoon heat, save the traffic whizzing like gnats past signs of welcome to Mills County, Meat Goat Capital of America. A curious boast, perhaps, but preferable to the county's nineteenth-century reputation as a region so overrun with horse thieves, army deserters, and errant mobs that the Texas Rangers came galloping in to introduce the concept of order.

The Mills County of today has long since shed its unruly past. To begin with, it is drier in ways beyond the weather. ("We got this deal called Baptists," a local explains.) It behaves, and adapts, and endures. Cotton farming got picked clean, a turkey business flew the coop, and the discovery of oil led to a bust before any real boom could stake a claim. Now many people get by on making farm equipment and raising goats and sheep, lots and lots of goats and sheep. The animals outnumber the five thousand people of Mills County by a factor of ten.

On a quiet ranch a few miles north of that Johnny Reb standing sentry, the choral clicking of grasshoppers aswarm in the dry grass is answered by a solitary *clack, clack, clack.* It is the sound of a man inching his aluminum walker through stillness toward a long, narrow one-story building.

His name is Kenneth Henry, and he moves with the prideful regret of a once-imposing man diminished now by age and illness, though imbued with the assuredness of having found Jesus just in time. He used to be just terrible, what with the drinking and the profanity, but the good Lord took hold of him and changed his life — saved him — on the exact date of December 12, 1999. So he soldiers on, directing his former big self into the musty coolness of the empty building's cafeteria-style dining room. A life-size poster of John Wayne in full cowboy attire, kerchief around his neck, long rifle in his hand, adorns a wall. This Iowa son of a drugstore clerk is squinting upward, as if

40

posing for his own monument to some inchoate American value: patriotism, individualism, true grit — opportunity.

Other items on display suggest the good intentions of a business that ended badly in the heartland. Here, for example, is a bronze plaque that features an illustration of a towheaded boy wearing an inscrutable expression.

PRESENTED TO
JOHNSON TURKEY & SHEEP RANCH
GOLDTHWAITE, TEXAS
SELECTED AS
EMPLOYER OF THE YEAR
BY
THE NATIONAL ASSOCIATION
FOR RETARDED CHILDREN
FOR THE WISDOM, FORESIGHT AND
UNDERSTANDING WHICH HAS LED TO
THE HIRING OF THE MENTALLY
RETARDED
OCTOBER 26, 1968

Here, too, are many color photographs, arranged in framed collages and blanched by decades of sunlight. They depict dozens of men in baseball caps and cowboy hats, coveralls and denim — and even, in one instance, clown costumes. Most everyone is smiling.

"That's Willie Levi," Henry says, one hand gesturing at the images, the other clutching firm to his walker. "Gene Berg. Joe Morrell right there. L. C. Hall, when LC was younger. Well, here's Frank Rodriguez. This is the guy that I can't think of his name that's in Midland. He's an angry rascal right there. He's still in Waterloo is my understanding. Let's see. This is Jeff Long. Robert O'Bier. I can't remember his name, and I can't remember his name. And then here's some that are even older. These are boys that are long gone. . . ." His slow recitation of names sounds like a priest asking congregants to remember the following people in their prayers. Carl Wayne Jones. Billy Penner. Bobo. Tommy House. The names blend together, the individual lost in service to the team. The 1955 Brooklyn Dodgers. The 1981 Boston Celtics. The Henry's Boys.

He spots another recognizable someone among those staring back at him from another time. " 'Tiny,' we called him," he says. "A colored boy, was here for several years."

Henry directs his walker to a dark office,

and clack-clacks his way to a seat behind a desk. It is the summer of 2013, four years after everything fell apart, but he is eager to tell his side again — to defend the company he co-owned, a company dedicated to training and employing young adult males with intellectual disability whom no one else wanted. Teaching them skills. Transforming them from burdens on taxpayers to societal assets.

Making men of them.

Henry's Turkey Service treated its young charges like family, he says, and all these interlopers — these lawyers and social workers and bureaucrats — who accuse the company of exploitation, well, they've just been hoodwinked by the boys themselves.

"They got conned," Henry says. "Some guys with IQs of sixty and seventy conned them. And they never even knew it."

The man with the walker takes a seat, and a breath, and then tries to explain how dozens of vulnerable men from Texas, all with cognitive challenges, wound up living for decades in virtual servitude in Iowa, more than a thousand miles from home.

It begins with his old business partner, he says, a Texas rancher with the honeyed name of Thurman Harley Johnson.

But he was known, simply, as TH.

43

Yessir. All begins with TH.

Larger than life. That's what everyone says about T. H. Johnson, and in some ways this was true. He was tall, maybe six feet, but he grew two, three, four inches, depending on the person doing the remembering. He often wore khaki pants that he'd scribble on, calculating the costs of running a ranch, or scratching out his next big moneymaking idea. In his shirt pocket he kept a leather billfold chock-full of money, leaving no doubt who was in charge.

He could have a heart as big as all of Mills County, and he could be one tough son of a bitch. Yessir. TH. You could love him, hate him, or love and hate him at the same time, but damn didn't he make his presence felt on this earth.

He grew up a dozen or so miles outside Goldthwaite, in a place that now is all but gone. Like so many other vanishing dots on the American map, it cropped up in the late 1800s in service to the almighty railroad. The Gulf, Colorado, and Santa Fe Railway needed a shipping point for crops and livestock in that general area, so pick a spot, name it after a local ranch foreman, and there you have it: Scallorn.

To reach what's left of Scallorn, turn onto

44

a dirt road just off US highway 183. Wait for the leisurely passing of a Burlington Northern Santa Fe freight train, its many cars forming an ever-moving art installation of cross-country graffiti. Drive through the bump and dust for a few miles until the top of a fire-scorched building bobs above the overgrowth. This was the Baptist church. When you ask what happened, people around here just say "meth heads," leaving you to deduce the rest.

Scallorn once had two dozen residents, a country store, a schoolhouse, and dipping vats near the tracks to kill the ticks off cattle. Now all that remains of what Johnson might have remembered are charred remnants of a church and shreds of birdsong in the brush.

His father, Leon, was an old-school rancher, working his animals while on horseback, using the gunfire cracks of a bull-whip to command attention. Leon and his wife, Hazel, had a daughter and twin boys, Thurman and Herman. That's right: Thurman and Herman. But the similarity between the two ended with their names. Herman was short, about five feet four, although he often exaggerated his height by two inches. Thurman was tall and strapping, with a shock of dark James Dean hair that

45

only added to his stature. Here he is in old Lometa High School yearbook photographs, posing with the basketball team, the tennis team, the track team, flashing a cocky smile that said he had all of Texas by the short hairs. And, as an old friend puts it, all the girls would go ooh-aah.

T. H. Johnson went to Texas A&M, of course, and joined the air force ROTC program on the College Station campus. A brief article in the local newspaper about his graduation, in June 1955, appeared just below an editorial cartoon that all but called out any godless Communists plotting away in the San Saba hills. "The Bible is the rock on which our republic rests," the caption declared, above a jumble of imagery that included Andrew Jackson, the Holy Bible, and a lighthouse beaming out the word "Freedom."

Later that month, the Baptist-born Johnson crossed the religious divide by choosing a Methodist as his wife, and, in doing so, married into the royal court of Goldthwaite. Her name was Jane Ann Steen, a school-teacher and daughter of the owner of the local hardware store. Walking up the aisle at the Goldthwaite First Methodist Church, the bride carried a white Bible topped by a white orchid, and wore a strand of pearls around her neck, a gift from her beloved.

Johnson served out his time in the air force, earning his pilot's wings along the way — which was funny, some say, because he didn't enjoy flying. Then he and Jane returned to Mills County to take their proper place in Goldthwaite society. One day they were competing in a local tennis tournament, the next they were hosting a graduation party of finger sandwiches and iced tea for a family friend.

With a ranch of his own, just like his daddy, Johnson had his good years and his bad. "Old Thurman can owe a million dollars and never lose a wink of sleep," the local doctor, M. A. Childress, once told the *Des Moines Register.* "He's a wheeler dealer, and if he's got $100 laying around somewhere, he'll probably invest it. The joke around here for a while was that Thurman had to go see his banker every day at two o'clock."

In a community of characters, T. H. Johnson stood apart: the bespectacled rancher in pencil-marked khakis, mind ever whirring, ambitions ever mounting. He even fancied himself a bit of a dowser. Every now and then he'd remove a forked tree branch he kept in a barrel of water and walk his expansive property with the long end pointed at the dry earth, like a metal-detecting scavenger on an endless beach. Sometimes, it was said, the end of his branch would curve down — twitch, almost — at the precise location of hidden, precious groundwater.

On his office wall hung a painting of Pecos Bill, the fictional embodiment of the outsize Texas sense of self, riding a mountain lion and using a rattlesnake as a lasso. This Paul Bunyan of the sage was said to have lassoed a twister, shot out every star from the sky save the Lone Star, and laughed himself to death at the sight of some city slicker posing as a cowboy.

Well, that's TH, one visitor recalls thinking. This is how the man views himself.

If Johnson told you to do something, he was not inviting you to discuss the matter. You just did it, if only to avoid the hell to pay if you didn't. But if he heard of a family in need, he'd have food delivered on the spot. And if a hard-up cowhand came rolling through town with his wife and kids, looking like they just drove out of one of Dorothea Lange's Dust Bowl portraits, Johnson would hire the man whether he needed him or not.

For a while there was a ranch hand so useless that one local described him as "eight-tenths of a sorry bastard." Johnson's managers wanted the man fired, but the boss countered by saying there were two good reasons why you can't fire old Flick, and listed the names of Flick's two young children.

Like many farmers and ranchers in Texas, Johnson relied heavily on the bracero program, a mostly forgotten government arrangement that allowed countless Mexicans to cross the border to work on American farms and ranches. The program developed during World War II, amid the realization that the attack on Pearl Harbor had not stopped crops and livestock from growing. Now that much of America's agricultural muscle was in boot camp or overseas, the United States established the Mexican Farm Labor Program, a name soon overtaken by "bracero" — Spanish for one who works with his arms.

The program continued even after the war, perhaps because it was too good to be true, offering farmers and ranchers an endless source of strong arms at minimal cost. Then came the Korean conflict and the resurrected fear of a shortage of agricultural workers at a time of war. Congress passed a law that formalized the bracero program, but with supposed protections for both American and Mexican laborers. The Mexican guest workers could be hired only during a labor shortage; they could not be used to break strikes; and they had to be provided with decent food and housing, as well as free transportation to the border when their contracts lapsed.

"You didn't have to carry him back into old Mexico where he lived," Kenneth Henry recalls. "All you had to do was get him to the border, and he'd go home and stay at least thirty days and he would meet you back at the border if you wanted him. And he'd come back and work for you again. It was a good program."

If you needed a rock mason, a fence builder, and a drywall man, you'd just call down to Del Rio. The next morning you'd go to the bus station and there, waiting, would be a rock mason, a fence builder, and a drywall man.

"That labor deal, it was the best thing in the world you could do," says Robert Womack, a former business partner of Johnson's. A heavyset man in coveralls, he sips coffee in the Mexican restaurant a few yards from his Goldthwaite welding business. "Put 'em in a decent place to live. Blanket, goat shed, grease, flour, and red beans. We called them 'wets' in the past."

But this controversial arrangement more than fulfilled its great potential for abuse, leading the former US Department of Labor official who oversaw the program to call it "legalized slavery." Highly skilled but desperate Mexican workers were accepting poverty wages and poor living conditions, while American farm laborers were struggling to find work at fair pay. The US government finally ended the program in 1964, much to the annoyance of the agriculture industry, which had come to enjoy the many benefits of cheap labor.

"It was too simple and too good," Henry says in conveying his disgust with the government. "They didn't have their finger in it, so it didn't work for them."

In trying to make do, T. H. Johnson often ran afoul of federal immigration officials, who conducted repeated raids on his ranch looking for undocumented Mexican workers. "We used to hit him once a month and get 10 to 40," a federal investigator once told the *Kansas City Star,* and Johnson did not dispute it. "We have wetbacks walking through here every day," he said.

But he had a two-thousand-acre ranch to run, a diverse operation with a concentration on inseminating and raising turkeys —

as many as a hundred thousand a year. Now he was shorthanded. If only his divining rod could lead him to laborers who could work turkey.

Funny how things turn out. Johnson had a lot of friends back then, and he knew somebody who knew somebody who worked at the Abilene State School, about 120 miles to the northwest. In Texas terms, just up the street.

Built at the turn of the century as a colony for epileptics, the facility sat on a 640-acre campus that included a powerhouse, ice plant, bakery, and mattress shop, as well as dormitories, two chapels, an occupational therapy building, and a special unit for "idiotic, imbecilic and feeble-minded epileptics." But as medication and treatment for epilepsy improved over the decades, the colony was transformed into one of the state's institutions for people who were then labeled "mentally retarded" — known in Texas as state schools.

By the mid-1960s, about the time Johnson was trying to operate a business without braceros, a few states around the country were beginning to embrace the concept of deinstitutionalization. The integration — or reintegration, when you think about it — of people with disabilities into the community was coming to be seen as more appropriate and, quite frankly, more cost-effective than maintaining beds at state schools. Although Texas was well behind other states in adopting this view, its department of education did have a division charged with "rehabilitating" people with physical disability, as well as those with what were once known as the "hidden handicaps" of mental illness and retardation.

The story told ever after was that a special-education counselor at the Abilene State School detected opportunity in the growing complaints of farmers and ranchers left shorthanded by the elimination of the bracero program. So, in 1966, he approached several ranchers, including Johnson, with a radical proposal:

Take on a few young men from the state school. Teach them basic agricultural skills. Pay them a nominal wage, provide them with room and board, and, simple as that, your labor shortage is solved and the state saves money. What's more, these "mental retardates" taking up space in the state school become useful citizens, contributing to the economy and paying taxes.

Just like the rest of us.

All but one rancher declined the offer, seeing little more than headache and risk in trying to train, feed, and house men with IQs between thirty-five and seventy. Only T. H. Johnson said he would give it a go. He did not know what kind of work these boys were capable of doing, but he needed hands, he already had a bunkhouse on the property, and what the heck: Yes.

But Johnson did have his reservations. That summer in Austin, about one hundred miles south of Goldthwaite, an architectural engineering student and former Marine named Charles Whitman carried a cache of firearms up to the observation deck of a twenty-eight-story building on the University of Texas campus. Firing away with a sniper's detachment, he killed or wounded dozens before an Austin police officer crept up to the tower with three colleagues and shot him dead.

How was this traumatic event pertinent to the possible hiring of young men from the Abilene State School? According to John Stowe, one of the school's vocational counselors at the time, Johnson was among many in the country who "didn't know the difference between someone who is mentally retarded and someone who is mentally ill."

His question to Stowe: *Are these folks the*

*ones who will do what happened down at that tower?*

No, Mr. Johnson. No.

# THREE

*Snapshot*

If their names had not been recorded in a ledger, who would remember them? The very tall Andy Sawyer, the very large Frank Wuritz, the very industrious Ardis Wilkerson, among others: the first men from the Abilene State School to move to Hill Country Farms, the Johnson ranch in Goldthwaite, where they were to learn all about working with hay, and sheep, and turkeys. Especially turkeys.

When the pilot program began in late 1966, the half-dozen new hires, known now and forever as "the boys," received encouragement and modest direction, free of pressure. A few months later, at a meeting to assess the arrangement, Johnson informed state officials that these boys weren't by any stretch carrying their weight. But the bracero program was gone, farmhands were needed, the boys were getting some things done, so — let's keep going.

Fortunately, the state schools of Texas had an ample supply.

As word of the Johnson ranch experiment spread, vocational counselors at other state schools — Austin and Denton, Lufkin and Mexia — seized on this rare opportunity and began recommending candidates who might also thrive at the ranch. Before long, Johnson was traveling to the state schools, sizing up possible choices, and saying: *Him, him, and him.*

The men who agreed to take a chance would undergo a few weeks of basic training to learn how to live life on the outside, since most had been institutionalized since childhood. After their boot-camp immersion into the world of the non-disabled, the candidates would spend a day or two at the ranch in Goldthwaite. Then, Kenneth Henry says, "The boy would decide, 'Do I want to do this or not?' "

Not everyone did. John Stowe, the vocational counselor at the Abilene State School, once delivered a hesitant candidate to the Johnson ranch, turned around, and headed home. By the time he reported to work in the morning, the young man he had dropped off the night before had already hitchhiked back to Abilene.

*I just wanted to get out of the state school,*

the man explained. If only for a day.

The anecdote reflects a harsh truth: most of these men wanted liberation from state school life. Abilene, for example, had become an institutional catch-all for many hundreds of infants, children, and adults with physical, intellectual, and mental disability. For reasons of convenience and hygiene, many of the men had buzz cuts, the women Buster Brown bobs. They lived in need-specific wards lined with dozens of beds, and were supervised by overworked state employees who were more warehouse custodians than attentive caretakers.

Among the 1,500 or so residents were more than a few people without disabilities who had somehow run afoul of the law. When Stowe first came to Abilene as a counselor in 1966, he sifted through the histories of the residents assigned to him, only to find case after case of country judges resolving a matter of delinquent behavior by simply sending the offender to the state school. The young man standing before the judge may not deserve protracted incarceration, but he was considered a nuisance to the community. So: Maybe a spell at the state school will get your mind right.

"You had a lot of people in the state school who didn't belong there," Stowe says. "Sounds cruel, but that's the way it was."

The school could crush the soul. Jaylon Fincannon, a consultant on developmental disability and a former Texas director of mental retardation services, began his long career in disability services as a recreation counselor at Abilene in the late 1960s. Some residents participated in sports, he recalls, while the most that others might do — those who were ambulatory — would be to walk to the park, toss a ball around, and return to their dormitories. Some had jobs in laundry and food services. Some went to the occasional movie or social in the gymnasium. Some could not talk and some could not stop talking. Some had families who remained in constant contact, taking their loved ones home for holidays and even for entire summers.

Most did not. Most had been dropped off at the school as children, and might see their parents once a year, or never again.

"Not a pretty picture," Fincannon says. "Over time, you care about the work, and you care about the people. But at some point, it hits you: this isn't the greatest setting."

Fincannon's understanding of the institutional oppression was as much personal as professional. He had married a hometown girl named Judy Fitzgerald, whose brother, Alan, was a resident at the state school for nearly twenty years. In the Abilene context, Fitzgerald was considered especially fortunate: his vigilant brother-in-law worked on the campus, and his family always collected him for holidays and long summer vacations.

Alan Fitzgerald's family moved him out of Abilene long ago. But they have not forgotten how he would make clear his intense loathing for the school, even though he was and still is unable to speak. Whenever he would be returned to Abilene at the end of an extended break, he would leave the car only after intense coaxing, and the assurance that his family would be back soon to take him home for another visit.

Many residents at Abilene had no trouble at all in expressing their feelings. Nearly fifty years later, Fincannon remembers what they would say as he walked the grounds:

"Get me out of here."

The program in Goldthwaite grew in size and in acclaim. By late 1968, T. H. and Jane Ann Johnson were living on the ranch with their three daughters and thirty-four former residents of state schools.

The arrangement was unusual, yet very much in concert with the fledgling movement toward deinstitutionalization. At a dinner in Detroit in 1968, Johnson was honored as "Outstanding Employer of the Year" by the National Association for Retarded Children, a prominent advocacy organization whose many name changes over the decades have reflected society's struggle to find the proper terminology when referring to people with intellectual disability (the preferred term as of this writing). Established in 1950 after an annual meeting of the American Association on Mental Deficiency — another term no longer in favor — the organization was first called the National Association of Parents and Friends of Mentally Retarded Children. Then the National Association for Retarded Children (NARC), the National Association for Retarded Citizens (NARC), the Association for Retarded Citizens of the United States (ARC), and, for now, The Arc of the United States (The Arc).

The award to T. H. Johnson became national news. Dr. Walter C. Alvarez, a syndicated medical columnist, praised the Goldthwaite program with a perspective that would be roundly condemned today: "A mentally retarded person is happiest in a job which does not require a lot of thinking and planning and meeting of emergencies. What he loves is a job that he has learned well and that then never changes from hour to hour or from day to day."

The President's Committee on Employment of the Handicapped also celebrated Johnson for "bucking the tides of convenience and prejudice." An article in the committee's magazine, carrying the inspiring headline of "A Ranch Where They Raise Spirits," described the Goldthwaite program as a win-win-win arrangement for Johnson, the men, and the state of Texas, which had gained thirty-four taxpaying residents and shed a $75,000 tax burden. Although acknowledging that Johnson's program had encountered some bumps along the way — mistakes on the job, adjustment issues, a few minor disciplinary problems — the article suggested that the many benefits more than made up for these challenges. The former state school residents were performing every chore imaginable on the turkey-and-sheep ranch, in addition to building their own quarters, preparing their own meals, doing their own laundry, and handling their own banking and personal needs.

If these claims were considerably overstated, no one seemed to mind. The government article noted that "patience, perseverance, and a dogged determination to make it work have paid handsome dividends for Johnson, for the community, and for 'the boys,' as he fondly calls his employees."

The plaque that T. H. Johnson received that night in Detroit is the one hanging in the ghostly office in Goldthwaite, where Kenneth Henry sits now, remembering. He is a bit more blunt in describing what the men actually did on the ranch:

"They basically caught turkeys."

Henry would know. Back then he was the king of turkey insemination.

Henry's father had turkeys on the family ranch in Comanche County, about fifty miles north of Goldthwaite, and for a while the Henrys retained a college boy to handle the insemination. But this college boy had a drinking problem, and the Henrys had to let him go. When the elder Henry asked his son whether they could do the insemination themselves, young Kenneth Henry responded with confidence: "Yeah. We can do it."

The teenager somehow found time to play half back for the Comanche High School Indians, serve as the vice president of the class of 1959, and be named the favored sweetheart of the Future Homemakers of America, all while building a business in the artificial insemination of turkeys. "Wasn't long 'til I was inseminating turkeys all over Texas," Henry says. "My senior year in high school, I artificially inseminated thirty-five thousand turkeys a week."

A measure of the young man's success is found in the columns of the local newspaper, the *Comanche Chief,* which solemnly chronicled everyday life in an agricultural county of about twelve thousand people back then. Headlines might include: "Visits Grandmother"; "Home from Hospital"; "Albuquerque Visitors"; and "Junior High School Honor Roll Cited." In late November 1963, near the inside-page headline of "More Kennedy Assassination," there appeared a roster of recently registered vehicles that included a 1964 two-door Corvette, just bought by the turkey-insemination wunderkind, Kenneth Henry, who was twenty-three.

Within a few years, Henry was providing his expertise to a larger-than-life rancher in Goldthwaite whose hired help included a growing number of men fresh from state schools. Together, Henry and his client, T. H. Johnson, did some hard-nosed calculations to assess the viability of Johnson's business model, at least when it came to poultry. For example:

Question: *How long does it take for an average man with developmental disabilities to learn to catch a turkey?*

Their answer, after some study: *About two months.*

"There's not really an easy way to handle a live turkey, because they're going to flap their wings, and they don't want to get caught," Henry says. "Some people never learn."

Others, though, have a gift for it. Take Willie Levi, Henry says with clear admiration. "He could sound just like a turkey."

Domesticated turkeys, as opposed to the wild turkeys sometimes seen strutting with false bravado on the wooded fringes of the interstate, have been bred to maximize their breast meat, creating that exaggerated dowager effect. As a result, the top-heavy toms can damage the hens during mating and are not as efficient in delivering semen, leaving their procreation to be best achieved through outside assistance.

This does not mean these turkeys have been stripped of their natural behaviors. They fly in short bursts, break out into brief frolics, flap their wings, ruffle their feathers, and bathe in dust — acts of apparent joy. They are also quite social, if social means being unwelcoming, even violent, to birds new to the flock, sounding off in times of tension and aggressively attacking opponents with their beaks and claws. Behavior not much different, then, than that of the species breeding them for food.

At turkey ranches similar to the Goldthwaite operation, thousands of hens are raised in a separate facility in which careful modulation of temperature and light prevents the premature laying of eggs. Then, after twenty-eight weeks of growing to about thirty pounds in this contrived environment, the hens are ready. Consummation nears.

In the nearby tom house, workers corral the toms, forty and fifty pounds of muscular wings and jagged edges that do not want to be held. A worker will grab a tom by the legs, flip him upside down, take hold of a wing and a leg, and place him on a bench in front of the "milker," who extracts the semen. With the tom clamped in place, the milker massages the lower abdomen, stimulating the bird, then quickly collects a few white drops of semen with the vacuum-pumped suction of a strategically placed aspirator. One after another, tom after tom, with syringes filling up with semen and "extenders," a combination of saline solution and nutrients.

The valuable semen is then hustled to the undulating, white-feather sea of the hen-house. Several dozen hens are penned off at a time, with workers known as "drivers" forcing them down a chute and into a pit. There, an "inseminator" uses a machine that draws a measured amount of semen from the syringes and into a small straw, or pipette. With the hen held down, tail up, the inseminator presses with his thumb to open her cloaca, sticks the straw into the vagina, releases the semen, and sends her on her way.

Next.

It is grimy, repetitive, shit-and-feather-filled work — work that few want to do. Fortunately, T. H. Johnson and Kenneth Henry now had pliable workers they could train for their business, which came to be known as Henry's Turkey Service. Maybe a man from a state school needed two months to learn the elemental and brutal skill of how to catch a turkey. Maybe he needed more time, or maybe he needed less. But he learned.

"They trained me how to catch semen," says Willie Levi, who came to Goldthwaite from the Mexia State School.

"Shoot that stuff in 'em," says Henry Wilkins, who came from the Austin State School. "Mash that cum in 'em. That make 'em lay eggs."

Willie Levi, Henry Wilkins, and many other men from the state schools became proficient. They caught these birds. They milked the ornery toms. They held down the terrified hens.

■ ■ ■ ■

# FOUR

■ ■ ■ ■

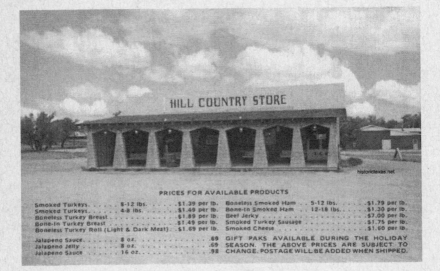

**PRICES FOR AVAILABLE PRODUCTS**

| | | | | | |
|---|---|---|---|---|---|
| Smoked Turkeys | 8-12 lbs. | $1.39 per lb. | Boneless Smoked Ham | 5-12 lbs. | $1.79 per lb. |
| Smoked Turkeys | 4-8 lbs. | $1.49 per lb. | Bone-In Smoked Ham | 12-18 lbs. | $1.30 per lb. |
| Boneless Turkey Breast | | $1.89 per lb. | Beef Jerky | | $7.00 per lb. |
| Bone-In Turkey Breast | | $1.49 per lb. | Smoked Turkey Sausage | | $1.75 per lb. |
| Boneless Turkey Roll (Light & Dark Meat) | | $1.69 per lb. | Smoked Cheese | | $1.60 per lb. |
| Jalapeno Sauce | 8 oz. | .69 | | | |
| Jalapeno Jelly | 8 oz. | .69 | | | |
| Jalapeno Sauce | 16 oz. | .98 | | | |

GIFT PAKS AVAILABLE DURING THE HOLIDAY SEASON. THE ABOVE PRICES ARE SUBJECT TO CHANGE. POSTAGE WILL BE ADDED WHEN SHIPPED.

*The Hill Country Store in Goldthwaite*

The faces changed over the years, thin and chubby, clean shaven and stubble bearded, with searching eyes and eyes averted, some so good-looking that people said what a shame, as they might of a handsome Catholic priest. The young men came and went, by the dozens, by the hundreds, depending on what plans T. H. Johnson and Kenneth Henry had for them. Though united by gender, relatively low IQ levels, and a shared status as wards of Texas, each had his own story.

Pete Graffagnino came from the Mexia State School by way of Port Arthur, a gritty oil town that can smell like rotten eggs when the wind shifts. A slight, balding man who tended to melt away in a group, he had cheap glasses that magnified his eyes, and an unshakable devotion to Jesus.

When Pete was little, the family story goes, his abusive mother threw him down a flight of stairs.

Daddy: *What the hell's he doing on the floor?*

Mommy: *He wasn't listening to me, so next time he will.*

Maybe this was why Pete had developmental problems, and maybe not, but it is the story told by his older sister, Rose Barton, who lives now in a one-story house somewhere in Houston's suburban spillage. Her living room is chockablock with collections of Mother's Day plates from Avon, salt and pepper shakers, angel figurines, and bottles of various notions and unguents covered with dust. Look this way at a portrait of Jesus on the cross, and his eyes are closed; look that way, and his eyes are fixed on heaven.

Rose sits in her housedress on a worn couch, its stuffing billowing from a breach. She opens a photo album adorned with small American-flag stickers and inscribed on the cover with one word: "Family." Some of the black-and-white photographs, dating from the late 1940s and early 1950s, feature grinning young men in short sleeves and smiling young women in light blouses and skirts, holding small Coca-Cola bottles wrapped in napkins. This handsome woman with a bottle is their mother, Rose says, and this dark-haired man holding baby Pete is their father.

Pete looks like any other cute-as-a-button toddler in any other American album from the Truman era, in coveralls and a striped shirt. Rose has a short loop of repeating memories from that time — of Pete, for example, chasing her around and around the house. She told him to stop, but he wouldn't, so she tried to kick him, missed, and cut her knee so bad she needed stitches. And Pete, poor Pete, crying and saying he didn't mean to do that.

Some things you remember real good, Rose says. Other things just slip the mind.

Their father never learned to drive, so he would bicycle several miles to his job at the Texaco plant. While he was gone, Rose says, their mother would drink and collect boy-friends. Some days, she'd tell Rose to stay home from school and watch her younger brothers, Pete and Billy, while she went out. Other days, she'd tell the three kids to wait outside this motel while she went in to talk to Uncle So-and-So. Then she'd give Rose a dollar and say, Don't tell Daddy where we went today.

Many times, after their dad had cycled home from the plant, his children would be waiting, their mother absent, so he would do his best to make light of it.

*Guess your mom's gone again.*

*Yup.*

*Guess what we're having for dinner tonight!*

*What?*

*Potatoes and eggs!*

*But we had that yesterday!*

*No, we didn't. We had eggs and potatoes.*

The moments loop in Rose's mind. Going for ice cream one time. Having her dad balance all three kids on his bicycle, one on the back, one in the middle, one on the handlebars, and taking a spin. Watching him try to help Pete with his homework, doing the lessons over and over and over. The divorce.

The three kids all went into foster care. Billy, who was only about three, went one way, and Rose and Pete wound up in a tiny Texas place called China.

Rose finished the eighth grade and made her way to Austin, where she got a job at a furniture factory, putting couches together. And twelve-year-old Pete went to the state school in Mexia. Rose wouldn't see him again for many years, but never did he leave her mind.

Gene Berg, from the Abilene State School, was brawny and square-jaw handsome, with a confident way of walking that said he knew he was one of the best workers around. You tell Gene to do something and he'd get it done, simple as that.

"He was just a small boy when he left home," his mother, Wanda Berg LaGrassa, says over the telephone.

The Bergs of Rhome, outside Dallas, did what other families did back then, going on lakeside vacations, getting saved together in a local Baptist church. But Gene fell behind in his lessons and speech development. His mother took him to some special education classes at a public school in Boyd, about six miles away, but his learning didn't improve much. A good, good boy, who gave his parents no problems at all. Just a slow learner is all.

The couple struggled with what was best for their son, and worried about where he would go after they died. Who would take care of their Gene? Their only option, they finally decided, was the Abilene State School. "My husband and I thought it was the best thing for him," his mother says. "To learn something that he could do and be on his own. And where he would be watched after we were gone."

The school, covering several hundred acres on the outskirts of Abilene, held a forbidding aura. When it opened in 1904 as the State Epileptic Colony, the best treatment for epilepsy was believed to be contentment — or, put another way, an avoidance of mental stress. Although the institution had been repurposed as a residence for people with intellectual disability in the late 1950s, some in town still called the Abilene State School by its old name: the Colony.

On June 7, 1968, the body of Senator Robert F. Kennedy, a champion of the rights for people with disabilities, lay in state at Saint Patrick's Cathedral in Manhattan. On the other side of the country, in Los Angeles, his killer, Sirhan Sirhan, was indicted. And in Abilene, somewhere in the American middle, the Berg family arrived at a campus of new dormitories and old brick buildings, intent on doing what was best for their boy, Gene.

The administrators told the Bergs to give it a while. Don't come visiting every weekend. Allow Gene some time to adjust to his new environment, and you to yours. Let it take.

Wanda and Clayton Berg said good-bye to their twelve-year-old son, and drove the 160 miles back home. "The hardest thing we ever did in our life," his mother says now, pain informing her every word.

"It killed him," she says. "It killed us too."

After that wrenching day of separation in Abilene, she and her husband visited Gene regularly at the state school and — in contrast to many other families who never returned to see their institutionalized children — brought him home for vacations and holidays.

Gene adapted. He adjusted well to living in a dormitory with other boys. He attended classes, excelled in physical education, and participated in vocational training. He learned about laundering and grounds-keeping and building maintenance.

And when he was twenty years old, Gene left Abilene for Goldthwaite, where he acquired a new and particular skill.

"Inseminating turkeys," he remembers.

Keith Brown, with piercing eyes and the moody air of forever being misunderstood, came from the Lufkin State School. His father had a good federal job at the Red River Army Depot, a munitions storage facility up in Texarkana, and his mother drank. The second of four children, he had a profound speech impediment — one of the reasons for his sometimes sour disposition — as well as intellectual disability, which some family members thought might be linked to fetal alcohol syndrome.

Although family photographs show a giddy Keith jostling with his older brother on the lawn, and a bow-tied Keith smiling for a portrait with his siblings, there was just too much going on. His mother's drinking problem would lead to a breakdown, a divorce, and an early death. His younger sister Sherri had EEC syndrome, a genetic disorder that left her with a thumb and two fingers on each hand and a big toe and two digits on each foot. And here was Keith, with behavioral problems and a clear need for constant attention that no one could provide. "My dad just couldn't deal with it," Sherri says.

Keith was sent first to the Denton State School because of its close proximity to a speech-therapy program. "I think I was about twelve," he says. "My mom and dad wanted me to go, and I said yeah. I thought it would help me."

Then he went to the Mexia State School, farther away. When the family would come to visit, their parents would lock Sherri and her sister in the car before entering a boys' dormitory to collect their little brother. "We were terrified," she says. "We didn't understand Down syndrome. We didn't understand retardation. They would go in and they would bring him out. I just remember sitting in that car."

Keith went on to Lufkin and, finally, to Goldthwaite, where he tended to the baby calves and inseminated the turkeys.

"It was something to do," he says.

There were so many young men.

Henry Wilkins, big-eared and with a hangdog look off-set by the touches of mischief and need in his eyes, from the Austin and Mexia State Schools. A self-described "country boy" from Sulphur Bluff, a boom-and-busted place of about three hundred, he liked being with other children, especially younger ones, and playing checkers and dominoes, though he wasn't very good at either. He enjoyed getting lost in television and hillbilly music.

If you asked young Henry to mow the church lawn, or to do the dishes at home, he might or might not finish the job. He was even-tempered most of the time, but could get upset when his widowed mother denied him cigarettes, or forced him to attend Sunday school. By the age of thirteen, he was deemed a problem in his community, wandering into other people's homes when they were not there, taking things now and then, doing pretty much anything for a cigarette.

He could not keep up at school, even though local educators took a special interest in him, and kept promoting him so that he could remain with his age group. But by the seventh grade he was performing at a third-grade level, while enduring everyday ridicule from his classmates.

If Henry remembers those difficult days, he prefers a different narrative. He says he used to run out of the school on the dares of classmates. One time, the principal chased him across the grassy expanse of the Sulphur Bluff Cemetery, caught him, and tore his butt up but good with a hole-dappled paddle.

"I didn't do it again, you know it," Henry says. "And I got sent to the state school."

Frank Rodriguez, who didn't quite seem to belong in Goldthwaite, and was often mistaken as just another ranch hand who might head to his own home at the end of the day. He was tall and boyishly good-looking, with a shock of black hair under an ever-present ball cap and a way of observing without comment that granted him a certain gravitas.

Born in Bismarck, North Dakota, the son of Cyril Frank Rodriguez and Velma Bear

Ghost, Frank wound up on a small ranch outside San Antonio, living with a grandmother who spoke no English and a grandfather who stopped his heavy drinking after crashing his car. He remembers fetching water for his grandparents, feeding the chickens, and suddenly being sent against his will to the Austin State School — a decision based mostly, it seems, on a slight speech impediment. He whiled away his state school time by washing dishes, until one day someone promised him the life of a cowboy in a place called Goldthwaite.

Chasing turkey is what it turned out to be, he says, but he didn't mind too much. "Somebody had to do the job, I guess," Frank says.

Billy and Robert Penner, brothers who shared the same hefty build and the same searching, owl-like eyes. Growing up in Amarillo, they were a handful, sitting still only long enough to pose for the occasional black-and-white photograph — in front of the family's big old sedan, or in cowboy hats while propped on a horse. Their father drove a truck, hauling cars to California, and their mother just tried to keep after them and their sister, who also had intellectual disability.

Their older brother, Wesley, married and

85

moved away. One day he came home, and things were too quiet. Turned out his little brothers had gone to the Abilene State School. "She couldn't keep 'em, basically," he says. "She said she had to put the boys in the home. She couldn't handle them."

But their mother, determined to stay in touch with Billy and Robert, sent imploring letters to Goldthwaite.

Dear Billy and Robert,

I'm trying again, it seems like there's no way anyone answers the letters. Well anyhow. . . . Our weather is really great here. I am asking about seeing you either Thanksgiving or Christmas, would it be possible? Wesley would get you cause he lives in Dallas and we would probably take you back and we could spend it at Wesley's.

Tell me how these things are worked out. . . .

Please write.

Love, Mother

Excitable Raymond Vaughn, who was abandoned by a foster father at a county court one day, and John Hatfield, who dreamed of being a ballet dancer, and so many others, pulled from the state schools of Texas for this grand experiment of fresh air and poultry procreation. The brothers Barefield, Leonard and James; the brothers Jones, Carl Wayne and Leon; James Fowler and Paul Hayek and Douglas Barco, on and on, including, of course, Willie Levi, formerly of Orange.

Levi arrived by bus with his sister, Idabelle, who would not be staying long. It was the second day of the summer of 1965, in the nineties already, and the top three songs on the radio conveyed a shared longing for connection: "(I Can't Get No) Satisfaction"; "I Can't Help Myself"; "Help Me, Rhonda."

His new home, the Mexia State School, had been built not as a colony for epileptics, or an institution for the feebleminded, but — of all things — a prisoner-of-war camp.

During World War II, military success for the Allied forces carried the logistical complication of where to house hundreds of thousands of captured enemy soldiers. Many were sent by Liberty ships to the United States, where dozens of POW camps were hastily constructed around the country, including one amid the needlegrass and pastureland just outside Mexia, another oil-depleted town losing its population and sense of purpose. At the very least, a POW camp meant jobs: barracks and warehouses, kitchens and mess halls, utility lines and a water system — they all sprang up to accommodate thousands of German officers and enlisted men from General Rommel's Afrika Korps.

A nine-year-old Mexia boy, committed as any American child to joining Little Orphan Annie and others in protecting the home front against the Axis powers, would never forget the sight of a few thousand Nazis disembarking at the downtown train station. Actual Nazis! Sunburned, fresh from battle, still wearing their khaki uniforms and large-billed cloth caps, the Nazis lined up for as far as a boy's eyes could see, and began goose-stepping the three and a half miles up Tehuacana Highway to a new home with barbed-wire fencing.

The German prisoners of war picked cotton, pruned trees, baled hay, and took quiet note of the poor treatment of the African Americans they saw working in nearby fields. They formed orchestras and staged theatrical productions, played soccer and watched weekly movies, and made homemade liquor from whatever fruit they managed to cadge. Some annoyed locals called the camp the "Fritz Ritz," since these enemy soldiers seemed to have it better than the average guy on the street.

One prisoner painted a mural-size map of the United States, with an outsize representation of Texas — "224 times larger than Rhode Island," it said, in cheeky reference to the Texas ego. Another painted a triptych drinking scene, very Three Musketeers, that would vanish and then reappear, decades later, during a demolition project. Another would write a letter to his girlfriend, Dory, back in Germany, wondering about the coming Texas summer, wishing he could travel with his letter back home to her, and signing it, "All my love, with hugs and kisses, from your Heinie."

People in town kept track of the Fritz Ritz, and shared a good chuckle whenever another Nazi tried to escape into the great Texas unknown. A couple of fleeing prisoners rode a freight train four hundred miles to Corpus Christi, then tried, while speaking no English and still wearing their German uniforms, to check into a motel. Another escapee stowed away for two days in a boxcar that sat on an unused spur in downtown Mexia. Yet another had to be rescued after being chased up a tree by an annoyed Brahma bull.

With the war's end in 1945, the prisoners vanished as suddenly as they had arrived, a

Nazi mirage, leaving an empty encampment with no clear purpose. But the elders of Mexia, sensing an opportunity for job creation, convinced the federal government to deed the former POW camp to the state of Texas. In 1946, buildings that had housed enemies to the American way of life became home to dozens of boys and girls with intellectual disability.

By the mid-1950s, a young college graduate named Randall Bryan — the boy who had watched that parade of Nazi humiliation and defiance up to the new POW camp — was working on the campus in the state school's supply department. While checking furniture and other inventory one day, he went out to a female barracks called East Lake. What he saw would stay with him forever: women tied with sheets to a post, lying in piles of shit.

"All women," he says. "Severely retarded. Bad. It was a tough situation."

Things changed. By the time Willie Levi arrived in 1965, Texas was working to improve its services to people with intellectual disability. The Mexia State School was one of the first to establish a vocational rehabilitation program to help residents find jobs and adapt to mainstream society. The school was changing in other ways as well;

an audit had uncovered various financial improprieties at Mexia, forcing the resignation of the school's longtime superintendent-cum-overlord, a man known as "Papa Jones."

By this point, Mexia was the largest state school in Texas, with new dormitories — enough for more than 2,800 residents — mixed in with leftover POW-camp buildings, a sixty-bed hospital, a volunteer fire department, and more than 700 employees. It was also Levi's new home, though he would never stop reliving that disconnecting moment when his sister boarded the bus bound for Orange, and he did not.

"I wanted to come back home," he says. "And she didn't want to leave me."

But she did.

Gradually, Levi adjusted to life in an institutional setting, an unusual environment made even odder by the occasional visits of middle-aged men with German accents, reminiscing as they wandered the campus. He slept in one of the dozens of cots, arrayed as if in an army barracks, in dormitory number 749. He found a girlfriend whose name was Mercedene. He played baseball. He donned a choir robe and sang with the school's famed Sunshine Singers, who performed around the country and recorded several albums, including one called *Bless This House,* which was dedicated to "God's Glory" and to "sharing with the public the accomplishments of the mentally retarded."

He also ran track, he says. "First place. Gold medal."

Sure, Levi, sure.

But here is a copy of the *Mexia Daily News* from May 1970, reporting that at the track and field state championships for special schools, Willie Levi won a gold medal. Actually, two.

And the next year, he won three.

"He was one of the big wheels on the relay team," remembers Randall Bryan, who by then was the school's recreation director, deeply involved in establishing Special Olympics events in Texas. "I remember him leaving. He had to be replaced on my coach's relay team."

In December 1973, Levi left for a tryout at T. H. Johnson's ranch in Goldthwaite. "I was on the inseminating crew, catching toms," Levi says. "They trained me how to catch semen."

Chasing and grabbing the toms. Stimulating them. Catching their semen in little bottles. And running it like the track star he was, over to the hen pen.

A few months later, the superintendent and the director of social services at the Mexia State School sent a letter to Mr. William Ernest Levi, c/o T. H. Johnson Ranch, Goldthwaite, Texas.

Dear Mr. Levi:
Since you have demonstrated the ability to care for yourself and are no longer in need of institutional care and training, you are being discharged from Mexia State School, effective July 5, 1974. . . .
May we take this opportunity to wish you success in your future endeavors.

Whether Mr. William Ernest Levi ever received these good wishes is unclear. For one thing, he could not read.

# FIVE

*Photos on the wall of the vacant Goldthwaite bunk-house*

The magic of simplicity.

A mysterious element that enabled an ordinary Texas rancher with no training in special education to transform these state school boys into competent ranch hands — and the best turkey catchers in Mills County, if not all of Texas. Who knows how many times T. H. Johnson was asked to explain his program's success, but the catchphrase he developed seemed to carry an antigovernment subtext: Here were the uncomplicated minds of those close to the land succeeding where the overcomplicated minds of those in bureaucracy could not.

The magic of simplicity.

Simple.

Johnson believed that an environment like his, one combining nonjudgment with a "touch of old-fashioned authoritativeness," could lead to personal growth and semi-autonomy. That most people with intellectual disability "want to be 'normal,' and will make extraordinary efforts to perform accordingly." That the transformation of a dependent, often heavily medicated person into a dignified man with pride in appearance and achievements took about eighteen months to two years at his ranch. A few might take six months; others, five years.

Johnson's partner, Kenneth Henry, recalls the philosophy of their business that became Henry's Turkey Service:

"If you're exposed to something, then, it doesn't matter whether you got an IQ of two hundred or fifty, if you do it repetitiously, you can get better at it. And they got better at it. Did that mean that they learned to read and to make change and to do all those things? No, it doesn't. But they can do a job."

The man's eyes tear up as he makes another point. "The boys had a lot of pride in what they did," he says. "If they could learn a task, any task, it was a victory for them. Any task. If they learned how to drive turkeys — they were prideful in that."

They wore western gear, with cowboy hats, cowboy boots, and blue jeans. They slept in metal bunk beds arranged in rows in a cinder-block building, and shared dormitory-style showers and toilets. They sat on benches in the television room, played table tennis on the screened-in porch, and ate better than they ever could have imagined back in the state school system. A strong believer in the importance of a good diet, Johnson made sure the men had good food, and plenty of it. A second slice of beef, a second scoop of beans, all for the asking.

Most of the men worked with turkeys. Then, when the local turkey market all but collapsed, they worked with hay, with calves, with whatever Johnson could come up with to keep things going. After broadening his operation to include a chicken-egg business in 1969, he joked that if it didn't work, "we're going to have to give some bankers some shock treatment."

But there were also jobs in the bunkhouse, cleaning beds and preparing food, as well as in the Hill Country Store, a restaurant and general market that the Johnson family established along highway 84. In addition to selling assorted turkey products, the roadside store also offered hams and tamales, jalapeño sauces and jellies, cheeses and candies, and pies so good, one local says, they'd "make you want to slap your mama."

The economics of the overall operation,

which the company said saved taxpayers hundreds of thousands of dollars in institutional care, was fairly basic. The Texas Rehabilitation Commission, which focused on finding jobs for people with disabilities, paid the ranch $165 a month per person for the first six months of training. After that, the men were paid a sub-minimum wage, thanks to a federal labor law that allowed employers to pay people with disabilities at a rate based on their productivity, as when compared with the work output of a non-disabled person. Some of what the men earned, of course, was spent at their employer's company store.

Keith Brown liked to buy his tins of Longhorn chewing tobacco there, while Levi sampled just about everything. "They had hamburgers, and peanut brittle, and some soda water," Levi says, smiling at the sweet memory. "Them long candies, butternut."

Now and then, complaints leaked out that the men weren't getting paid. But Nan Shaw, who worked as a nurse on the ranch, told the *Des Moines Register* that T. H. Johnson always kept his word. "Even when Thurman was broke, the boys got their pay," she said. "Thurman and his family went without during that time. Their diet was turkey sausage or stuff off the farm — the same as what the boys ate."

So many years have passed since those days, and so much has happened, that one of the ranch's former supervisors, Robert Womack, sits at that Mexican restaurant in Goldthwaite, next to his welding shop, and jokes about the men's treatment at the Johnson ranch. "Everybody got lined up in the morning, and we kicked 'em in the nuts."

In truth, he says, a family dynamic developed among the men, who had been all but abandoned by their own relations. Even with decades of distance, Womack remembers them. Big Bear, for example, also known as Leonard Barefield, whose speech was so garbled that only Womack and a few other people could understand him. Henry Wilkins, who was "always where he wasn't supposed to be." Frank Rodriguez, who didn't belong at the ranch, to tell the truth, and who used to make the most exquisite artwork using colored sand and glue. In fact, Womack still has one that Frank gave him. . . .

"I wouldn't give a million dollars for my experiences with the boys," he says. "You can't help but be their friend or their buddy."

As for Johnson, well, you never knew exactly where you stood with him. You'd see him one day up at the company store, and your money'd be no good — everything on the house! You'd see him the next day, and he'd be in such a foul mood he wouldn't even look up when you greeted him.

But Johnson cared for these boys, Womack says. Like a gruff den mother, he'd do bed checks at night to make sure they were safe and well, and not quarreling or staying up too late. "He was one of those people you could love real easy and hate at the same time," he says. "The son of a bitch is dead and gone, but he cared about those boys, and he took care of them."

Defensive and uncooperative around inquisitive professionals, with a particular loathing for nosy social workers — that's how Nan Shaw remembered her former boss. "I won't say he's a saint and I won't say he's the devil incarnate," she told the *Des Moines Register.* "But I've worked with psychologists and social workers since I worked at the farms, and Thurman Johnson just seems to have a way with MRs" — shorthand at the time for "mental retardate."

Whether he had "a way" with the men was not the concern of some of those professionals he so detested. They chafed, of course, at Johnson's refusal to avail himself, and the men, of the social services available in Mills County, particularly since he had no training in working with people with special needs. More important, they began to ask questions that delved beyond those of possible financial exploitation. Questions about basic human rights.

Cynthia England, a caseworker at the Texas Department of Human Services in Brownwood, argued early on that a central tenet in special services — a belief in the innate rights of all people, regardless of race or intellectual ability — was not evident at the Goldthwaite ranch, where the business practice of using the men for cheap labor was being masked as a beneficent endeavor.

"Some of the men are timid and infant-like," she told the Fort Worth *Star-Telegram*. "They have no sense of themselves as persons with decision-making rights."

True, Johnson had a large paddle displayed on his office wall, and the rumor was that he might spank you if you misbehaved. Just a joke, he said. One of the boys had made the paddle for him as a gift, in fact. "I don't even spank my own kids," he once said. "I'll stand in front of the same judge the rest of them stand in front of one of these days."

One time an out-of-town rancher pulled up with a truckload of sheep and shouted for these blankety-blank guys to unload the animals. His face scarlet with rage, Johnson ran up to the visitor and gave him hell, telling him to never talk to the boys that way again, and to unload his damn truck himself.

"I don't think that guy ever brought another load of sheep to the ranch," says John Stowe, the Abilene State School counselor, who witnessed the moment.

The men were rewarded for their hard work when racing the clock in the time-sensitive business of turkey insemination. Beers all around, maybe, and then a pig roast on a Sunday. Goldthwaite became a family, Womack says. "The family they never had."

Take sweet J. W. Brown, for example, who was much older than the other boys and fresh out of the Abilene State School. He served as a sort of nursemaid in coveralls for one of Johnson's daughters; wherever he was, she was. And if you asked JW to recite statistics from, say, the 1934 World Series, out it would come from the deep reservoir of an inscrutable mind: Dizzy Dean and Hank Greenberg, Joe Medwick and Goose

Goslin, and the Gashouse Gang of Saint Louis crushing Detroit in the seventh and deciding game, 11–0 . . .

David Johnson, T. H. Johnson's nephew, befriended some of the men as a boy, playing games and swapping baseball cards with them. Whenever he'd pull into the ranch in his father's pickup, the men would hustle from every direction just to talk to the boy — about anything, often repeating what someone else had just said, finding validation, even comfort, in the repetition. The boy sensed that they looked up to him for some reason, even though he was only in grade school. But he took his role seriously, and made sure to treat them like anyone else, because they were.

"And they remember you forever," he says. "Anybody that's ever been nice to these guys, they'll remember them forever."

Christmastime was extra special at the ranch, with no expense spared for food, fireworks, and presents, including those big net stockings filled with fruit and candy. Johnson always made sure that Santa Claus, who also moonlighted as the local postmaster, paid a visit, charming the men by using their first names as he handed out gifts.

"Christmas belonged to the boys," Robert Womack, the former ranch supervisor, remembers.

The Hill Country Farms program grew in reputation, with various officials and chambers of commerce stopping by for tours, and Johnson traveling around the state to give speeches about the magic of simplicity. How the boys on his ranch underwent medical and dental checkups annually. How they had their own accounts down at the Mills County State Bank. How those with a higher degree of maturity might occasionally be allowed to have a few beers with friends — or even develop a relationship with a woman. How the town of Goldthwaite was a place where the boys could run errands, get haircuts, and be accepted. How the whole operation had the approval of the Texas Rehabilitation Commission, the Social Security Administration — the very government he held in mild contempt. Lastly, how working with these boys had affected Mr. T. H. Johnson personally.

"They really get under your skin," he'd say.

Some aspects of the Goldthwaite operation went unmentioned, though, at all the Rotary Club luncheons and award-banquet dinners, and in all the admiring articles with titles like "A Ranch Where They Raise Spirits."

The prostitutes, for example.

As the bossman father to these men, Johnson concerned himself with their diet, interpersonal skills, work production, and even the satisfaction of their natural urges. Every once in a while, a crew chief took some of the men for a three-hour drive down to a notorious brothel in La Grange known as the Chicken Ranch — in keeping, perhaps, with the poultry motif of their circumscribed lives.

This brothel, the inspiration for the musical *The Best Little Whorehouse In Texas,* derived its nickname from the desperate years of the Depression, when the madam established a "one chicken for one screw" policy to keep her employees well fed. A visit to the Chicken Ranch became a rite of passage for many a buzz-cut freshman at Johnson's alma mater, where young Texas A&M colts routinely piled into cars with six-packs of Lone Star courage and drove the seventy miles south from College Station for the eight-dollar Aggie Special, a discount from the standard fifteen-dollars-for-fifteen-minutes rate, in support of higher education.

And now, in the parlor, where chitchat was

awkward and a Coke cost a dollar, where college boys fidgeted and truck drivers took brief breaks from the road, there sat some visitors from Goldthwaite, showered and shaved. It is unknown whether they enjoyed a Henry's Turkey Service discount.

Years later, Johnson framed such visits as an ordinary part of life, a matter of choice. "If a boy wants to go to a cathouse, it's his own thing," he told the Fort Worth *Star-Telegram.* "We try to meet as many of his needs as we can. I don't condone it, but it's like beer. If he wants one, he can have one."

In this spirit, Johnson also arranged for discreet visits to the ranch by a woman or two. Decades later, several of the men still remember by name a particular Mexican American woman. Keith Brown blushes at her memory. Frank Rodriguez says he used to have a photograph of her somewhere, but he got rid of it. On second thought, maybe he didn't. He reaches for a photo album, flips through a few pages, comes to a stop. His forefinger hunts over an image of several people gathered around a picnic bench, before lingering just below the image of a young, attractive woman, dark-brown hair to her shoulders.

The photograph cannot convey who she was, or how she came to provide fleeting, ten-dollar moments of intimacy for men who might not otherwise have known a woman. She sits among them, like someone's sister, or girlfriend, or wife, and more than forty years later, her name is remembered and said with near reverence.

Also left unmentioned at all the hail-fellow-well-met gatherings where the Goldthwaite operation was lauded: the runaways. The men who bolted from the ranch and vanished, if only briefly, into the endless flat landscape of mesquite and pasture.

One of the Penner brothers took off one time — Billy, or Robert. Probably Billy, though you never knew, they looked so much alike. Anyway, Billy either had a fight with his brother or got homesick for his mother in Abilene, so off he went, with no one the wiser. That is, until Robert Womack got a call from the sheriff's office down in Fredericksburg. Home of the Texas German dialect and some very tasty peaches, it's ninety miles to the south and in the opposite direction from Abilene.

We got a vagrant here in the lockup, the sheriff said. You want him?

It was a Sunday, Womack remembers. He drove down, had some of that famous Fredericksburg barbecue — "They do a good job," he says — and collected a bedraggled and hungry Billy Penner at the sheriff's office, where the jail food was intentionally unappetizing and, perhaps mercifully, in short supply. No sense in attracting vagrants with some fine barbecue and peach cobbler.

As they began the long drive north to Goldthwaite, Womack chewed out the runaway for a while, then asked:

*Did they feed you good?*

*No sir.*

*What'd you have for breakfast?*

*Water.*

*When's the last time you ate?*

*Thursday morning, when I run off.*

Womack stopped at a market and bought a loaf of white bread, a package of lunch meat, and a quart of milk. He handed the bundle back to Billy Penner. By the time they reached Goldthwaite, all that was left were three slices of bread.

Another one who took off was Willie Levi. He loved the many benefits to living on the ranch, from those candies at the company store to Jane Ann Johnson, TH's wife, who occasionally took him with her to go shopping. But Johnson himself was another matter entirely, always annoyed, always barking out orders. One day, Levi decided he had had enough and took off for Orange, the hometown he had never wanted to leave in the first place.

"TH wasn't treating me right," Levi explains.

He got pretty far, by his estimation: thirty-five miles up highway 84, right to the bus station in Brownwood, where maybe, just maybe, there might be a bus bound for Orange. But Horace Brooks, the longtime sheriff of Mills County, tracked him down.

*What are you doing here in the bus station?*

*Looking for work.*

*Well, I know a fella who needs help. He runs a turkey place.*

*I'm allergic to turkeys.*

*Come on, Levi, let's go.*

Levi remembers that when he was brought back by sheriff's car to Goldthwaite, Johnson gave him a hard time, saying, "How come you didn't keep a'going?" And Levi answered: "Well, you called Sheriff Brooks on me."

Sheriff Brooks, it seems, had a preferred term for the boys at the Johnson ranch: "nitwits." Not that he was entirely unsympathetic. "Any ol' boy would rather be a-walkin' along the river pickin' up acorns," he once said, "than rockin' on the porch of the state school."

One day, two disgruntled men bolted from the Johnson ranch and supposedly managed to steal food, guns, and even a garbage truck before being arrested. They further tested the community's patience by promptly breaking out of the Mills County jail in Goldthwaite, only to be caught again.

This time, Sheriff Brooks had a plan. A deputy sheriff drove the two men more than 450 miles north, past Amarillo, to the town of Dalhart, in the northwest corner of the Texas Panhandle. Then he turned around and drove back to Goldthwaite. Alone.

Most of the men had been erased from familial memory, a mistake best forgotten. But now and then, a letter would arrive at the Goldthwaite ranch, its handwritten scrawl revealing glimpses of the home life left behind, such as one received by quiet, apologetic Pete Graffagnino, whose hard-drinking mother had once knocked him down the stairs for not listening.

My Dear Son Pete
    Darling, how are you? Hope fine. I am doing fine. Feeling good. . . . What have you been doing lately? Some day I'll come over and get you home. I have a

nice apt. I stay by myself. I have a cute little dog. His name is Peanuts.

I might come over for Christmas. I hope. I went to Houston to see Rose and the boys. When I get you home me and you will go to Houston and go see Rose & the boys. Would you like this?

I wish I was living in a pretty town like you. I'm so tired of this town I hate it. I like to move but I can't find a place in Houston.

I want you to write me a letter. I'd love to hear from you. I don't live with Bobbie no more. He is BAD. He is no good.

Guess I'll close for now. May God bless you darling.

Love, MaMa

Other letters, though, sought connection . . .

Dear Billy and Robert,

Since I never hear from you even if I write I'll try again. I'm just doing fair, because I'm not able to work.

How are you both? Fine, I hope. Now boys I know it's been a real long time, but would it be possible to see you in May if I came down there. Have somebody write me and let me know. . . . It is awful lonesome cause Grandpa and Grandma have both died and I sure miss them. So please let me know if I can see you.

Love, Mother

P.S. Do you boys need anything. I would try and get it. . . .

And received a response — from the company:

Dear Mrs. Penner,
As of this early date, we do not know when the boys will return to the ranch. The boys are working on a turkey inseminating crew so the work is finished when the turkeys stop laying, which is usually around the last of June or the first of July. . . .
The boys are in good health and have matured a great deal. They are pleasant and get along well with the other boys. . . .

Yes, the work revolved around the turkey, always the turkey: its artificial insemination, its eggs, its hatching, its feeding, its slaughter.

But the turkey market was shifting away

from that part of Texas. T. H. Johnson and Kenneth Henry decided the time had come to send the boys of Henry's Turkey Service out into the wider world, beyond the Texas border. To contract them out as turkey-savvy laborers, willing to do those high-turnover jobs no one else wanted to do, because the work was hard and low-paying and repetitive, a bloody, filthy, feathery mess.

But before leaving the mesquite and brush and mess hall of the Goldthwaite ranch, some of the men sought out David Johnson, the small boy who was always there to swap baseball cards and talk about everything and nothing. They took his small hand into their large mitts and gave it a good shake, saying so long, they were leaving Texas.

In short order, Henry's Turkey Service secured contracts in several states, including one at a meat-processing plant in some Iowa place called West Liberty. Now all the company needed was a building to house dozens of men just a couple of years out of the state schools of Texas. A building, then, that would protect that rarest and most magical of elements. Simplicity.

■ ■ ■ ■

# Six

■ ■ ■ ■

*A godsend on a hill in Atalissa*

A scout from the Hill Country of Texas wandered the verdant flatlands of southeastern Iowa, searching. Leave it to the rest of the country to obsess over the scandal of Watergate, the resignation of a sitting president, the stability of the republic in 1974. This man was intent on his mission, having been dispatched one thousand miles north by his employer, Henry's Turkey Service, to find the nearly impossible amid the boundless fields of soybean and corn.

A building immediately available for rent. Large enough to provide dormitory-style living arrangements for dozens of men, but also close enough to the Louis Rich turkey-processing plant that dominated a modest town of 2,300 called West Liberty.

The explorer from Texas, Robert Womack, sought assistance in his reconnaissance from a few local people, including a Louis Rich executive and a real estate agent, but nothing they found was quite right. Frustrated, he headed out on his own one day, driving the back roads of rural Muscatine County, through and around hamlets named Nichols and Fruitland, Stockton and Conesville, seeking serendipity.

He found himself on US Route 6, one of the least relevant and most curious highways in the federal transportation system. Stretching from Provincetown, Massachusetts, to Bishop, California, the route has neither inspired a finger-snapping song to celebrate its hipness nor summoned a singular moment to the collective American mind — other than, perhaps, the denouement of the classic Chaplin film *Modern Times,* with the silhouettes of the tramp and his girl following its path into the future's promising glow. But in its lackadaisical unspooling of 3,205 miles across the continent, Route 6 meanders right through a seed spit of a place called Atalissa. And there it was, visible from the road and just five miles from the turkey plant: A temple on a hill. A realized mirage.

"Like God opened the heavens to me," Womack recalls.

The inspiration for his spiritual moment was an old public schoolhouse, looming from a rise over the quarter-mile square that was Atalissa. The town had a dozen short streets, a couple of churches, a tavern, a grocery store, a grain elevator, a post office, and not much else, other than this old schoolhouse.

Built in 1911, the tan building had two stories and a bell in its tower to summon generations of Atalissa children for uphill lessons in the twentieth century. Over the years, a class might have three students or it might have ten, with the recurrence of the same surnames creating a kind of Atalissa-specific chant come graduation ceremonies: Garvin and Hepker, Lindhorst and McKillip, Passmore and Spilger. Go Indians!

By the late 1950s, though, Atalissa had decided to merge with the West Liberty school system, making the Atalissa High School class of '57 its last. So ended the building's purpose as a repository of youthful memories, from the starchiness of the white orchestra uniforms to the dramas within the drama club. The time that wintry conditions forced the cancellation of the baseball season, and the players walked in snow and ice to the homes and farms of school board members to plead, in the name of holy baseball, to let the season continue. Or that time a train struck the school superintendent's car, and the entire student body attended his funeral in the gymnasium. Boys from the basketball team serving as pallbearers. A sextet from the girls' basketball team singing "The Old Rugged Cross."

All those school plays in that gymnasium; all those barn-dance frolics and banquets and family get-togethers . . .

For a few years, Atalissa rented out the schoolhouse building to neighboring towns in need of classroom space, then briefly used it as a youth activities center to provide distractions from the everyday monotony of rural life. Nothing seemed quite right, though, until a fellow with a Texas accent and a fondness for barbecue inquired about the availability of the building, which seemed to suit his purposes perfectly. It had communal showers, communal bathrooms, plenty of classrooms to subdivide, and a large kitchen.

A godsend, Womack remembers. "I could see my people took care of here."

The turkey service and the town struck a rental deal of six hundred dollars a month. In came dozens of military-style bunk beds, new plumbing fixtures, a stainless-steel sink, and buckets of paint. Out went generations of scholastic memorabilia. A second-place Muscatine County basketball trophy from 1950. A pair of gym shorts, blue and white

122

with orange striping. A copy of a 1923 play called *Betty, "The Girl o' My Heart."* A large red varsity letter — "A" for Atalissa.

These mementoes are now kept behind glass and just above a snowblower in the Atalissa volunteer fire department building, which becomes a community center when the trucks are pulled out of the bays. The scuffed trophies and game balls, the cobwebbed class portraits of unlined faces feigning preparedness for what is to come — they are the relics of another Atalissa, of another American time.

The life story of the town's founder, an adventurer named William Lundy, reads like several Jack London stories crammed into the same novel. Born in Pennsylvania in 1811, Lundy left home at sixteen to seek his fortune as an itinerant tailor, joined the navy to sail the South Seas, participated in the battle of Quallah Battoo in 1832 (a response to a massacre aboard an American merchant ship), boarded a whaling ship bound for the States, and returned home by steamship and stagecoach to stun his family, who had all but buried him in their minds. He took up the uneventful life of a Pennsylvania tailor, married, fathered four children, then abruptly moved his family to Iowa, where he bought 1,300 Muscatine

County acres to farm. Three years later, in 1850, he suffered a relapse of wanderlust and left his family to pan for gold in California. He returned to Iowa a couple of years later without gold but with a mellifluous nugget — the name of an Indian queen in local California lore — on his tongue:

"Atalissa."

In 1856, Lundy and a partner subdivided some of his land to create a town he named in honor of an Indian monarch with no historical connection to Iowa. He also promised a corner house lot to the first baby girl in the community to be christened Atalissa, to the eventual benefit of a Miss Atalissa Davis.

The town grew at a measured pace befitting Iowa — not too fast, not too flashy. The natural gift of a twenty-five-foot-wide spring drew iron horses to water on their runs between Davenport and Des Moines, helping the community grow. But Lundy expressly prohibited the other kind of watering hole. There would be no demon rum for sale in Atalissa.

In 1867, a local citizen, miffed by a reporter's dismissive description of Atalissa in the *Davenport Gazette,* wrote to the *Muscatine Journal* in protest. He decried the failure by this "knight of the quill" to mention the two physicians in town, the Atalissa Hotel, and the considerable commitment by Atalissa residents to the "boys in blue" during the Civil War — by everyone, it seems, save one.

"That one individual, so kindly excused for his 'simplicity' (imbecility), who neither fought nor voted right, I presume feels quite relieved to learn that his neck is safe from the effects of a h—p string."

The town followed the all-American arc, the entwined necessities of commerce and faith determining the development of its dozen streets. By the time its new schoolhouse rose from the hillside, Atalissa had become a thrumming business center, boasting a Masonic lodge, two temperance clubs, three Protestant churches, two general stores, a decent hotel, a drugstore, a butchery, a blacksmith, a grain elevator, a cement factory, an all-important railroad depot — and a clutch of Civil War veterans who routinely gathered beneath a large maple to talk about things no one else could understand. Overall, the town's residents "give every evidence of prosperity and contentment," one turn-of-the-century visitor wrote, an impression seconded by a local newspaper: "No one in sickness or distress suffers for want of care in the community if their wants are known, and the kindly ministrations of friends and neighbors are often spoken of with highest praise."

The community gelled around the small moments and the large, though rarely the outright violent. The Colt .38 Special bought in 1901 for local policing remained the official Atalissa gun for so long, nearly seventy-five years, that it rusted from disuse and required oil to be removed from its holster. The ordinances the weapon was intended to help uphold were shoved into various drawers, more apt to be nibbled by mice than to be read by citizens.

The men gathered in the office warmth of the grain elevator and the women at Tuesday quilting bees, engaging in what was not so much gossip as the telling and retelling of their distinctive, ever-evolving story, the story of Atalissa.

*Anyone been by the schoolhouse? Seems some mischief makers have gone and put a horse buggy on the roof of the boys' outhouse. Who did it, no one's saying, but I got a suspicion. . . .*

*So the school superintendent's car stalled again, and they brought it down to the garage. Turns out some rascal shoved a corncob into the exhaust pipe. Again . . .*

126

*Did you hear what that Turner boy did? The twelve-year-old? He sees little Thelma Conner stuck on the railroad tracks on her tricycle, and he runs over and grabs her just as the number 8 train is coming through town. Never says nothing, but a train agent saw the whole thing, and now there's gonna be a write-up in the papers. . . .*

Still, the outside world at times would intrude, piercing the eight-foot barricade of corn that surrounded the town.

In the very last days of World War II, a naval cruiser called the USS *Indianapolis* docked in Tinian, in the Northern Mariana Islands. The ship delivered its top-secret shipment of enriched uranium — for the atomic bomb that would soon devastate Hiroshima — then stopped in Guam to swap out some sailors before continuing on to its next mission. But shortly after one midnight, a Japanese submarine buried two torpedoes into its starboard bow. Within twelve minutes, the massive cruiser rolled over and sank, a quarter of its 1,196-member crew instantly drowned, its Mayday call missed or ignored.

With few lifeboats or lifejackets, the rest of the men were left to float in the open waters for nearly four days, as saltwater poisoning and heat exposure took their toll, as hallucinating brothers turned on one another, as sharks feasted. Finally, an American bomber on a routine patrol spotted the men by chance, and a rescue mission began. By then, only 316 men were alive, in what is considered the worst naval disaster in US history.

Among the 880 Americans lost to the Philippine Sea in this tragedy was a Marine named Arthur Thomsen, of Atalissa, Iowa, eight thousand miles away.

Three other men with Atalissa ties were also killed during the war, including one with a familiar local surname. Corporal Leslie McKillip died in combat in Belgium in the fall of 1944. Soon after, the local chapter of the Royal Neighbors of America, a women's organization that sponsored those Tuesday quilting bees, presented his mother with a gold star, which was what you did when there was nothing you could do.

After the war, people tried to pick up where they had left off. Parents trundled their children up to the cemeteries on Memorial Day to place flowers and pine branches at the graves of veterans. Neighbors came together to help other neighbors too frail to harvest their corn and soybeans. There were barn dances and Sunday picnics and church concerts — and even a bar now, on Cherry Street.

A diner called Dick's Cafe opened, and a young daughter of its owners would sing a song to the tune of "Little Brown Jug":

My Dad and Mommy busy are
Feeding folk from near and far
They serve the finest pies and cakes
Also hamburgers and steaks.
Ice cream, malts, and things they fix
Cleanest place this side of heaven
But hurry, folks! We close at seven.

But things just weren't the same. As if war had obliterated the cornfields protecting the self-contained town, exposing it to inevitable conquest by outside forces. The Atalissa Hotel and the Atalissa Savings Bank and the Atalissa railroad depot were already gone, and now interstate highways and big-town supermarkets and television were rubbing away at what had been. Then came the shutdown of the most prominent reflection of Atalissa pride: its school.

This does not mean that the clutches of men had run out of things to say down at the grain elevator, or that groups of women quilted in silence, or that children ran around the short streets shouting nothing

129

more than "You're it!" For one thing, they could all muse about the activity taking place up at the old schoolhouse. Dozens of men were living there now — a Texas invasion that, overnight, had increased the town's population by nearly 20 percent.

Clanging school bells and gymnasium dances receded further from the collective Atalissa memory, as townspeople wondered about the mysterious tenants up on the hill, living like show-and-tell exhibits in rooms once reserved for math and science and English; in rooms where students once learned of a Shakespearean tale told by an idiot, signifying nothing.

Two yellow school buses took these men in the early morning into West Liberty, and returned them to the schoolhouse in mid-afternoon. You'd catch glimpses of them sometimes, working on a flower garden, lingering beside an old weeping willow, sitting on a swing as if waiting for something to happen. But they never left the yard.

■ ■ ■ ■

# SEVEN

■ ■ ■ ■

*Awaiting slaughter in West Liberty*

So it began, a looping reel of existence.

Well before dawn's light, the former state school residents were roused from bunk beds spaced three feet apart. They dressed and made their beds. They ate a light breakfast: cereal, maybe, and some coffee. They piled into a yellow school bus that rocked and rattled them along the bump and rut of Route 6, through the black-and-blue night, over a railroad track, past the darkened storefronts of West Liberty: the funeral home, the small grocery store, the old Independent Order of Odd Fellows building, the ancient Strand Theatre, where the lobby featured vintage posters from the 1930s for movies like *The Good Earth* and *Easy Living.* On to the massive plant rising from ten downtown acres, its grass speckled with telltale white feathers.

Once on site, each man was handed a white lab coat, a pair of rubber boots, a hairnet, a plastic helmet, and, if he wanted them, earplugs and gloves. The protective gear equipped them for immersion into an industrial realm of bright light, loud noise, and poultry gore, where they would perform one of the least-desired jobs in American industry — all for a dead man whose name they would say over and over, perhaps more frequently than their own, and always with a touch of formality. It was never Lou, or Louie. It was Louis. Louis Rich.

The name sounds like the conjuring of slick Manhattan ad men trying to evoke all-American wholesomeness: Betty Crocker, Aunt Jemima, Louis Rich. But Louis Rich lived and breathed and strived, a short, bald immigrant who, before he died at seventy-four in 1970 — four years before these men from Texas began working at his plant — had changed what and how we eat.

In 1906, at the age of ten, Rich traveled mostly in steerage to the United States from the small Ukrainian city of Zhytomyr following his father, a kosher butcher who had fled the persecution of Jews in the Russian Empire. The father came first to Chicago, but, on whispers of greater opportunity, moved south to the suitably named Rock Island, Illinois, a hard-edged city across the Mississippi River from Davenport. For many years a gangster lawyer named John Patrick Looney pretty much owned Rock Island: the local Democratic Party, a newspaper, scores of brothels and gambling dens — just about everything short of the river water beyond its banks. But Louis Rich was above or below all this, working in factories and delivering bread before starting his own provisions business.

The Yiddish-speaking immigrant became a chicken-and-egg man, traveling to area farms in a battered truck to negotiate the purchase of products he would then provide to butchers and grocers. "Then he hired a man for a truck, then two trucks, then three, four, five," his son Martin says. "Finally, he had thirteen trucks."

A workaholic who allowed himself only the occasional game of cards, Rich zeroed in on the opportunities to be found in his adopted country. He began selling dressed poultry — feathers and blood removed, but the rest of the bird largely intact — to distributors in the East, a gambit so successful that by the early 1940s his business had outgrown its Rock Island facility. Looking to expand, he bought a tomato canning factory in West Liberty to convert into a chicken processing plant. But with the chicken business migrating south, and with massive producers locking up the growing supermarket trade, Rich made the switch to another fowl — and soon disabused a nation of relegating turkey to a meat served only on the fourth Thursday of November.

He and his sons, Norman and Martin, became meat-industry pioneers by developing the technique of "further processing" — that is, finding a use for nearly every inch of the bird. Parts and trims became lunch meats, bacon, and sausage, while other fully cooked products included whole turkey breasts. The meat became a year-round staple, with the Louis Rich corporate headquarters in West Liberty receiving, killing, and processing as many as twenty thousand turkeys a day.

"We developed and changed the turkey industry," Martin Rich says, with justification.

The company proclaimed itself "the largest further processor of turkey in the world" — a distinction surely lost to most consumers — and publicized in roll call advertisements the many products it was able to derive from a single creature:

Rich's Oven-Roasted Catering Breast. Rich's Turkey Breast Filet. Rich's Turkey Thighs. Rich's Young Hen Turkey Breast — Self-Basting. Rich's Turkey Meatloaf. Rich's

Turkey Roast White. Rich's Turkey Breast (Crown Imperial). Rich's Turkey Salami. Rich's Turkey Ham. Rich's Turkey Bologna. Rich's Turkey Pastrami. Rich's Turkey Summer Sausage. Rich's Smoked Turkey. Rich's Turkey Franks (The Leaner Wiener). Rich's Turkey Roll White & Dark. Rich's Chicken Breast Roll. Rich's School Lunch Quality Rolls. Rich's Pure Ground Turkey. Rich's Turkey Breakfast Sausage. Rich's Fresh Turkey Parts . . .

Leave it to others to joke that Rich's "Crown Imperial" turkey breast sounded more like a Ford sedan, or that its "School Lunch Quality Rolls" gave no indication of the presence of actual meat. In addition to transforming an industry through "further processing," the Louis Rich company had also created year-round, day-and-night employment for hundreds in Muscatine County.

In 1963, the town of West Liberty proudly held its first Turkey Day celebration, with ten-cent lunches, entertainment, and a drawing for valuable prizes. Presiding over the festivities was the old chicken-and-egg man, Louis Rich, wearing a deli counterman's white paper hat and standing before a large banner with an invitation that sounded more like a command:

The poultry trucks were always waiting. Lined up outside a bay called the "live dock," they were loaded down with stacked coops jam-packed with turkeys that had been crated the night before, when the birds tended to be calmer. You might detect movement in this breathing cargo — a barely perceptible shift in the tight confinement, a nudge. Then again, you might be seeing merely the breeze-fluttered tremble of a feather protruding from a crate, a disturbed wisp in the fluffy rectangular stillness.

Certain aspects of the process have changed over the years, as have certain names and faces. The fundamentals, though, have remained constant, like rituals central to a religious belief.

As each truck pulls to a stop in the bay, some of the men, standing on height-adjustable platforms, reach into the crate, grab the forty-pound toms by the legs, and hang them by their feet on V-shaped metal shackles that dangle along an overhead conveyor. The birds are generally not happy with this proposition, perhaps sensing that no good can come from being hung upside down, and they fight back with their surpris-

138

ingly powerful wings. The trick is to grab a foot with one hand, swing that plump body almost behind you, grab the other foot, and hook it.

"It'll beat the hell out of you, black and blue," one of the men, Danny Miles, recalls. "But you get used to it."

Who knows what it was about the stray-eyed black man named Willie Levi, but he could just about coo the turkeys to slaughter. He liked to brag that he could talk turkey, and there was no reason to doubt him, as his guttural gobble found obvious resonance among the fowl, creating a call-and-response dialogue between man and bird.

*Quieten down, Tom, quieten down,* he'd advise, before giving the upside-down turkey the final rites of a reassuring pat on the belly.

The conveyor carries the shackled turkeys inside the plant to be stunned in a shallow pool of electrically charged water, after which a device slits their throats to make them "bleed out." The carcasses are then immersed into a vat of scalding water, so hot that fans are needed to at least stir the humid air, and then pass through a series of mechanized rubber fingers to beat away the feathers. A worker called a "cutter" removes the hocks, while others, called "pinners," pluck away any stubborn feathers.

The birds, fat and pink, plop onto tables, and the evisceration begins. Workers called "rehangers" attach the carcasses by the legs to the shackles of a second conveyor — a critical moment in the process, dictating the pace of the assembly line. A missed shackle means idle moments, lost revenue.

Next in line, the "three-pointers." These workers grab the tail with one hand, the neck with the other, and put the head in the V of the shackle. Then a cutter slices a hole under the breast.

Once cut, the shackled turkey moves on to the "drawers," who reach into the carcass to pull down the viscera — the heart, intestines, liver, gizzard, and spleen — ever mindful, though, to keep it attached for examination by the US Department of Agriculture agent, usually sitting in a raised chair along the assembly line.

A worker with the evocative job title of "heart cutter" grabs the heart, still attached to the viscera, and cuts away the organ and the valve stem with air scissors. The heart is then sent down a pipe to join its visceral mates in the "giblet cooler," while the valve is thrown in the "river," the water-fed trough that carries away the offal.

The turkey then swings to the "croppers," who remove the bird's feed-filled digestive system. A company document described the cropper's job as follows:

SUMMARY:
Crops are part of the digestive system of the bird. The crops are required to be removed from the bird. While the bird is hanging upside down by both legs, the Cropper will reach under the neck skin and grab both windpipe and the top of the crop and pull down until they come out. Crop and windpipe are sent to offal.

JOB DUTIES:
[1.] Reach under neck skins and grab the windpipe and top of the crop.
[2.] Pull down until both the windpipe and the crop come out of the bird cavity.
[3.] Place the windpipe and crop in the trough to go to offal.

There was a trick to pulling crop — or pulling guts, as it was sometimes called. "Two fingers," Henry Wilkins, who became an expert, explains. "Take this finger up there, pull the skin apart, take both your fingers up there, pull it straight down. The crop's out and you throw it in the trough."

Over and over and over again. "Makes your fingers sore, aching in pain," he says.

In the eyes of their overseers, the repetition of the work — the unloading, the rehanging, the cropping — was key to the men's workplace success. *You see,* the argument went, *what might bore you and me after a while is just fine for these boys.* It also provided a seamless workplace solution for the Louis Rich plant, which had trouble finding and then keeping anyone willing to pull turkey guts all day.

Martin Rich, the younger son of Louis Rich, recalls that "these handicapped boys" were unable to handle skilled work, such as operating machinery, but they excelled at repetitious jobs. "Once you showed them what to do, they could do it," he says. "They were proud of what they were doing."

The din, the feathers, the blood, the guts. Raymond Vaughn did it. And Frank Rodriguez. And Gene Berg. And Tommy Johnson. And James Fowler, who shakes his head at that one, long, standing-over-the-trough memory.

"Nasty job," he says.

The nastiness could extend beyond the work at hand. Perhaps it was too much to have expected hundreds of turkey-plant workers to accept with universal grace the sudden addition of dozens of Texas men with intellectual disability. In through the door in their lab coats and hairnets came Douglas Barco, nicknamed Snoopy, wearing Frankenstein-like shoes to accommodate a physical impairment, and John David Hatfield, forever smiling no matter what was going on, and Willie Levi, seeking connection by telling you again and again about his birthday. Some of these men could work as fast as anybody, while others needed more time, extra instruction, patience.

Retards.

"They didn't quite accept the boys too well," recalls Segreta Davis, who, with her husband, Warren, worked at the bunkhouse for several years, supervising the inhabitants.

Some of the plant workers played pranks on the Texans. Tried to get them to goof up. Goaded them into bad behavior. Pelted them with turkey slime, as plentiful in a turkey plant as snow in an Iowa winter. The abuse became so intense that Warren Davis complained to the plant's superiors, to no avail. He reported it to his bosses down in Goldthwaite, but says he was told not to do anything rash.

Davis could not abide the mistreatment of his boys. One day he rounded them up in the middle of their shift and loaded them back on the bus. He told the plant supervisors that he was keeping his guys home until he received assurance that they'd be treated properly from now on.

Frantic calls between Goldthwaite and Louis Rich ensued. The walkout ended. Point taken.

The truth was, many of the plant's employees admired the work ethic of these men from Atalissa. A guy like Gene Berg? A guy like Frank Rodriguez? They locked into the task put before them, no matter how grisly — no matter how *repetitious* — and got it done.

Dave Meincke, an easygoing man who would rise to become the plant's evisceration supervisor, remembers his first day working turkey, back around 1980. Fresh out of Durant High School, he had no work experience other than at a Hy-Vee supermarket, and now here he was, on the line beside the men from the bunkhouse, blown away by their kindness in teaching him the brutal art of evisceration. They put this soft-spoken kid at ease, taught him to keep up the pace — took him in. Snoopy, and Leonard, and Levi. Bill Murray, always cramming his pocket protector with pens. Henry Wilkins, always prattling on about NASCAR.

"We grew up together," Meincke says.

All the while, the bunkhouse men were making less than their nondisabled colleagues, even though they were no less skilled at some, if not many, of the tasks. Henry's Turkey Service was taking advantage of an exemption in the Fair Labor Standards Act of 1938 — section 14(c) — that was designed to encourage the employment of people with disabilities. With the proper certification from a federal office in Fort Worth, Henry's could pay the men at a rate commensurate with their productivity, rather than at the minimum wage, which in 1974 was $2 an hour. Their wages were supposedly based on their output when compared with that of the nondisabled workers around them, which meant that one of the Henry's men might be earning $1.35 an hour, while a bunkhouse colleague beside him might be earning 70 cents an hour.

The system was ripe for abuse.

Everything went through Texas. The tally of the hours the men worked went to a bookkeeper in Texas. The savings accounts for the men were kept in a Texas bank. Henry's Turkey Service was the representative payee for each of the men, so their Social Security benefits were controlled in Texas. The two hundred dollars for their monthly room and board, a figure that rose steadily through the years, was deducted — in Texas.

This left the men with about sixty-five dollars a month, which was doled out in weekly portions. Ten dollars here and fifteen dollars there, for men who, Meincke recalls, "came in and got it done."

Sometime in midafternoon, after the last of thousands of turkeys had been unloaded, killed, and gutted, the men threw their blood-flecked lab coats into a hamper, stored their rubber boots, and filed back onto a waiting bus. On Wednesdays, they might stop on the way home at the Jack & Jill grocery store for a treat. Willie Levi loved his Mountain Dew. Keith Brown needed his Longhorn tobacco. Gene Berg swore by his Duchess Honey Buns, those massive swirls of pastry straining against frosting-smudged cellophane. And on Fridays, those who drank could buy themselves some beer. Beer was for Friday and Saturday nights only; drink during the week, and that three o'clock wake-up call might split your head open.

Back at the bunkhouse, the men showered before anything else, some of them hustling off the bus to be first under the nozzle; hot water was in short supply. They had dinner. Cleaned up. Took turns vacuuming, sweeping, and changing the bedsheets. In those early years, they were also summoned to the gymnasium to be lectured by a supervisor on that day's performance at the plant. Invariably, there had been a problem or two: a missed shackle, a crop not properly yanked free. If a man did something wrong at the plant, he was made to stand in a corner of the gym. Sometimes you'd see two or three of them with noses pressed against the cold wall, mortified.

"I didn't like that," Segreta Davis says. "They were grown men."

The men were not permitted off the bunkhouse property without supervision, at least not in the beginning. So they killed the time until lights out, listening to country music or watching television, an old western if they were lucky.

Or they might sit out in the Iowa quiet, spraying arcs of tobacco juice into the dirt, maybe, or drawing on orange-tipped cigarettes in their rough hands. Just sit there, in the silence, peering at the bright pinholes in the dark blanket above.

# EIGHT

*Ed George, circa 1974*

*Tap. Tap. Tap-tap-tap. Tap-tap.*

The impassioned hunt and peck of a young social worker disturbed the after-hours quiet. Each press of his finger sent the silvery ball of an IBM Selectric typewriter pivoting and rotating in the creation of his audacious memorandum. He tapped out the name of his superior in Davenport, then the recipient, then the memo's subject:

Henry's Turkey Service, Inc.

Hill Country Farms, Inc.

*Tap. Tap. Tap.*

Outside, the city of Muscatine was bidding good-night to a December-crisp day. Down at the Montgomery Ward department store, where this social worker's mother worked as a clerk, the convenience of artificial Christmas trees was on display — just hook the branches to the pole and get yourself some eggnog. Bud's SuperValu was reminding housewives to save their valuable

S&H Green Stamps, redeemable for that toaster they'd had their eye on, or maybe that hair dryer. And Bart's clothing store was advertising men's bell-bottom pants "in swinging solids and super stripes" — ideal for a stylish Christmas.

But here, in a cramped two-story house across from the county courthouse, a building used as the local office of the Iowa Department of Social Services — later renamed the Department of Human Services — Ed George typed away in the solitary fury of a twenty-four-year-old on a mission. A bantamweight with long blond hair, he was ever mindful of the public trust, of conducting only government business on government time, and so he had waited until day's end to begin writing. True, the issue easily could be justified as central to his job's mission. But he wanted his missive to be unassailable. A clean shot across the bureaucratic bow.

Besides, something else was driving him, something well beyond his state job. You see, Ed George knows this guy, a guy not from Muscatine, or even from Iowa.

Billy.

It's personal.

Ed George's wife was waiting for him at home, and his green AMC Hornet was parked just outside, on darkening Walnut Street. But he had to meet his self-imposed deadline tonight. Over the steady hum of the machine came the hesitant, rhythmless strikes of keys, as words and phrases formed on the page.

"Obscene."

"Exploiting."

"Not since the days of slavery."

George knew this memo he was composing would send his supervisor into apoplectic shock. He did not care.

Ed George was as Muscatine as the mussel shells he threw around while growing up a few blocks from the murky Mississippi. His was a small river city, clinging to its dated claim as "The Pearl Button Capital of the World," a reference to the time when community life centered on that small, round, taken-for-granted fashion accessory: the button.

Panning for thick-shelled mussels, punching out blanks with lathes, transforming these river bits of calcium carbonate into polished gems, and sewing them onto cards for retail displays around the world, offering modesty to a gentleman in woolen pants, or a lady in her Sunday finest. Muscatine men, women, and children, working amid heaps of mussel shells to make and sell buttons, buttons, buttons.

Billions of buttons, all of them nearly, but not quite, the same.

By the time of George's birth in 1949, Muscatine had all but picked the riverbed clean of suitable mussels, while other markets were opening up and cheaper materials being found. In 1937, a device known as the zipper beat the button in the "battle of the fly," and *Esquire* magazine swooned, saying that this innovation would eliminate once and for all the "possibility of unintentional and embarrassing disarray."

So much for Muscatine buttons.

Now this city of twenty-two thousand kept moderately busy as the seat of rural Muscatine County, its elders forever trying to capitalize on its billions-of-buttons past and its slight connection to a young Mark Twain, who spent a few months there in the early 1850s. In the two paragraphs dedicated to Muscatine in *Life on the Mississippi,* the celebrated author marveled at how the city's magnificent sunsets painted the river "with every imaginable dream of color."

"The sunrises are also said to be exceedingly fine," Twain concluded. "I do not know."

■ ■ ■ ■

Young Ed George was so scrawny that Sister Ludmilla at Saint Mathias grade school would force him to sit in the cloakroom every afternoon and eat peanut-butter-and-jelly sandwiches and vitamins, in hopes of putting some height and bulk on him. At Bishop Hayes High School, he developed into a prankster possessed of a rebellious idealism. A fierce Chicago Cubs fan, he once climbed two city water towers to spray-paint "Ernie Banks" — the name of the team's superlative infielder — on their tank bellies. Another time, he submitted an application to enter the Chicago Golden Gloves boxing tournament as an undefeated heavyweight weighing 186 pounds. This was only a sixty-pound exaggeration, and besides, it was absolutely true that he was undefeated, since he had never boxed. The joke led to a comical chain of mishaps and misunderstandings that soon became Muscatine lore — although, thank the Lord, he did not step into the ring.

George graduated from the University of Iowa and became a state social worker stationed in his hometown, in this white house with steep steps and a wide front

155

porch. On its first floor, supervisors and secretaries for the Department of Social Services worked in offices carved from the dining room and living room, while on the second floor, social workers sat at desks squeezed into former bedrooms. Old case files were stored in the bathroom.

He shared the smallest bedroom-cum-office with another social worker named Jan Soboroff, mostly because they were the only employees who didn't smoke. But they also shared the empowering rush that comes from the confluence of youth, fresh independence, and the belief that you can change the world, that you *are* changing the world. Working hard to protect children at risk all morning, heading to Cohn's Newsland for a quick lunch and some can-you-believe-it office gossip, then back to fighting the good fight — Ed and Jan loved every minute.

In his free time, George was also working to establish much-needed group homes and sheltered workshops, sparring with the county board of supervisors and touring area buildings that might, just might, be suitable for people with disabilities. In the spring of that year, in fact, he accepted the invitation of some town officials in Atalissa, about eighteen miles to the north, to consider its old schoolhouse as a possible site for a teenage group home. Although the townspeople seemed well intentioned, the schoolhouse was in disrepair and a long way from being suitable for habitation. He wished Atalissa the best.

Then one autumn night he received a telephone call from Sister Molly Munoz, one of three firebrand Mexican American siblings, all members of the Congregation of the Humility of Mary, who had dedicated their ministry to championing the rights of migrants toiling in the fields and factories of eastern Iowa. While helping migrant families find their place in West Liberty, Sister Molly had heard some ghost-story whispers: about the old schoolhouse in Atalissa, filled with men, all from Texas, all with disability, all working the lousiest jobs at the Louis Rich turkey plant.

Somebody ought to do something, Sister Molly said, which is a nun's way of saying: Ed, you ought to do something.

George didn't quite believe what she had told him, in part because he had been in that building just a few months before, and found it uninhabitable. Effectively deputized by Sister Molly, he drove to Atalissa one afternoon and knocked. Several men appeared at the schoolhouse door and invited him in. Soon he was at the center of a welcoming mob, as more men stepped from the shadows to greet him and show him around their new home. In their generous spirit and eagerness to connect, they reminded him of Billy, of course. Billy.

If we are shaped by those we love, then Billy Bunce helped shape Ed George.

George's childhood summers were often defined by the vacations his family spent with relatives in Maywood, Illinois, including Billy, his first cousin, who was six months older, a little bigger, and much more gregarious, always there with a smile and an extended hand waiting to be received. Through the wondrous grace of boyhood, the two bonded over the Chicago Cubs, the University of Iowa Hawkeyes, and who knows what else. They became Billy and Eddie, Eddie and Billy, two peas in an all-inclusive pod.

Billy's parents had decided early on not to have their only child institutionalized. Although the local public and Catholic schools refused to accept him because of his intellectual disability, he was eventually able to attend the Kennedy School, a Chicago facility for students with special needs, which helped him immensely with his communication and other skills. These days he was living at home, working and socializing at a sheltered workshop, and attending Sunday Mass at Saint Eulalia Catholic Church, where he and his father served as ushers.

Now here was Eddie — Ed George — surrounded by men who reminded him so much of his beloved cousin, in age, friendliness, yearning for connection, and intellectual impairment. But the profound difference in their circumstances took him aback: having spent their formative years in institutions, separated from families, these men were now sleeping in bunk beds shoved into the filthy crannies of an unkempt old schoolhouse.

"I was just in shock," George remembers.

A pissed-off supervisor with a Texas drawl hustled up to ask just who the hell he was and just what the hell he was doing here. George was no fighter; his claim to Golden Gloves glory, after all, had been a prank. But he was a representative of Iowa, a state social worker with a growing sense of something terribly awry, and he had a few questions. His shock only deepened, though, as the supervisor answered with boastful candor: Yep, we get these boys out of the Texas institutions, but we look for ones with no family ties, because families can be meddlesome. Many of them get Social Security, but I don't know too much about that, and on Saturdays we take them out to buy supplies and such, and maybe a movie.

George was flabbergasted. This was 1974. In his worldview, people with disabilities belonged in the community, exercising their basic rights, along with the rest of us. Yet here was this affable man with a honeyed way of speaking, describing indentured servitude as a progressive, beneficent act.

Ed George returned to his Hornet, and wept.

The next morning he reported his Atalissa experience to his supervisors, including the district manager in Davenport, and they seemed to share his outrage. For days and nights afterward, he conducted his own private investigation into this company called Henry's Turkey Service, running up his telephone bill with long-distance calls to learn more about its operations in other states. He lived and breathed Atalissa, confiding in his colleagues, meeting with state legislators, laying out his concerns for the county board of supervisors, only to develop the growing sense that it was all for naught. His superiors were only patronizing him, he suspected, and had no intention of cracking down on an apparent case of human trafficking in Atalissa.

Which is why Ed George, social worker II with the Iowa Department of Social Services, was hunched before an IBM Selectric on this December night. His immediate supervisor had informed him earlier in the day that the district manager was coming from Davenport in the morning to speak with him. The district manager was driving thirty miles? To meet with a grunt social worker? George deduced that the big boss was about to tell him to leave it alone, and not put anything in writing about Henry's Turkey Service. So that is precisely what he was doing: putting it all down on paper before being told not to, in what you might call an act of anticipatory rebellion.

I am concerned that if the Iowa Department of Social Services does nothing to stop corporations such as Henry's Turkey Service, it will be condoning this type of operation by its apathy. If this happens, the Department is, in fact, saying that the principle of normalization, which it has encouraged, does not apply in Iowa. It is saying that the retarded adult does not have a right to a self-directed life, and that future generations of mentally retarded in Iowa will not have the community-based

161

services which they will need. . . .
   Specific Complaints:
Education is not available (basic skills or academic)
No professional services available
Lack of adequate housing
Too few persons supervising
Untrained persons supervising
No religious freedom
No community involvement
No parental involvement
No privacy
No choice in food or clothing selection
No set-up for people to advance into independence
No freedom to quit without threats of being returned to institutions
Lack of recreational activity
No freedom to inter-relate with opposite sex
No say in financial matters
Forced to live in company's house to maintain employment
No choice in where you work or live
No one outside of company with whom you can talk about problems
No accountability for an individual's money spent by company
No provision for outside client advocate . . .

Not since the days of slavery have we had an example of the antithesis of normalization as Henry's has provided. Their list of violations of this principle is endless.

Their residents are deprived of the following:

Family
Home community
Professional service
Education
Involvement with the community
Normalized and adequate housing
Selection of food and clothing
Selection of work experience. . . .

Once the resident becomes an employee of Henry's Turkey Service, he for all practical purposes loses most basic human rights. He loses control of finances, the location where he lives, the type of work he does, and the type of housing in which he must dwell, as well as with whom. If he dislikes any of these arrangements his only way out is to return to an institution. By allowing Texas to ship out their handicapped citizens we are not encouraging the communities in which those adults have a right to live, to develop the needed community-based programs. If you can ship them out, it is cheaper than programming for them. . . .

The idea of implementing any program like this in Iowa is obscene. There is absolutely nothing worth saving in their program. True, we must get more handicapped people employed in the community, and work must be done in this area, but not in Henry's exploiting manner.

When the district manager from Davenport arrived at the cluttered Muscatine office the next morning, George shared his damning conclusion that the Atalissa schoolhouse was a slave-labor camp, a human rights horror in our midst that should be immediately shut down. George also informed the manager that he had laid out his conclusions in a long letter to him, copies of which had been mailed to both him and the Iowa commissioner of social services in Des Moines.

Apoplexy achieved.

The district manager had no choice but to conduct some kind of inquiry, but the findings of his final report were predictable. The Texas company's operation appeared to be legitimate; it had the proper certification to pay their men below minimum wage, and its concern for them seemed genuine.

164

So far, the report noted, "only" one man had run away from the bunkhouse, the district manager noted, and that runaway "was found and flown back to Texas, according to Mr. Johnson, and this is the appropriate handling of this kind of situation, he believes."

The Atalissa schoolhouse may not be "tastefully decorated, in good repair, or maintained in high standards of housekeeping," the district manager wrote — Ed George had not been hallucinating — but this was consistent with the company's philosophy that the men care for themselves and their belongings as much as possible, so, yes, the rooms and floors "are not immaculate or as tidy as might be."

But in general, the men share a "good group spirit" and their quality of life seems acceptable. They receive "adequate" servings of good-quality food, and on Saturdays they walk to the local grocery store and go into "town" — Muscatine — but always with supervision.

Still, the district manager concurred, the men were indeed being segregated, and could benefit from "better community acceptance" and exposure to "social, religious, educational and other opportunities." As a result, he would be appointing a "project monitor" to follow up with the Atalissa schoolhouse, ensuring the men's safety and fair treatment.

The supervisor's overall message was implied rather than stated: No problem here. Let's move on.

More than forty years later, Ed George has forgotten nothing. The threats of a lawsuit from an attorney for Louis Rich, who called him a long-haired son of a bitch. The nagging feeling that it was all a conspiracy, a heartland cut of *The Parallax View,* or *All the President's Men.* The deflating sense of betrayal. Most of all, he remembers the hollowed-out feeling of helplessness. The realization that these men in the Atalissa bunkhouse were, in a way, shackled to a conveyor belt that was moving inexorably toward tragedy.

"I always thought that if people knew, they'd correct it," he says, his voice catching. "To this day, I never understood, and I never will."

George's former office mate, Jan Soboroff, shares his bafflement. She remembers watching the men from Atalissa file out of old school buses in front of the Hy-Vee supermarket in Muscatine, a couple of blocks from her home, to begin their Saturday outing. A chain gang bound together by invisible manacles.

"And we basically had been told: 'Butt out: You're not seeing anything inappropriate,' " Soboroff recalls. "It was pretty disturbing."

After the district manager's report put an end to his holy mission, George mourned. He also moved on, his career of more than forty years dedicated to helping others — working as a social worker, operating the Muscatine County Sheltered Workshop, helping people with mental illness find housing after leaving institutions.

Throughout, George remained close to his cousin, Billy Bunce. He would take Billy to Cubs games and to the Brookfield Zoo, and visit him at the group home he moved into after his parents died. Billy would often ask after Eddie's family and the people he had gotten to know over the years in Muscatine, once the capital of buttons, buttons, buttons.

It didn't matter how many times Billy was softly told that these people had long since passed away. He'd still be sad, and he'd still keep asking, until his own death, in 2013, at the age of sixty-four.

Billy and Eddie, Eddie and Billy. And billions of buttons, all of them slightly different from one another, all of them the same.

# NINE

*John Orange, Robert Penner, and Henry Wilkins, studying photos from their bunkhouse past*

The opening of the crinkled manila envelope releases the musk of cloistered mysteries. Hundreds of photographs skitter across the varnished dark wood, the past spilling from the envelope's mouth. The four men around the dining room table hesitate. But soon they are sorting through the square and rectangular images like partners working on a familiar jigsaw puzzle they're not sure they want to reassemble.

Combined, they gave nearly 150 years to Henry's Turkey Service, and here now are stray snatched moments from their time as Henry's boys, twirling like playing cards before them. Scratch-covered photographs, taken with types of cameras no longer even manufactured, their spectral negatives tucked into small Kodak envelopes labeled "Magic Moments."

"He used to be in the bunkhouse with us," Henry Wilkins says, his finger resting on a frozen face. At seventy years of age, Wilkins remains boyishly lanky, but he has emphysema, and works hard to mask the trouble he has with his balance. "I know him but I can't think of his name. What was his name, Johnny?"

John Orange, fifty-four, the only black man at the table, so disconnected from his roots that no one is sure whether his true surname is Orange or Owens, takes a look. "John . . . Novack," he says.

"John Novack," Wilkins says in confirmation. "He had his fingers . . ."

"Sewed together," Billy Penner says, because these men often finish one another's sentences. "Just like this."

"His fingers were like that," Wilkins agrees, holding up two fingers as though they were one — the hand gesture, also, of inseparability.

The men peer deep into these photos of then. Billy Penner, seventy, stocky, with long white hair swept back, has his trademark toothpick jutting from his remaining teeth. He always keeps several pens arrayed in his shirt pocket and a keychain dangling from his belt, conveying authority, a man in charge of things. His younger and quieter brother, Robert, sixty-six, wears coveralls, and his sparse gray hair is long and wild, forever windblown.

For them, the past is one dark swallow of time. Maybe because it's been so many years, or maybe it's because of their intellectual disability, but they cannot point to a picture and say, This was from a Christmas party in the early '80s, or late '90s, or last December. When Billy Penner says, "I ain't seen him in ages!" he could be talking about months, years, decades.

"Charles Ponzo," says Owens, or Orange. "He used to work in the kitchen."

"He died right in his bed," Billy Penner says. "I tried to wake him up. I don't know what he died of. I didn't ask him. But he died in bed."

"He died in bed," Wilkins says in punctuation.

"He died in bed!" Robert Penner trumpets.

They move on. Here's a woman who used to smoke all of Billy Penner's cigars. Here's Tommy Johnson, sprawled on his bed in coveralls, passed out, and someone says the bosses used to handcuff him to that very bed. Here's a poster of an Elvira-style model in a slinky red negligee, hanging beside a plastic chair in some dingy strip joint they were taken to once. Here's a man they called Oliver Dipshit, for reasons forgotten,

173

but Billy Penner says that Oliver Dipshit "knows how to work, and he knows how to hit, too," speaking as if they were on the evisceration line, still.

Here's the kitchen in the bunkhouse. Here's good old Pete Graffagnino, smiling with his glasses slightly askew, and James Fowler, on a trip to the Adventureland amusement park in Des Moines, and that young woman named Terry, who was one of the nice supervisors over the years, and Willie Levi, and Willie Levi, and Willie Levi, so many pictures of Willie Levi, and that guy who used to wet himself on the assembly line, and Carl Wayne Jones, who had a brother named Leon, who was sent to a turkey plant in South Carolina, and a glowering Leonard Barefield, whose verbal skills were so poor that few ever knew what he was saying, but everyone listened, he was that strong.

"Hey, this right here was in the parade," Wilkins says. He holds a photograph of one of the parade's floats: a long trailer with more than a dozen men — Henry's boys, many in baseball caps, some wearing suspenders — sitting at picnic tables arranged on a flatbed gussied up with a fringe of silver tinsel.

"All of us was in the parade," Billy Penner says.

"All of us was in the parade," Wilkins repeats.

"All of us was on a trailer," Billy Penner says.

"A van pulled us," Wilkins says. "That's Atalissa Days."

"That's Atalissa Days," Billy Penner repeats.

Atalissa Days.

The people of Atalissa took their time warming to the men who had moved into the old schoolhouse, and who could blame the locals for being leery? For one thing, the population of their little hamlet had ballooned overnight with these new residents — fifty, sixty, seventy of them — and for another thing, they were clearly not from around here. Also, they were . . . how do you say it? Not quite right.

What was conjured in the minds of most Atalissans by this sudden influx of not-quite-right men? What did they think when they caught glimpses of Henry Wilkins and John Owens, Willie Levi and the Penner brothers? What latent images and old stories, stray impressions and corny jokes, rose from the deep recesses of the nondisabled

175

collective memory?

It reaches back, way back, to ancient Sparta, whose citizens left for dead any newborn male showing signs of physical or mental feebleness. To the medieval jesters, in jingling hats evoking the ears of an ass, prancing about for the enjoyment of kings. To the days when the city of Hamburg relegated people to a tower nicknamed the "idiot's cage," and Renaissance artists might use the facial characteristics associated with Down syndrome to depict cherubs — and, on occasion, the infant Jesus.

The passing generations struggled to categorize people with intellectual disability — to identify their place — as in this ancient legal definition: "He that shall be said to be a sot and idiot from his birth, is such a person who cannot count or number twenty pence, nor tell who was his father or mother, nor how old he is, so as it may appear that he hath no understanding or reason for what shall be his profit or what for his loss."

They were called innocents. And cretins — from the Swiss French word for Christian. And simpletons, like "Simple Simon," who met a pieman going to the fair. And idiots, who, like Johnny in Wordsworth's poem "The Idiot Boy," were never quite lost, never quite found. When his mother, Betty, asks Johnny what he has heard and seen after a night spent in the forest, he speaks as if for the natural world:

And thus, to Betty's question, he
Made answer, like a traveller bold,
(His very words I give to you,)
"The cocks did crow to-whop, to-whoo,
And the sun did shine so cold!"
— Thus answered Johnny in his glory,
And that was all his travel's story.

In the years after the American Revolution, these idiots, for that was what they were called, were just another strand, slightly frayed, in the rural community fabric. Those fortunate enough were cared for by families and neighbors, while most were indistinguishable from the poor; that is, invisible.

By the mid-1840s, the French physician Édouard Séguin was asserting that physical exercise and sensory development could improve the cognitive abilities of idiots, while the American physician Samuel G. Howe proclaimed that idiots deserved care and instruction. "Their bodies were fed and clad," Howe wrote. "As for minds, they seemed to have none. They were therefore kept out of sight of the public as beings, the presence of whom seemed only to do harm to the beholders."

The Massachusetts School for Idiotic Children and Youth, a family-like facility established by Howe in Boston, became the template for other schools around the country. Its purpose: to train and return students to their communities as contributing members of society. But with few jobs available for the graduates of such schools, these institutions shifted in purpose from education to custodial care of those now commonly referred to as "feeble-minded." Residents were expected to work on the school farm, make furniture, and do whatever else was needed to support the facility and the many jobs dependent on the institutional model.

By the early twentieth century, the pseudoscience of eugenics had taken hold, with its adherents arguing that these morons, for that was what they were called, posed enough of a threat to the country's superior American stock that they should be sterilized and perhaps even banished to an island somewhere. A 1912 case study by the psychologist Henry Herbert Goddard purportedly traced the descendants of an American Revolutionary War soldier whose pseudonymous surname — Kallikak — combined the Greek words for beauty (*kallos*) and bad (*kakos*). The Kallikak patriarch was said to have fathered children with both his virtuous Quaker wife and a feebleminded barmaid. His "legitimate" progeny became upstanding citizens, Goddard wrote, while the "illegitimate" products of his union with the barmaid tended to be criminals and dull-witted wastrels. His methodology would not withstand scrutiny, and Goddard would later repudiate some of his findings. Still, in an era when Kansans staged "Fitter Family" contests at their state fair to celebrate "a goodly heritage of well-bred families, free of defects," the Kallikak narrative seemed to provide a hereditary link between feeblemindedness and immoral behavior.

This supposed link provided justification for the sterilization of the likes of Carrie Buck, a plump seventeen-year-old girl with short-cropped dark hair who had been raped while in foster care. After she gave birth at the Virginia Colony for Epileptics and Feebleminded, the state determined that Buck, her mother, and her newborn daughter were intellectually deficient, and it petitioned to have her sterilized as a way to test a new Virginia law, the Racial Integrity

Act of 1924.

In his majority opinion upholding that law, United States Supreme Court associate justice Oliver Wendell Holmes wrote, in part: "It is better for all the world, if instead of waiting to execute degenerate offspring for crime, or to let them starve for their imbecility, society can prevent those who are manifestly unfit from continuing their kind."

Carrie Buck was sterilized and released. Her daughter, Vivian, died of intestinal complications at the age of eight, and Carrie herself died at the age of seventy-six in 1983. Both were of normal intelligence.

*Do you know why little Moron was standing on the street corner holding a loaf of bread? Because he was waiting for the traffic JAM!*

*Do you know why Little Moron punched his eyes out? Because he had always wanted to have a BLIND DATE!*

*Eight little morons went to bed, but only seven of them got up — 'cause they just set the alarm for SEVEN!!*

People laughed and laughed at "retard jokes" like these, found in a popular 1940s comic book that centered on the antics of "Little Moron," a dull-eyed, bucktoothed character with a bad haircut. They laughed, too, when cartoon characters mimicked tragic Lennie from Steinbeck's *Of Mice and Men.* ("Which way did he go, George? Which way did he go?") All the while, experts recommended that the targets of this brand of humor should remain institutionalized. Better for them, their parents were told, and better for you.

Soon, though, newspaper and magazine exposés were revealing the execrable conditions in institutions reserved for the mentally retarded. Soon the country was reading a 1953 book by Dale Evans, the wife of singing cowboy Roy Rogers, called *Angel Unaware,* about the couple's daughter, Robin, who was born with Down syndrome and died before the age of two. Evans described Robin as a "gift from God" — a precious being who belonged in her family's embrace, and not in an institution.

Evans's work became a manifesto of liberation for many families trapped by the accepted wisdom that having a child with a disability signaled a hereditary, even moral, failing. At book signings and performances, the author noticed a marked increase in the attendance of children with Down syndrome and their families, as if emerging together from behind a musty veil of shame. And in the face of each child, she saw her Robin.

But as Roy Rogers and Dale Evans, then among the world's most famous couples, argued that children with disabilities belonged at home, the demand for residential facilities was on the rise — at least in Texas. The state converted a hospital in Abilene into a state school, and opened other institutions in Denton and Lufkin. In 1951, Texas had about three thousand state school residents; by 1962, that number had grown to nearly ten thousand.

Nationally, though, the emphasis slowly shifted from warehousing residents to returning them to the community, where their potential could be nurtured through education, recreation, and training. Those who had long been kept out of sight were suddenly in the spotlight. Here, in 1963, was a movie called *A Child Is Waiting,* with Burt Lancaster and Judy Garland, followed five years later by *Charly,* starring Cliff Robertson. And here was American royalty: President John F. Kennedy, appointing a panel on mental retardation whose legislative recommendations would help lead to deinstitutionalization; Senator Robert F. Kennedy, decrying the unspeakable conditions in the state institutions of New York; Eunice Kennedy Shriver, championing the rights and joys of the mentally retarded with the establishment of Camp Shriver, which would evolve into the Special Olympics.

The country knew these Kennedy siblings were motivated, at least in part, by their sister, Rosemary, who was mentally retarded. That was still the preferred term in the early 1970s, when the television reporter Geraldo Rivera exposed an abominable Staten Island asylum called Willowbrook, and the creation of outpatient treatment programs, sheltered workshops, and assisted-living arrangements helped remove people from the stultifying confines of institutions.

Court jesters and idiots in cages, Simple Simon and cherubs with Down syndrome, the Kallikaks and Carrie Buck, the Little Moron and the angel unaware, the girl down the street and the son just dropped off at a state school. The sister of the martyred president. These were the images and connections percolating in the collective subconscious of the people of Atalissa, as they adjusted to their new neighbors on the hill.

At first, the men remained separate, forbidden by their supervisors to leave the bunkhouse property. They existed as if in a snow globe, to be observed more as curios than to be received as neighbors. You might see a couple of the men sitting on a swing, or tossing a ball around, or puttering about the yard, transforming the grounds into a floral spectacle at springtime, a glittering light display come the holidays. On Fridays, you might run into them at the small market in town, a handful at a time and always under supervision, buying sodas and snacks and maybe six-packs of beer. On the occasional weekend you might find them exploring the wonders of the relatively new Muscatine Mall, although they were often instructed to replenish their toiletries first before stopping for ice cream.

Here they were, at the bowling alley and the movie theater, among us but apart. Leave it to children and Christmas, then, to pierce that translucent snow-globe divide.

It began with local kids daring to come onto the grounds to play with the children of bunkhouse supervisors, only to wind up joining the men in throwing a ball around, or taking a lazy evening's rock on the swing. As word of these innocuous playdates spread, some trepidation evaporated, making room for a kind of guarded acceptance. But the gauzy goodwill of the Christmas season is what allowed Atalissans to fully claim the men of Henry's Turkey Service as their own.

Christmas had always been the central day on the T. H. Johnson calendar, especially when it came to the state school boys. Just as he had done in Goldthwaite, Johnson spared no expense in creating an outsize Christmas celebration for the men, as if to compensate for the rest of a year spent working blood-simple jobs, for little pay and far from home.

The bunkhouse supervisors were instructed to go all out. Someone would be dispatched to a nursery in Wilton to find the tallest tree that could fit in the cavernous gymnasium, but always with enough room for a treetop ornament. After each man filled out a list, a couple of Henry's employees scoured the stores in Muscatine and Iowa City to find the items, then spent long hours wrapping gifts for sixty or seventy men — so many gifts that Johnson sometimes hired locals to assist with the wrapping. As the days passed, the pile of presents beneath the tree would rise and topple over, but the men never peeked, never snuck in to shake a present and try to guess what was inside. There were rules.

The drab gymnasium became a holiday wonderland, with the rafters draped in garlands and lights, the cinder-block walls adorned with name-inscribed stockings, and that massive tree soaring toward the ceiling. Here was Gene Berg's stocking, and John Hatfield's, and Frank Rodriguez's, and Raymond Vaughn's, and don't worry, Levi, yours is here somewhere. There would be food, and soda, and beer, plenty of beer, and sentimental Christmas carols oozing from a stereo system.

Then one year the town of Atalissa received a cordial invitation into the snow globe. To everyone, from Henry's Turkey Service: Please join us for a Christmas open house.

Flattered, curious, and a little apprehensive, the town returned its RSVP: Yes.

The men put on their "Cadillac clothes" — the nickname given to their finest threads, kept in cubbyholes in a back office — and played the perfect hosts, handing out small Christmas treats to their guests. They could not wait to show their new friends where and how they lived, now that the company had invested some money in the schoolhouse: an updated kitchen; a laundry room; a Jacuzzi; a barbecue pit; a heated garage; even a few playful dachshunds darting about. They seemed to want for nothing.

Dennis Hepker, a local farmer, businessman, and proud member of the West Liberty Jaycees, felt the flush of envy the moment he walked through the schoolhouse door. Here he was, a young bachelor, living with few amenities in a big old farmhouse several miles outside town — and these men had a big television, a pool table, exercise equipment. Just about everything a man could desire, short of female companionship.

There was even a barber chair for the men to sit in for their haircuts, given regularly by a barber from West Liberty. Better this, maybe, than having dozens of these fellows with intellectual disability descend on his shop on a busy Saturday.

"I was living on popcorn and Falstaff," Hepker remembers. "I thought these guys had it made."

Their Christmas parties became an annual highlight in Atalissa, filled with dancing and drinking and merriment. Executives from the Louis Rich plant made appearances. Local women dressed as if for a semiformal event. Names would be drawn, and each man would be called up to receive his gifts, which ranged from the practical (socks, underwear) to the cozy (handmade quilts, homebaked cookies) to the personalized. Vaughn liked his country music tapes, Wilkins his Jack Daniel's.

These early Christmas gatherings made warm first impressions on the townspeople of Atalissa that would endure: a clean and friendly household; a family atmosphere created for those with no families of their own; men with disabilities being given a purpose in life, working hard and paying their own way. And did you see the look on Levi's face when he opened his present? Priceless.

Having witnessed such goodwill and such good works, few residents put much stock in two investigative reports about Henry's Turkey Service that appeared in the *Des Moines Register* in late 1979, two days before Christmas. The main story, with the arresting headline of "Retarded Texans Labor in Iowa Turkey Plant," began:

ATALISSA, IA. — Sixty retarded Texans, 1,000 miles from home, will spend Christmas here as many of them have spent the last four years, living in an abandoned school-turned-bunkhouse.

The men pay $350 a month room and board to sleep on sagging iron bunks and eat in a Quonset-hut mess hall.

They'll feast on turkey Christmas day; ironically, because it is the holiday bird that brought these men to Iowa in the first place. They're employees of Henry's Turkey Service, a Texas labor broker that legally hires the men out to turkey farms and processors across the country at half the federal minimum wage.

All of the men are retarded and many of them are former residents of Texas institutions.

In Iowa, they work for Louis Rich Foods in West Liberty, one of the nation's largest turkey processors.

After deductions for room, board, supervision and a ration of beer provided by Henry's, the men get less than $70 a month.

The men sleep together, eat together, ride to work together, apparently giving up many basic choices in return for their jobs and room and board.

On the job, they work side by side with other Rich employees. But while Rich workers earn $4.58 an hour and up, the Texans are paid $1.45 an hour. Rich pays Henry's more, but just how much more isn't known. . . .

The stories, written by Margaret Engel and Mike McGraw, captured the disarming Texas charm of the man behind the program, T. H. Johnson: his soft green eyes and

189

syrupy way of speaking, his seemingly bottomless reservoir of patience — except when it came to government regulations, which he said wasted money and did more harm than good. Johnson described his operation as a threat to bureaucrats and busybodies who would rather see people with disabilities doing "Mickey Mouse things like packing little plastic forks and spoons into little plastic bags."

The *Register* reporters also interviewed several of the men, though always with a Henry's supervisor present to stop them from mentioning wages. Some of the men expressed satisfaction, even joy, with their lives. Others seemed to ache with homesickness. "I want to go home for good and see my mamma," said one of the men, L. C. Hall. He was twenty-seven.

The stories reported that various government agencies, including the federal Department of Labor, were conducting inquiries into the men's compensation and living conditions — the very same concerns raised five years earlier by Ed George, the passionate Iowa social worker whose damning memorandum had been ignored almost as soon as it was written.

History repeated. The government inquiries and the newspaper's exposé changed almost nothing. If anything, they prompted Henry's Turkey Service to solicit letters of support from a few grateful parents:

I am very pleased with Mike's improvement since he has been under the supervision of Hill Country Farms. His jobs at the various turkey farms and turkey processing plants have had a good effect upon him, as follows: (1) given him worthwhile work to do; (2) given him self-confidence and happiness by being busy; (3) taught him how to dress properly & take care of his personal grooming. . . .

John has really improved and now has a future to look forward to. He is excited about his capabilities and all the new and exciting things he can do. Without your program, he would not have the clothes or medical attention he needs. His behavior has greatly improved since being at Hill Country Farms and he has a sense of worth. . . .

This letter is to let you know that I am pleased with the program and the job that Keith is involved in. The last four years have shown a marked improvement in his behavior, maturity, and knowledge. The proper supervision and housing he receives, plus the fact that he feels he is earning his living, have made him much happier. . . .

The men in the schoolhouse were now accepted as Atalissans. They walked in pairs, buddied up, along the never-busy streets of a town small enough to be a movie set: the train tracks, the post office, the struggling grocery store, the two churches matched by two bars, the modest houses, all framed by fields of corn and soy.

They greeted people by name, even if Carol's name wasn't "Cheryl" — a friendly misunderstanding that went both ways. John Hatfield, a slip of a man who viewed life with a grin and a slight tilt of the head, was called "Smiley." Big, square-jawed Gene Berg, who often carried a boom box on his shoulder, was "the good-looking one."

On Friday afternoons, after another brutal week of unloading and eviscerating turkeys, more than a few of the men hustled into the bunkhouse, showered, and rushed out. Maybe to while away some time at the small grocery and gas station on Route 6, where much of their sixty-five dollars a month was spent on soda and tobacco, chips and Honey Buns. Or maybe to one of the two bars, the Corner Tap or the Old University, for a couple of drinks, some more potent than others.

Give me a beer, Willie Levi would tell Poopsie the bartender, down at the Corner Tap. "But this would mean a root beer," she says. "And just one. Because two would get him hyper."

The men loved to socialize, yes, but most of all, they loved to dance. To hold a woman's body, or just her hands, for an Elvis-infused minute or two, even if it was under the watchful eye of a half-smiling husband leaning against the bar, gripping his long-neck Bud. They liked country and western, they liked oldies, they liked just about anything with a beat they could move to, especially when the moment was enhanced by whiffs of perfume.

Vada Baker, who remembers with a smile how one of them said, helpfully, "Mrs. Baker, you're getting fat," is forever indebted to the men for teaching her the Texas two-step. She repeats, almost verbatim, what more than a half-dozen local women recall: "And if you danced with one of them, you danced with all of them."

They could play coy, though. Jeff Long and his best friend, Brady Watson, were a bit younger than the others, and saw themselves as the schoolhouse bad boys. Watson adopted the nickname of "Texas Wolf," while Long called himself "Lone Wolf." They'd lean against the walls of the bar or community center, feigning disinterest in dancing while just waiting to be asked. Like this one time . . .

"I was standing by the door," Long remembers, "and Brady said, 'Watch out, you might get grabbed.' " And he was.

"Bye, Jeff, nice knowing ya," Watson remembers saying. "Send me a postcard."

But Watson got drawn onto the dance floor too. "Many a times I got grabbed," he says. "By many other ladies too."

Long adds one more detail. "He had a beer in his hand, and I had a Pepsi in my hand."

"Tattletale," Watson says, pulling his red, white, and blue baseball cap over his eyes. "Rebel," it says.

The men were treated like anyone else, in the full understanding of this tired phrase. Most of the town accepted and even embraced them, while others could not abide them. A few locals dreaded to see any of the "boys" walk through the tavern door to whoop it up, dancing by themselves if they

194

had to, banging on tambourines, trying to fit in.

"Some people frowned on them, some people shunned them," says Lorna Pahl, who used to deliver the shopper newspaper in town. "They liked to socialize with people, and some people didn't want to be bothered by that."

Sometimes the men reeked of turkey-plant slaughter. Sometimes they interrupted conversations between friends trying to catch up over a few beers. Sometimes the locals didn't want to hear about what Gene Berg and his John Deere all-terrain vehicle had been doing that day, or about Willie Levi's birthday coming up again, or how much beer Henry Wilkins expects to drink at the Muscatine County Fair.

Sometimes, Atalissa just did not want a hug.

But don't think for a second that you could come in from Wilton, or Durant, or Muscatine, have a few drinks at the bar, and then start making fun of these distinctive characters on the dance floor. If anyone ever teased or picked on the men — well, that did not happen. "They were stopped immediately," Carol O'Neill, also called Cheryl, says. "The townspeople took care of them."

These were the Henry's boys, yes, but they were Atalissa's boys as well. "Even though they were adult men, they were boys to us," O'Neill says. "They were, like, our boys."

That is why the men always "hit" the target when they threw balls at the dunk tank set up by the local Jaycees at the Muscatine County Fair every summer. No Jaycee would ever say the game was rigged, oh no. But you could, if you wanted to, trip the device whether the ball hit the little dot or not, sending some insurance agent or John Deere salesman into the drink. The Henry's boys never missed.

And why the Jaycees always gave the boys an early tour of the haunted house they built for charity every Halloween. The men looked forward to being frightened. Willie Levi would be brave, so brave, walking up to the house, and chickening out at the last second. He'd agree to go inside only if Dennis Hepker accompanied him, and then he was clear up inside the man's jacket. "But when he got back, he was very brave," Hepker recalls. "He was just telling them what a great experience it was."

And why a local woman named Dorothy Garvin, a diminutive, grandmotherly woman who taught Sunday school and folded the weekly bulletins at the Zion

Lutheran Church, gave John Hatfield the use of a three-wheeled cycle. He would pedal up and down, policing the streets and collecting litter that he'd toss into a basket attached to the trike. After a while, you couldn't find so much as a candy wrapper on the Atalissa ground.

The city council was so grateful for Hatfield's civic sensibility that they voted to grant him special status. They attached a strobe light to the back of the trike, and presented him with a plaque.

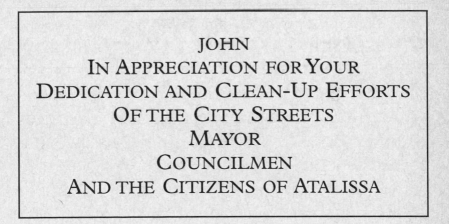

JOHN
IN APPRECIATION FOR YOUR
DEDICATION AND CLEAN-UP EFFORTS
OF THE CITY STREETS
MAYOR
COUNCILMEN
AND THE CITIZENS OF ATALISSA

It was John Hatfield's proudest moment.

When Hatfield's trike was stolen one day, the outraged word spread to all parts of Muscatine County. It didn't take long. Soon a police officer was driving Hatfield to a house in West Liberty with an item on its front porch.

*That the bike?*
*Uh-huh.*
*Well, then. Go get it.*
Case solved.

The men became as Atalissa-present as the huge grain elevator near the railroad tracks, or the weekly euchre games down at the Corner Tap. You might answer a door knock one December night, as the postmaster, Dyann Roby, did, to find a clutch of Henry's boys singing Christmas carols. Even after saying good-night and closing the door, her tears continued.

At moments like these you were reminded of how removed the men were from their Texas homes, and how alone. Only a fortunate few had families they could visit come Christmas, or during the brief summer break. Through correspondence with letters, the company would try to facilitate these reunions, as long as they did not disrupt the productivity of the turkey-plant assembly line.

Every now and then a concerned parent would send a letter to the company's office in Goldthwaite, asking about a son's welfare — and receive a letter in return. In August 1975, for example, a company representative told a worried mother that her son gets "real homesick" at times and could use a telephone call from home to cheer him up. "He will get to come home for Christmas, but he needs all the encouragement you can give him," the representative wrote.

A year later, the mother received another letter from the company, providing an encouraging update. Her son had matured in his behavior and was no longer nearly as homesick. In fact, the company representative wrote, "He seemed happy."

Based, then, on the whims of their employers and the close proximity of a turkey-processing plant, the men now called Atalissa, and the state of Iowa, home.

Atalissa: a small town that, each year, staged an annual weekend celebration of itself, a way of announcing to all concerned that despite the closing of the high school, despite being bypassed by the construction of Interstate 80, despite the various socio-economic forces nudging it toward becoming another spectral community of the Midwest, we're still here.

These yearly events, called Atalissa Days, were equal parts neighborly silliness and community pride. Antique cars and modern fire engines, bed races and horse-drawn carriages, neighborhood floats and *Hee Haw* satires and an outhouse plopped on top of a tractor, with a sign saying PROGRESS: DO-

ING TWO JOBS AT ONCE.

At some point, the men of Henry's Turkey Service became as central to the annual Atalissa Days parade as the grand marshal and the 4-H contingent. Gene Berg might ride down the main street on a John Deere utility vehicle. Other men might sit stoically on floats. Many dressed as clowns.

A local woman named Wilma Rock, known for her big heart, sewed those clown costumes. Taking the men on as her special assignment, she also made sure they received homemade gifts at Christmas and something nice on their birthdays. But those costumes — here they'd come down the street in crazy wigs and white gloves and grease paint, earning cheers and laughs from spectators. Willie Levi with his tambourine. John Hatfield dressed as a girl. Tommy House in a conical hat, the black Pagliaccio of the cornfields. ("We had that white paint all over our face," House recalled.)

Did these costumes set them up for ridicule? Or did it make them feel accepted, welcomed into the local foolishness? After all, Wilma Rock was always beside them, also decked out as a clown, her gloved hand twirling a silly, silly umbrella.

Oh, Atalissa Days.

■ ■ ■ ■

Henry Wilkins holds up the Atalissa Days snapshot to show to the other men gathered around the dining room table. John Orange, and Billy Penner, and Robert Penner.

Did they dress up as clowns?

Billy Penner and Wilkins say nothing. Robert Penner says no-o-o-o-o-o, but Owens says yes, and laughs.

The photograph of clowns on a silver-fringed float is tossed onto the table without further comment, soon to disappear under other stop-time moments.

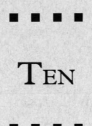

# TEN

*Terry Senn in Atalissa, mid-1980s*

Dinnertime at a McDonald's that could be anywhere, so universal are the aromas of sizzling beef, the discomfort of bolted-down furniture, the absence of anything to savor. This particular McDonald's sits beside an interstate that cuts past a small South Carolina city called Newberry, home to a massive Louis Rich meat-processing plant. The drive-thru crackles and deep-fryer beeps compete with the television secured to the wall, which is shouting the news that half of Buffalo is paralyzed by a freak November storm.

"Just look at this snow!" a manic reporter is bellowing on screen. "I can't blink!"

In the half light of the hard-plastic dining area, a quiet conversation eventually turns to mention of a man named Alford Busby, one of the Henry's boys. He worked on the live dock at the West Liberty plant, lived in the Atalissa bunkhouse, and, very early one frigid morning, ran away.

Hearing that name — Alford Busby — the woman at the table asks, "Do you know I was involved in that?"

And with her "that" the beeps and crackles of a McDonald's beside an interstate seem to fall away, replaced by a reverent silence.

Alford Busby.

"This is what has shaped me into the person that I am today," she says.

Her name is Terry Senn. She is fifty-four, a brown-haired, youthful grandmother with the air of one who accepts that, yes, life can be hard, but no one said it would be otherwise. She finds comfort in Scripture and the music of Reba McEntire. She's from Little Mountain, South Carolina. She'll get by.

Seeing no clear path after high school, Senn went to work at the Louis Rich plant here in Newberry, weighing and packaging turkeys on the production line, and getting to know a couple of young people who were supervising some workers living in a mobile home–style bunkhouse across the street from the plant — all with intellectual disability, all from Texas, all employed by a company called Henry's Turkey Service.

Before long, Senn was spending some of her free time at this South Carolina bunkhouse. Before long, one of her new friends, Vicky Benton, was moving back to an Iowa town called Atalissa, where her parents, Leon and Shirley Benton, were supervising a bunkhouse packed with men with disabilities. Then came a call from Vicky, presenting a life-altering proposition:

*Do you want to come work with these special men here in Iowa? The company will even pay for your flight.*

Senn was already leaning toward a career dedicated to people with special needs, and now here was an opportunity for some hands-on experience. It was also a chance to leave the one-horse town of Newberry and see the world. Look out, Iowa, here comes Terry. She was twenty-one.

On the drive from the airport, Senn took in the flat nothingness of the Iowa landscape. Nowhere near as lush as her hometown corner of South Carolina. And if Newberry was a one-horse town, well, by the looks of it, Atalissa didn't even have a horse. But the farm town did have this old schoolhouse, home to several dozen men who needed help navigating the world.

She moved into a trailer at the back end of the property and began to work as a troubleshooter, helping supervise the assembly line at the plant, stepping in to spell a man if he needed a bathroom break, making sure that shackles did not swing past empty.

Senn joined others in believing that the men in the bunkhouse had it made. The building seemed relatively clean and warm, and everyone seemed relatively happy. She was twenty-one, she emphasizes again, and didn't know much. "The men were not treated with dignity and respect, as in an age-appropriate manner," she says in retrospect. "No one had any formal training. You did the best you could."

Leon and Shirley Benton, a Missouri couple who had assumed the roles of house supervisors — house parents, really — harbored genuine affection for their adult charges. There were no more dress-down lectures in the gymnasium after every workday, no more making a man stand in the corner with his nose pressed to the cold wall. Leon, his combed-back white hair offset by thick black glasses, could be stern when the occasion warranted, and Shirley, her brown hair coiffed, was a stickler for clean bedsheets and spick-and-span rooms. But they also fostered a one-big-family atmosphere. Judging by photographs from that time, Shirley was everywhere: shooting pool with Charles Ponzo, dancing with Jeff

Long, playing a board game with James Fowler — and, most often, just enjoying cups of coffee and a cigarette or two with a few guys gathered around her, the way a mother might with her children after another whirlwind weary day.

"The nicest crew chiefs we had," Willie Levi says.

"Leon Benton was nice to me," Gene Berg agrees. And then he says what all the men say, in their matter-of-fact way of mourning. "Shirley Benton died," he says. "Died of cancer."

Yes, she did. In 1992.

Also appearing in many of those snapshots is a sprite of a young woman who could be fifteen or twenty-five, hard to tell. Here she is, working in the garden behind the school-house, smiling in front of the Christmas tree, sitting on a man's lap and sharing a joke. Posing arm in arm with one man after another, everyone's crush, and you could just hear them saying: Me next, Terry, it's my turn for a picture with you.

Terry Senn grows silent as she studies some of the photographs splayed across the McDonald's table. She smiles the smile that dams tears.

"Tippy was the cook," she says. "This is Tippy right here. There was another little guy named Ponzo. They were both just as sweet as could be. Loved Ponzo to death."

Henry Wilkins; always stirring stuff up. Leonard Barefield; his nickname of "Big Bear" suited him perfectly. Willie Levi; that man had a musical gift. So many men she hasn't seen in so many years, men once as close to her as brothers, for whom she would spend days and days shopping and wrapping Christmas presents. One time, she drove a half-dozen guys with nothing to do on their summer break to a Barnum-like tourist spot in Wisconsin called the House on the Rock. These Atalissa vacationers forgot all about hanging birds and pulling crop as they took in the attraction's singing robots and flying angels, automated instruments and theater organs and "the world's largest indoor carousel" — all in a house balanced, like theirs, on a precipice.

Terry Senn was the mother of a baby boy and married, unsteadily, to one of the Benton couple's sons, but still she kept working at the bunkhouse, never giving much thought to the daunting responsibilities for which she had received no formal training. Her common sense and heart guided her.

Rising early and driving the men to the plant. Ensuring the smooth running of the evisceration line. Overseeing lunch in the plant cafeteria. Returning to the line, to the feathers-and-blood repetition. Henry, stop your fooling. Levi, you need a bathroom break? Almost done, boys, almost done. A stop at the Jack & Jill grocery store in town for some soda and beer, some snacks and some tobacco. Back to the bunkhouse. Raymond, you take your shower yet? Come on, now. Who left this mess in the kitchen? What're we doing this weekend, boys? Anyone up for bowling?

Terry Senn gives a half smile as she returns in her mind, her McDonald's coffee now a tepid gray. These were her Atalissa Days.

Tippy. Ponzo. Snoopy. Raleigh Binnion. Cullen Murphy. Pete Graffagnino. Alford Busby.

Alford Busby.

And she asks: "Do you know I was involved in that?"

Alford Busby is the ever-present blur of the bunkhouse, defining yet undefined. Records and memories conflict. He was born on October 22, 1942; October 22, 1943; or September 13, 1949. His middle initial was "J," or maybe it was "E." He was tall, or he was short; he had a pronounced limp, or he didn't limp at all; he was a puppy dog, following around supervisors he called Mama and Papa, or he was a fiercely proud black man, who grumbled that the boss, TH, favored the white guys.

But Terry Senn remembers Alford Busby as if he were sitting beside her. About five feet five, a little stocky, and with a smile that you could not resist returning. Had a good sense of humor, loved attention, but hated those times when you got on to him. He'd lower his head, pop his bottom lip out, and give a pout that would just melt you.

"One of my favorites, in all honesty," she says.

He was an expert crop puller, a very good worker. That is, when he wanted to work. One time he told a supervisor he didn't want to touch any turkeys that morning, so the supervisor said fine, you just sit there in the snow while I catch these turkeys. After a while, though, Alford Busby had had enough.

*Papa, could I catch some turkeys?*

*I thought you was crippled.*

*I got cold in my ass.*

*All right then, come along.*

*Okay, Papa.*

On another day — the day before *the* day — in January 1987, Alford Busby did some-

212

thing egregious at the turkey plant. Terry Senn can't quite recall his transgression, although he might have urinated in the "river," the trough that receives the offal. Stipulated: Urinating in the workplace, especially when in close proximity to food products, cannot be abided. It needed to be addressed.

That evening, Senn's father-in-law and no-nonsense supervisor, Leon Benton, told her to handle it, since the incident had occurred on her watch.

*Okay. But how do I handle it?*

*You need to talk to him, you need to be very firm with him, and you need to tell him that after supper he has to go to bed.*

Senn may have scolded a man or two now and then, but she had never disciplined any of them. She did what she was told. She was young, and up for the challenge.

Where did she dress down Alford Busby? Was it in the dining room before supper, with just the two of them sitting at one of the long boardinghouse tables that always featured bottles of Tabasco sauce, the bunkhouse condiment of choice? Was it in the gymnasium, under the steer skull and other Texas memorabilia hanging above the massive radiator? Was it in his room, while he sat, compliant, humiliated, at the foot of

213

his bed?

No, wait. It was in the back office. That's where it was. Away from the other men. Senn had no desire to embarrass Busby publicly.

Her exact words have long since gone from her head. But she remembers coming down hard on the man, probably too hard, cussing and fussing at him and telling him that after supper he needed to go straight to his room. He was in his late thirties or early forties, who knows, and she was sending him to his room. No TV.

Head lowered. Bottom lip popped out.

Oh, Alford.

"Should we have done that?" Senn asks, already knowing the answer. "Probably not. These were grown men. You don't punish grown men. Although there has to be natural consequences for your actions too. So. You know?"

That ended the matter, she thought. Tomorrow was Friday, the close to another long week. More trucks would be waiting outside the plant. January winds would ripple the feathers of anxious turkeys, the shackles would swing, life would go on.

When Friday's sun rose to reveal the Iowa tundra, the temperature was six degrees below zero, and Alford Busby was gone.

■ ■ ■ ■

Men had fled the bunkhouse before. If you ask Gene Berg, for example, how many times he ran away, he holds up several fingers.

"Six," he says proudly, as though counting medals.

The first time was after his father's premature death, at forty-nine, in 1981. The family paid for Berg's flight back to Texas for the funeral. But when it came time to return to Atalissa, he did not want to go back to days of killing turkeys and nights stuck in an old schoolhouse. He wanted to stay with his mother, who, though heartbroken, had to tell him this could not be.

"Okay, Gene, you need to go back," Wanda Berg LaGrassa, his mother, recalls saying. "You need to go back to work because I do."

"I didn't want to go back," he says now.

Sometime after her very reluctant son flew back to Iowa, she received a telephone call from his employer, T. H. Johnson; a "real stern type of person," she recalls. He had distressing news. Her Gene had either disappeared from the bunkhouse or had never made it back from the funeral.

Her frantic worries ended when a truck driver, calling from a rest stop in Dallas, explained that he had picked up her son hitchhiking on Interstate 35, and was treating him to a meal. She rushed fifty miles that night to the truck stop to collect her twenty-six-year-old son, whose only possessions were a piece of paper with her telephone number, twenty-five cents, and a Bible.

"He was nice to me," Berg says of the truck driver.

But there were other times, he says. One day the supervisors were accusing him and the other crop pullers of not working hard enough at the plant. " 'You're too lazy to do this, too lazy to do that, you ain't doing your job right,' " he recalls them saying. So: "I gave up on it and I left."

One escape is so very vivid in his mind. The time he took in planning it. The buying and stowing away of soda, cookies, and a case of his beloved Duchess Honey Buns; nine boxes to a case, he says, six to a box. The packing of his bag, including his winter coat. The wait, the wait, the wait, until late night, until all in the bunkhouse had fallen asleep. Then his assumption into the cool pitch of the Iowa night, down Route 6, bound for the interstate.

"It's fifty thousand miles to Texas," he says.

A deputy sheriff eventually found him, he says. Cuffed him, tucked him into the backseat, and returned him like a lost dog to the bunkhouse, but not before imparting some words of warning: "That he'd shoot me in the leg if I run off again."

The details never change whenever Gene Berg tells the story of this aborted escape. He takes delight in the derring-do of it, in the involvement of law enforcement, and, most of all, in the still-lingering aftertaste of sweet freedom.

Hiding in the ditch. Balled up in his coat to stay warm. Ducking the headlights of passing cars. Laughing to himself, as he ate Honey Bun after Honey Bun.

Terry Senn cried when she learned that Alford Busby was missing, cried when she was ordered to stay in the bunkhouse while search parties set out, cried when she heard the *whop-whop-whop* of the helicopters above, scouring the winter-stripped fields.

"Cried my heart out," she says.

The police quickly issued an all-points bulletin for an Alfred, not Alford, Busby:

*Mentally retarded man has wandered away from a group residence in Atalissa. Black male, five feet five, one hundred and fifty-five pounds, with black hair, brown eyes, and mustache. Last seen before five a.m. wearing light blue coat with white trim, brown-striped western shirt, blue jeans, black work boots, and camouflage hat. Suffers from epilepsy and needs regular medication to control seizures. Afraid of police. Has wandered away from the facility before.*

As the first full day of his absence emptied into the second, and the third, Senn's bunkhouse friends tried to reassure her. Alford has probably found his way back to Texas, they said. Remember how Gene Berg made it to Dallas after his father's funeral? Well, Alford probably thumbed it to his hometown of Woodville, a thousand miles away. She came to believe this improbable scenario because she wanted to believe it. She needed to believe it.

Yep, that's probably what happened. Old Alford just went back home to Texas, is all.

Little snow fell that winter upon the muck-colored fields, though gusts of cold barreled from the north and west to shiver the desiccated stalks and steal feeling from the extremities of the living. Winter then ceded the ground to spring, the permafrost giving in to the boot steps of farmers inspecting their fields. On a mild April day, a farmer came upon something along a fencerow in a field, about a half mile outside Atalissa.

A crumpled scarecrow. In blue jeans and a brown-striped Western shirt.

The death certificate laid it out:

Cause of death:
*Hypothermia*
Accident, Suicide, Homicide, or Undetermined:
*Accident*
Place of injury:
*Farm field*
How injury occurred:
*Mentally retarded man wandered away from home in sub-zero temperature*
Other significant conditions:
*Mental retardation*

Henry's Turkey Service shipped Busby's body back to Texas, back to a sixty-nine-year-old mother who would die two years later and be buried beside him in Tyler County. The men held a modest service on the sloping front lawn of the Atalissa schoolhouse, lowering the flag from the pole in honor of their dead bunkmate. A gray memorial stone was planted near a weeping willow. In one final misspelling of his name, it read:

IN MEMORY OF ALFRED E. BUSBY

In the years to come, the stone plaque would keep the cautionary tale fresh in the minds of the men, some of whom came to believe that their old housemate was actually buried in the front lawn. Henry's Turkey Service would adopt the position that you never can tell what these boys might do from one minute to the next — "And away he went," Kenneth Henry, one of the co-owners, says. "We never did know why" — while Atalissans would keep to a fairy-tale narrative: this Henry's boy overslept one morning, missed the company bus to the plant, and tried walking the six miles to work by following the train tracks.

But the men in the bunkhouse held firm to a different truth.

"Put him to bed by six o'clock," Willie Levi says. "He say, 'No, I'm not going to bed, I'm going to watch TV like everybody else.' That's what made him mad."

"They pissed him off and he walked out," Henry Wilkins says.

"They made him stay in his room," Keith Brown says. "He did something he wasn't supposed to. He ran away, it got cold, snow on the ground. And he died."

Terry Senn holds to that truth as well. Having deluded herself into believing that Alford Busby was all right — that he had just gone back to Texas — she was devastated by the discovery of his body, and more tears flowed. She decided that she could no longer do this kind of work. It was time she went back to South Carolina.

Senn did go home, eventually, but it took a while. When Leon and Shirley Benton retired, T. H. Johnson put Senn in charge, making her the so-called CEO, responsible for the work schedule and welfare of several dozen men with special needs. She was twenty-five. Crazy when you think about it, no?

But Senn and her estranged husband wanted to give their marriage one last shot, in fresh surroundings. There was the baby boy to consider. Besides, when she was honest with herself, she knew she was too young and inexperienced for the formidable challenges of the job.

Time to go.

Some of the men helped load up her red Chevy Cavalier. She secured her son in his seat, exchanged many hugs, promised to come back for a visit, and said good-bye. Then down the gravelly hill, away from the schoolhouse, a watery blur through her tears, never to see it, or them, again.

"I bawled my eyes out from Iowa to Missouri," she says. "They were my family. I loved those guys."

When the reconciliation with her husband did not stick, Senn moved back to South Carolina, where she has spent the last quarter century working with people with disabilities. For many years she supervised a sheltered workshop in Newberry, about three miles from the Louis Rich meat-processing plant, and only a few miles from this McDonald's.

Every year, she and her staff would take refresher classes on client interaction, and she would tell again the story of her role in the life and death of a certain man in Iowa, long ago. The lessons she would impart included a strong reminder to take care in your words and tone when addressing clients. But her central message was this:

"You should not, *ever, ever, ever,* be mean to the clients," Terry Senn says, her voice rising above the noise of the television behind her. "You *always* treat them with dignity and respect."

By then, everyone in the room would be crying. Everyone.

■ ■ ■ ■

# ELEVEN

■ ■ ■ ■

*Atalissa Days*

The dozen obedient men sat on red-brown benches at the Muscatine County Fair, dressed in button-down shirts and slacks, as if for church. Although a few also wore baseball caps to ward against the summer sun, the formality of their outing was reflected in the watches worn by Raymond Vaughn, one on each wrist. The men stayed put, as instructed, though they could not help but look about in anticipation at the midway, the Ferris wheel, the step-right-up jazz of it all.

The county fair in West Liberty, a turkey call or two from the evisceration line at the Louis Rich plant, was *the* event on the men's limited social calendar. They talked about the July fair the year round: what rides they would muster the nerve to attempt this time, which games of chance would be worth their quarters, how much they would drink in the beer garden. Several of the men routinely asked their bosses to sock away a portion of their small earnings every month, so that when the time came, they could swan about the fairground like squires of the county, clearly succeeding in the game of chance called life.

With their days spent in a turkey-processing plant and nights cheek by jowl in a dimly lit schoolhouse, how could they not be drawn to the sugar rush and neon dazzle of a county fair? The demo derby and the tractor pull, the dog show and the horse-and-pony show, the chain saw artist and the stilt walker, the crowning of the Muscatine County Queen and the naming of the finest goats, mules, rabbits, swine, poultry, turnips, rhubarbs, beets, tomatoes, marigolds, hydrangeas, tea roses, quilts, scarves, taffy, fudge, pecan rolls, fruit pies, zucchini bread, frosted chocolate brownies, unfrosted chocolate brownies, canned apricots, blackberry jam, and, among hundreds of other items, corn, of course, corn, from the longest ear to the tallest stalk.

Gone were the county fair days of the 1920s, when believers in eugenics — in the eradication of the physically and mentally defective — would have their own booths, when "fittest family" and "beautiful baby" contests were in vogue. This was the late

1980s, after all. Raymond Vaughn and Henry Wilkins and the Penner brothers and all the rest were free to lose themselves along the midway, to fail with the rest of us at knocking over the weighted milk bottles with a softball, or to pause at the apex of the Ferris wheel and imagine themselves the kings of all they surveyed.

And there was that one concession, the dunk tank run by the West Liberty Jaycees, where they had the best luck of all: *every time* they threw the ball at the bull's-eye, the seat would collapse and the taunting man would fall into the water. *Every time!*

But today's visit to the fair was extra special. The men were a featured attraction. Not exactly headliners performing in the Midway Pavilion, but they weren't appearing in the Swine Pavilion, either. Some folks had already taken seats in front of a small stage near a bank of trees. Willie Levi nervously beat out a rhythm on his tambourine (*DUH-duh-duh-duh-duh, DUH-duh-duh-duh-duh*), while Charles Giffey, an Austin State School alum now dressed in the stovepipe hat and red, white, and blue shirt of Uncle Sam, fiddled with his fake white beard. Standing nearby was Wilma Rock, the men's "grandma," the one who bought them Christmas and birthday gifts and occasionally dressed them as clowns. Today, though, she was the only one in clown attire, an umbrella in one gloved hand, a small American flag in the other, her wig the color of pink cotton candy.

Showtime. The performers filed onto the stage in close formation, Levi in the lead and Grandma Rock at the rear, their summer colors and her garish costume stark against the black backdrop. Like basketball players huddling with a coach, they gathered around the Reverend John Beck, a stocky, bearded man in khaki shorts and sneakers who had just finished adjusting the microphones. Beck, the thirty-nine-year-old pastor of the Zion Lutheran Church in Atalissa, spoke briefly to the men, who nodded to his every instruction. He then turned to address the audience of women with gray-white haloes and men with the distended stomachs of retirement.

"We're very, very glad to be here today," the pastor said. "This is one of the choirs from Zion Lutheran Church in Atalissa, and this is our most special choir: the fellows from Henry's Turkey Service. And they sing with some regularity at some of our special programs.

"They put the program together today. And one of the ways that they want to start the program is with a special tribute to our country. So at this time I'd like to ask Charles Giffey and Levi to come forward, and I'd like you all to please stand."

With an earnestness befitting the moment, Levi and Giffey raised their kazoos and began to play the national anthem, with Levi also shimmering his tambourine to the beat. Tommy House, an Abilene State School graduate whose large size earned him the nickname "Moose," kept his baseball cap on, but placed his right hand on his chest. Grandma Rock waved her flag.

Sitting now at a piano, his back to the audience, Pastor Beck played the first strains of the African-American spiritual "Do, Lord," and the men began to sing, some in a key of their own:

Do Lord, O do Lord, O do remember me
Do Lord, O do Lord, O do remember me
Do Lord, O do Lord, O do remember me
Way beyond the blue

The men clapped to the words of a song rooted in servitude, a song in which the shackled beseech God to please not forget them in the next life, for this life has been so very hard. Do Lord, O do Lord, O do remember me.

The variety show continued. The members of the Schoolhouse Choir, as they were known, performed solos during the singing of "Old Time Religion," its lyrics implying close familial ties as unattainable for these men as a carousel's brass ring. " 'Twas good enough for daddy, 'twas good enough for daddy, 'twas good enough for daddy, then it's good enough for me," sang Levi, who had not seen his alcoholic father or troubled mother in decades. John Orange, whose very surname was in doubt, sang of his brother, while Paul Hayek, a man-cherub in a long-sleeve shirt buttoned to the neck, sang of his sister. And bruising Tommy House sang of his daddy while keeping his hands on his hips, as if daring someone out there to say he ain't got no daddy.

What memories that Raymond Vaughn might have had of his birth parents were confused by a succession of foster parents in Houston, including a man who brought him to a courthouse one day, said he'd be right back, and disappeared, bequeathing the child to the system. He was raised by the Mexia State School, truth be told, and now he stood before the microphone, a watch on each wrist, to begin his own solo. It was "The Old Rugged Cross," written in 1913 by the Reverend George Bennard in wounded response to being ridiculed by some youths at a revival meeting:

So I'll cherish the old rugged cross,
'Til my trophies at last I lay down;
I will cling to the old rugged cross,
And exchange it someday for a crown.

When Vaughn finished his hesitant rendition, Pastor Beck thanked him and turned again to the audience to introduce one more solo, by John David Hatfield, well known in Atalissa for cleaning up litter while riding about on his tricycle. Less known was his penchant for dressing in a tutu and performing his own private ballet — something the pastor might have thought too daring for the county fair crowd.

"We had to make one change in our program," the pastor said. "John David had a special dance routine. And he practiced on it for many months. But it wasn't going to work because of some staging and technical difficulties, and so he is going to substitute for that a version of 'Silent Night.' You listen very closely and you will hear all the words."

The audience did have to listen closely even to discern lyrics everyone knew by heart. Still, they sang along, injecting a

231

refreshing breath of winter into the wilting summer heat, as kazoos kazooed, a tambourine shook, and the rest of the choir sang backup for a waif of a man who kept his head at a tilt, as if expecting to be hit.

When they were done, the men turned to the bearded pastor at the piano in search of guidance, but he was too busy applauding them.

John Beck had come a long way to stage a performance at the Muscatine County Fair. A Seattle native, he graduated from Pacific Lutheran University in Tacoma, then came east to work for the Lutheran church in Minneapolis. He earned a master's degree in journalism at the University of Minnesota and another master's, in divinity, at Dubuque's Wartburg Theological Seminary, where his liberal, even radical, leanings were often on display, and where he met his first wife, Jackie. After returning to Tacoma for his ordination, he promptly received his first posting as a pastor: the Zion Lutheran Church, Atalissa, Iowa.

When John and Jackie Beck pulled up to the parsonage on Fourth Street, congregants were waiting on the front porch to unload the truck, reminding the new pastor of a few basic lessons drilled into him at the seminary. Never assume that your ministry is more important than the calling of the garbage collector or store clerk. Do not obsess over the many lies you will be told. Develop an interest — horticulture, stamp collecting, baseball — that has nothing to do with your ministry. And finally: beware of the people who help you to unpack.

In other words, the people who exude friendly graciousness to you at the start may, in the end, be the ones to thwart your every move.

The new leader and his flock needed time to adjust. Pastor Beck had grown up in the straitlaced and sober Norwegian brand of Lutheranism, and now he was the head of a German Lutheran church, where things were more informal: offers to join congregants for a beer were common, and an American flag hung in the sanctuary, continuing a practice dating to World War I, when German Americans felt the need to prove their patriotism. What's more, a handful of dominant clans shared control of the Atalissa congregation, adhering to a power structure established when the church was founded in 1903. There were certain unwritten rules about who was in charge of what. This family oversaw music, that family oversaw dinners, on and on.

Within the insular congregation, wounds remained raw. One family did not return to the church for years because their children had once been accused of inappropriately eating mints from a tray. Beck also sensed a smoldering enmity between his new congregation and that of Our Redeemer Lutheran Church in nearby West Liberty. The tensions went back decades: the Atalissa church had actually helped to establish Our Redeemer in 1953 — part of its Golden Jubilee celebration — but petty jealousies had gradually developed over money and, perhaps, the fact that the West Liberty congregation now dwarfed Atalissa's.

If Pastor Beck had to adapt to his new church, so too did its members to this strong-headed bear of a man from the Pacific Northwest. Although he respected church traditions forged by hardworking farmers over generations, he had no interest in having growth and renewal stymied by those same traditions. He was interested in true community, which is why, for example, he quickly adopted a predecessor's practice of inviting local Presbyterians, whose church in town had closed, to worship at Zion Lutheran. Bring your hymnals, he told them, and we'll sing one of your hymns every week.

Inclusion mattered to Beck, inclusion extending beyond the rare mixing of hymnody. Living now in downtown Atalissa, such as it was, he could not help but notice the schoolhouse men coming down from the hill to make their rounds, stopping at the post office, the firehouse, the taverns, the gas station. He saw orphans in his midst.

One day he walked up to the schoolhouse and invited the men to an outdoor Sunday service and picnic that his church was holding in a stretch of woods called the Spilger Timber. On the day of the event, a schoolhouse bus pulled up to disgorge nearly fifty men and tray after tray of food. A moment of grace, Beck recalled, a blessing, and a daring departure for Zion Lutheran to reach out to people with developmental disabilities — people who, by the way, had been a part of the community for a decade.

What he did not expect was to have a dozen of the men show up at church the next Sunday. And the next. And the next.

As the small congregation received these new worshippers, a routine developed. On Sunday mornings, several of the bunkhouse boys would walk down from the schoolhouse to the white clapboard church with the unassuming steeple. They would first attend Sunday school classes with Dorothy

Garvin, a resilient white-haired woman, maybe five feet tall, who had dedicated herself in retirement to volunteer work, which included doing just about anything that needed to be done at Zion Lutheran. With her new students, she found a purpose beyond the folding of church bulletins: by offering friendship along with lessons in hymns and prayers, she instilled in them a sense of belonging. After a while, a map of Texas in the Sunday school appeared on a classroom wall, with pushpins to denote that Willie Levi came from Orange, and Raymond Vaughn from outside Houston, and Jeff Long from Meridian.

After class would come the service inside the modest church, where the morning light filtered through mitre-shaped windows, and two ceiling fans stirred the air when the new air-conditioning system was not activated. The men would take their seats among the eighteen wooden pews arrayed in nine rows, usually toward the front, settling onto the gold cushions and opting not to use the red hymnals tucked into the pew backs. Before them, behind the altar, was a large painting of the Good Shepherd, a lamb safe in the crook of his arm.

A few of the men had trouble reciting the Lord's Prayer, so they hummed instead during its recitation, their rhythmic undertones enhancing the moment's sacredness. They took up offerings. They gathered for after-service coffee in the basement, using more milk and sugar than coffee. Most of all, they sang for the congregation, knowing full well that they were free to carry the tune with "la-la-la" if lyrics eluded them.

" 'What a Friend We Have in Jesus,' " Levi recalls. " 'Amazing Grace.' 'Surely Goodness.' 'Give Me That Old-Time Religion.' All that."

The men presented Pastor Beck with unique challenges. Some talked more than others. Some were easily wounded, requiring special attention. Some seemed disconnected from the moment, while others never hesitated to burst into his office whenever they felt the urge to share some special news. Then again, perhaps the men were like all the other congregants.

True, their exuberance could all but kidnap the service, testing the patience of members whose forebears had founded the church. Pastor Beck made a point of reminding visiting bishops not to include rhetorical questions in their sermons, because some of the men would shout out answers. And there was the delicate matter of Levi's enthusiastic use of his tambourine and kazoo, instruments that were not, shall we say, part of the Lutheran liturgical tradition. But Levi readily agreed when privately asked to play his kazoo only during certain songs, an accommodation the pastor took as a sign that an easy trust with the men had been established.

The presence of the newcomers provided many teaching moments — mostly, it turned out, for the pastor and the rest of the congregation. The men's concern for others seemed ever present. When one member returned to church after being absent for a while with an injury, the schoolhouse men surrounded him to say they had been praying for him, and was he all right, and did he need anything? "No one else in the congregation was paying attention, or even remembered that he had been hurt," Pastor Beck recalls.

On another occasion, the pastor had just delivered what he considered to be one of his finer sermons. Satisfied with himself, he raised his hands to begin the benediction — "May the Lord bless you and keep you" — only to have lanky Jeff Long step into the aisle and shout: *This has been such a good worship! Don't you think we should sing something else?*

The turkey worker then began to lead

everyone in the simple hymn "Jesus Loves Me."

Jesus loves me — this I know,
For the Bible tells me so;
Little ones to Him belong —
They are weak, but He is strong

Yes, Jesus loves me!
Yes, Jesus loves me! Yes,
Jesus loves me!
The Bible tells me so.

The congregants wept as they sang, so free of pretension was the moment, so powerful. It came to be seen as a lesson in essential truth, taught by men who were thought to be less functional than the rest of the congregation, yet in some ways seemed much more grounded. They remembered the important stuff.

Perhaps this is why the members of the Schoolhouse Choir were always given featured roles in the Nativity pageant that took place every Christmas Eve on the altar at Zion Lutheran. The 1989 service was typical:

A teenage Mary and a teenage Joseph knelt before a crèche placed on the altar, taking turns holding a baby doll in swaddling clothes, while another teenager fidgeted at the lectern and labored his way through a reading from Luke: "And in the same region there were shepherds out in the field, keeping watch over their flock by night . . ."

With that, a dozen shepherds and kings in colorful robes and head scarves filed onto the altar, some carrying staffs, others sporting fake beards and golden paper crowns. Jeff Long may have been in brown and John Hatfield in white, but they were all cloaked in solemn reverence, as if the baby doll before them were made of more than plastic.

Pastor Beck hunched over a small electric organ and led the men in song, "How Great Our Joy" and "Joy to the World." The last note struck, he stood and, with a sweep of his hand, directed shepherds and kings back to their places among the congregation.

When John Beck and his wife left Atalissa in 1990 for new assignments, he allowed himself the pride of accomplishment. The congregation had grown during his six years at Zion Lutheran, and not only in numbers. In the truest Christian sense, there was now in place an understanding of community that extended beyond the clapboard confines of the church on Fourth Street.

"I was naive," he says. "I thought that I had changed the world. I hadn't."

Those who disagreed with him, he says, simply waited him out. In the years after he left, the animosity and small-mindedness returned, the quarrels and power grabs playing out in a passive Iowa aggression evoking Meredith Wilson's *The Music Man.* The hiding of toilet paper so that underprivileged kids in a youth program couldn't use church supplies to make papier-mâché puppets. The aromatic cleaning of a nearby hog pen at choice times. The continuing tensions with the sister church in West Liberty.

Beck has since returned to the Pacific Northwest. He and his second wife, Joan, are now two of the three pastors at a Lutheran church north of Seattle. He has many, many memories of his own Atalissa days, but none more vivid than this:

The men kept inviting the Becks, Pastor John and Pastor Jackie, to the schoolhouse for some kind of "program." The couple repeatedly begged off, mostly because of the all-consuming demands on a pastor's time in a small community. Finally, though, after services one Sunday afternoon, the pastor and his wife paid a visit to the schoolhouse at the top of the hill.

They were led into the gymnasium, where

just two chairs were set out, facing the stage. Reserved for you, they were told. All the while, some of the bunkhouse men he knew from Zion Lutheran, along with others he had seen around town, were hustling about the gym, sorting out logistics.

Then the program began. It was a variety show, presented to Pastor Beck and his wife as a gift of thanks, with country-western songs and church hymns and silly skits and dancing, yes, dancing.

For here was slight John David Hatfield, head angled in that funny, inquisitive way, wearing his big glasses, his broad smile, and his tutu. Dancing an elaborate ballet on a stage large enough to accommodate his uninhibited expression of pure joy, his wordless sermon on grace.

■ ■ ■ ■

# TWELVE

■ ■ ■ ■

*The bossman, T. H. Johnson*

The winter fields hardened to earthen pavement. They gave again by early April, accepting the seeds. By summer, ten-foot stalks rippled like fresh sheets snapped over the bed of Iowa. Come late September, the harvesting combines cut, shucked, and shelled with straight-line precision, spraying golden streams of kernels into hoppers and spewing the chaff over the God-kissed soil.

Spring came again, and this time soybean was planted, in keeping with a belief in crop rotation that predated Christ. The plants sprouted. The harvest came. Corn, soybean, corn, soybean.

The surrounding fields marked the recurring loop of the seasons, the progression of the years. Yet all the while, the men in the hilltop schoolhouse remained the boys. Aging into their forties and fifties, they were graying adolescents. Those boys over in Atalissa. The Henry's boys.

In the world beyond the schoolhouse property that they mowed and dappled with petunias, ever diligent to clear growth from the memorial plaque beside the weeping willow, the use of the "R-word" lost acceptance. Media investigations, lawsuits, and government legislation led to a heightened national emphasis on inclusion, not exclusion, for people with disabilities; on strengths, not weaknesses; on fundamental rights of choice and self-determination.

In 1974, the year Henry's Turkey Service staked its Atalissa claim, a class-action lawsuit filed back in Texas challenged the conditions at the Austin, Denton, and Fort Worth State Schools: too many residents and not enough staff, excessive medication and unnecessary restraint, physical abuse and inadequate medical care — state-sanctioned pockets of hell. The protracted lawsuit, called *Lelsz v. Kavanagh,* eventually led to the shutdown of some of the schools and to the creation of homes in the community for hundreds of state clients with developmental disabilities.

In 1975, while the men acclimated themselves to what would be a lifetime of unloading and eviscerating turkeys for room, board, and sixty-five dollars a month, Congress enacted the Developmental Disabilities Assistance and Bill of Rights Act, which was broadened in 1990 and again in 2000, when it asserted:

The goals of the Nation properly include a goal of providing individuals with developmental disabilities with the information, skills, opportunities, and support to:
make informed choices and decisions about their lives; live in homes and communities in which such individuals can exercise their full rights and responsibilities as citizens; pursue meaningful and productive lives; contribute to their families, communities, and States, and the Nation; have interdependent friendships and relationships with other persons; live free of abuse, neglect, financial and sexual exploitation, and violations of their legal and human rights; and achieve full integration and inclusion in society, in an individualized manner, consistent with the unique strengths, resources, priorities, concerns, abilities, and capabilities of each individual.

The forceful declaration reflected the desires and expectations of a nation. By now, even prime-time network television, hardly fearless in challenging the accepted cultural ethos, was celebrating the obvious.

Mickey Rooney had starred in an affecting made-for-TV movie in 1981 called *Bill,* based on the true story of a man with intellectual disability who struggles to adapt after a half century in a Minnesota institution. And Chris Burke, an actor with Down syndrome, had played a central role in a prime-time television drama, *Life Goes On,* that enjoyed success in the early 1990s.

Horizons had broadened everywhere, it seems, except in Atalissa. Life there did not evolve; it revolved, like the gears of a combine, churning up the years and spitting out the husks of the days.

An Iowa social worker had denounced the schoolhouse arrangement as obscene, the state's leading newspaper had questioned its propriety, and various state and government agencies, including the US Department of Labor, had conducted inquiries, some more rigorous than others. Through it all, a largely unaffected Henry's Turkey Service stuck to a for-profit business model with a paternalistic overlay of limited freedoms and routine discipline.

No intimate relationships. No choice in where to live or work. No training in self-sufficiency as basic as learning to dial 911 in an emergency. And, despite that granite reminder of Alford Busby on the schoolhouse lawn — "Can't tell how many times I cleaned it off," one of the men, Brady Watson, says — the continuing practice of sending grown men to their rooms as punishment for minor transgressions.

Kenneth Henry, the co-owner of Henry's Turkey Service, denies that any link existed between productivity at work and punishment at home, but he admits that the contractual obligations with the turkey plant required a tight rein. "You know you're on a schedule," he says. "You need to be ready."

And the occasional banishment to one's bedroom, for example, was necessary to maintain order. "You had to do some things like that to make the boys bathe, to make the boys brush their teeth, to change clothes," Henry adds. "The same thing as you would do with a twelve-year-old."

But at least the men were working toward a life of leisure. They looked forward to the day when they would no longer have to get up before dawn to kill and gut turkeys. There was a retirement plan in the works.

They had been promised.

What little change there was came quietly. It came in the gray-white dusting of Willie Levi's black hair, in the creases etching around the mischief-seeking eyes of Henry

Wilkins, in the loss of nails on fingers damaged from reaching into freshly killed birds to yank out crops, countless times a day. It came in the renaming of the Louis Rich plant to West Liberty Foods, after an Iowa turkey growers' cooperative bought the operation.

And it came in the comings and goings of the pseudofamily inhabiting the schoolhouse. Men might leave for a while, sent to work at the Louis Rich plant in Newberry, South Carolina. Staff members might leave too, some of them overwhelmed by responsibilities for which they were never trained. Leon and Shirley Benton might have been missed, but others were not, including the crew chief who looted the men's rooms one night and disappeared.

The biggest change of all came when another man arrived from the ranch in Goldthwaite, Texas. The bossman himself: Mr. T. H. Johnson.

Why Johnson moved up to Atalissa was never made quite clear. Was he ducking a few business complications back in Texas? Had he come to stabilize things after that staffer stole from the bunkhouse? Some people speculated that he and his wife, Jane Ann, were simply a better couple when separated by one thousand miles. They would talk a few times a day on the telephone about business and family, but their marriage had become, at the very least, unconventional.

The charming but inscrutable Johnson converted some basement space behind the gymnasium into his office and living quarters, its clutter a kind of mirror to his idea-fertile mind: a paper storm of invoices, receipts, and government papers forever brewing on a desk, while CNN droned like Muzak from a small television. Surrounded by an inoperative stove, a dirty kitchen sink, and a refrigerator stocked with insulin for a couple of the men who were diabetic, he'd lay on his bed with his cowboy boots on, lending to the air a whiff of manure from the calves kept at the back of the bunkhouse property. And there was always alcohol around. Crown Royal, mostly, but also some Jack Daniel's. Wine, too.

This room was the space behind the curtain that concealed the great and powerful Wizard. Johnson's name was well known, but he was rarely seen, a recluse. He socialized so infrequently in Atalissa that many in the small town wouldn't know him to see him. He was not one to join the weekly euchre games, or attend services at Zion Lutheran, or chat weather nonsense over a cold one at the Corner Tap. If he had a hankering for something from the minimart, he'd summon one of the men and say: *Levi, here's five dollars. Fetch me a can of sardines, and keep the change.*

"He liked sardines," Brady Watson remembers. "Them things stink. I'll never eat a sardine."

"Makes me sick," Watson's best friend, Jeff Long, says. "TH gave me one one day."

"You turned green," Watson says, chuckling. "I couldn't help but laugh."

The men loved Johnson for these moments. He was more than their bossman, he was their daddy, walking the darkened halls with a cash-jammed leather billfold jutting from his shirt pocket, as if to announce his power. If you hadn't saved up enough for the county fair: Here's some money to tide you over, have a good time, and now don't tell anyone, hear? If you had a penchant for tattling: Here's a little something, so's you can tell me what's going on. And if it was your birthday, oh boy: Here's fifty dollars, many happy returns, and let's keep this our little secret.

"Gave me fifty dollars on my birthday," Levi says, smiling. "Yeah. Went to Hooter's. Yeah. The girls had me do the Funky Chicken with a bucket on my head."

Michelle Hahn, a young crew member, lived for several years in a bunkhouse bedroom beside Johnson's room, and shared his bathroom, with its balky shower and temperamental toilet. Raised nearby, she got to know some of the men at a local campground. Johnson welcomed her kind-hearted interest in the men, and soon she was juggling college courses, raising a young son, and living at the schoolhouse as a kind of a bosslady-nanny: preparing lunches, helping out at the evisceration line, listening to the men's late-evening woes, treating them to a day trip of swimming and inner-tubing at Wacky Waters in Davenport. Sometimes she'd take a few of the men with her to a laundry in West Liberty, the only place she could wash the turkey stench from her clothes. To kill time between cycles, she and the men would walk into a nearby Mexican bar, to be greeted by patrons genuinely delighted to see their plant co-workers in clothes not streaked in blood.

Hahn was impressed by Johnson's insistence that the men want for little — beyond, of course, their basic rights. Every week she would drive to Sam's Club in Davenport, with Willie Levi, Keith Brown, and James Fowler often in tow, to buy so many supplies in bulk that they'd create a ten-cart train snaking back to the parked van. Johnson believed in having enough of everything to go around, from Gatorade to beer. He also made sure that lunches at the turkey plant stuck to the men's ribs: spaghetti, hot dogs, pork and beans, sausage and onions, polish sausages wrapped in tortillas, corn dogs, chocolate pudding with crumbled cookies. A heavy spice to the meals always signaled that Johnson had gotten involved in the food prep. His chili gave you the sweats, and his white gravy had so much pepper it looked like a dalmatian's coat.

Sometimes he seemed like just one of the "boys," in on the craziness of it all. Around Halloween, for example, the men festooned the schoolhouse lawn with wooden tombstones bearing inside-joke inscriptions:

*Here Lies Gene: Gone for a Ride and Never Was Seen*

*Here Lies Henry: Puffed His Way to Eternity*

*Here Lies Moose: Ate One Too Many Honey Buns*

*Here Lies Preston: Lied His Way Out*

And one for the bossman daddy himself:

*Here Lies TH: The Father of 41*

Christmas, though, defined the schoolhouse calendar. Johnson would dispatch Michelle Hahn out to buy dozens — no, hundreds — of gifts for the men, as well as for the staff members and their children, the so-called bunkhouse brats, including her young son. His name was Terence, but half the men called him Clarence or Herm.

The boss lived for Christmas, a magical time when the Henry's boys were not the only adults being treated like children. So the money flowed. "Hardly ever did he tell me no," Hahn says. "He could be the kindest, sweetest person ever."

Johnson also took care of his "boys" in other ways. This wasn't a monastery he was running; this was a good-old-boy bunkhouse, pulsating with horny guys. He did what he could.

When men with no families spent their week of summer vacation back on the ranch in Goldthwaite, one of its employees would be handed several hundred dollars and told to take them somewhere special in Houston, say, or San Antonio.

"I was told to let them go where they wanted to, including X-rated movies and bars with hookers," one of those former staffers told the Fort Worth *Star-Telegram* in 1980. "We never went anywhere respectable. If they wanted a whore, we were told to let them have a whore."

The men received similar consideration in

Atalissa. Sometimes the visitor would be that attractive, dark-haired woman they all knew from Goldthwaite. The story was, she got ten dollars a man.

"She was a sweet, nice person," Segreta Davis, who once worked at the bunkhouse, recalls. "You'd look at her and you wouldn't think she was that way."

Former employees remember sitting on a bunkhouse stairwell, outside the room designated for assignation, trying to keep everyone calm as they waited their turn. Others recall a mobile home pulling up onto the property. Still others remember the rental of a motel room near the interstate.

"They'd have their health papers," recalls Danny Miles, who lived and worked at the bunkhouse for years. "TH was one man who took care of his guys, and he made sure they were well protected."

Keith Brown agrees. "We didn't know they'd be coming," he says. "And then, 'Uh-oh, uh-oh. Gonna have a good time."

Johnson maintained a matter-of-fact defense of these arrangements. "We're trying to create a normal situation and treat them like normal people," he told the *Star-Telegram.* "They should have that privilege. Some people will question the whole program, but it goes on in the rest of the world."

"It" being sex.

The occasional prostitute, then, and porn magazines and racy postcards — a redhead, say, with a tape measure around her bare chest, asking "Will I measure up?" — but these were poor replacements for a loved one's intimate touch. And a man risked paying a steep emotional price if he violated the bunkhouse's almost monastic code.

The company's most dependable worker may have been the tall and taciturn Frank Rodriguez. If a barn needed to be knocked down, or if the temperatures of calves needed to be taken, Rodriguez was the man; he could pretty much do anything but read. He might have a beer or two, but he spent most of his time constructing intricately carved wooden boxes to give away as presents. He knew the bunkhouse operation smelled as bad as Johnson's boots, but what can you do except get on with it. Do your work, have a beer, go to bed. He was the reliable, slightly distant older brother to the men, and they looked up to him.

At some point, while working in Goldthwaite, Rodriguez developed a relationship with a married crew member named Helen. "The rest of them were rowdy, but he was quiet," she recalls, explaining the attraction. "He kept to himself in his room, working on his woodwork."

Helen became pregnant by Rodriguez, and gave birth to a daughter. Two years later, she says, she came home to learn that he had been abruptly taken from the Goldthwaite bunkhouse and sent back up to Atalissa. Years of attempts to reunite followed — Helen even moved to Des Moines to be closer to Atalissa — but she was thwarted at every turn. If she visited, she says, Johnson would threaten to have her arrested for trespassing. If she telephoned, he would tell her that Frank was sick and about to die.

"It was terrible," Helen says, her eyes blurring with tears. "He was just determined not to let us be together."

She wrote letters to Rodriguez, but most of them were intercepted and shoved into a box. Another staff member once found a letter addressed to Rodriguez in one of Johnson's desk drawers. When she asked about it, he told the staffer to put it back and mind her business.

Sometimes, though, a letter got smuggled past the bunkhouse censor. "I seen some of them," Rodriguez says.

His friend Pete Graffagnino, the cook,

would occasionally be dispatched to the post office to collect the mail. He'd pluck out any letters addressed to Frank, and then he and Brady Watson would try to help their friend decipher the letters. Ardis Reyes, a kind but no-nonsense woman in her mid-forties who worked for several years at the bunkhouse, did the same. She knew that Frank worried about his daughter, and she could not understand why he was being denied this natural connection. So, every now and then, she would whisper:

*Frank. There's another letter. A letter for you.*

Then, huddled in some private nook of the sprawling bunkhouse, she would read Helen's words aloud to Frank, a secret dispatch, it seemed, from the unattainable outside world. A letter that slipped past, a phone call that somehow got through — for twenty years, this is how Frank tracked his daughter's journey from infancy to young adulthood.

One day, Reyes opened another envelope, pulled out the letter to read to Frank, and — *Oh look, Frank. There's a picture!*

Frank's proudest possession became not some wooden box that he had made, but a photograph of a young girl.

*My daughter,* he'd say.

Johnson might have been trying his paternal best to minimize the pain for all parties. After all, Helen was married to another of his employees, and her husband might come looking for Rodriguez. He also might have decided that Rodriguez was ill equipped to handle the responsibilities of parenthood, much less those of a relationship. Or it could be that he did not want to lose his best worker.

"He told me that Frank was the most dependable boy he had," Helen says. "And he was going to keep him."

This much is true: Johnson had an aversion to unwanted attention — he hated having his photograph taken — and preferred to keep things off the books as much as possible. For example, he refused to have the men apply for Medicaid in Iowa, so he did what he could to keep them from going to the hospital if at all possible. When his assistant, Michelle Hahn, asked what he had against hospitals, his answer was blunt: too many questions.

If someone got sick, he'd often pull out a large bottle of erythromycin, an antibiotic used to treat everything from pertussis to gonorrhea. Plagued once by a persistent cold, Hahn dutifully took the medicine given to her by Johnson. That is, until she finally took a good look at the bottle —

which had come from the vet's. Turns out that erythromycin is also used for foot rot and other infections in cattle.

*You're giving me goddam cow pills!* Hahn screamed.

Even the crude identification cards carried by the men made no mention of Iowa. Here, for example, is James Fowler's identification: a laminated index card that includes his photograph, fingerprints, date of birth, and Social Security number. He half smiles for the camera, above the mug shot marquee that says "Mills County, Sheriff's Dept., Goldthwaite, Texas." Left thumb print here; right thumb print there.

Whenever Hahn asked about his stealthy Iowa arrangement, which effectively denied the men access to the many Muscatine County programs available to people with disability, Johnson would recall the time he had been caught harboring undocumented workers on his Texas ranch. How they used to take food and supplies out to the workers who were hiding from the *federales* . . .

If Hahn persisted, he would say in condescension that this is just the way it has to be. "I was his little 'wet head,' " she says. "Because I didn't know anything."

The earth hardened, softened, hardened,

261

softened. Corn, soybean, corn, soybean, the fields harvested at the end of one millennium and into the next. As time passed, the people of Atalissa stopped receiving invitations to the schoolhouse to celebrate Christmas with the men. No reason given. Maybe the parties had become too cumbersome, or too rowdy. Frank Rodriguez remembers having his nose broken by a local man when a beer-fueled fight broke out.

Now, along with the petunias, there sprouted on the schoolhouse grounds a few signs that said NO TRESPASSING.

T. H. Johnson remained in that back office, a bunkhouse hermit, dung-flecked boots on the bed, CNN hyperventilating, liquor bottles within reach, dealing with the big thoughts of running a business that depended on the performance of a few dozen men with intellectual disability. Over the years he had burned through so many crew chiefs and employees that he'd just about run out of candidates.

At one point, he tried to groom a stocky young man from Goldthwaite, Kevin Poindexter, to be a foreman who would oversee the men during their shifts on the line at the plant. "I went in there unloading them turkeys," Poindexter recalls, decades later, while examining the innards of a go-kart on his front lawn in Goldthwaite. "The whole time, them turkey wings are beating on you. That was the hardest job that I did when I was up there. I did that for three days. Then he put me inside, pulling tenderloins. Made my arms sore."

Poindexter, streaked with engine oil, searches the ground for a tool. "He wanted me to be a foreman and live in the bunk-house," he says, finding the tool. "I stayed a week."

Eventually, a local couple, Randy and Dru Neubauer, took the job. They were paid ten dollars an hour to manage the Atalissa bunkhouse and oversee a staff that included their adult children. A race car enthusiast with longish brown hair parted in the middle, Randy had worked as a landscaper and in the cat food division at a StarKist plant. Short, slight, and beleaguered, Dru had initially been hired by Henry's Turkey Service to take the men on weekend fishing trips, but soon began sharing her husband's responsibilities.

Neither had experience in caring for people with intellectual disability, although Randy Neubauer had met the schoolhouse men before, he once said, "in parades and stuff like that." He received no company manual on how to discipline an employee, how to handle complaints of discrimination — how to manage, really.

Years later, he would be asked in a deposition about his qualifications for the formidable job.

Q. Prior to working for Hill Country Farms doing business as Henry's Turkey Service, did you have any seminars or training or other kind of education related to health care?

A. No.

Q. Did you receive any training or education related to counseling?

A. No.

Q. Before Hill Country Farms?

A. No.

Q. Psychology?

A. No.

Q. Speech therapy?

A. No.

Q. Occupational therapy?

A. No.

Q. Vocational rehabilitation?

A. No.

Q. Job training?

A. Just with — well, no, because when I started working for Henry's, TH, you know, told me how to handle, you know, different situations, but prior to that, no.

What Neubauer lacked in expertise went unfilled by his choice of a right-hand man: Danny Miles, a tall Marlboro Man with straggly hair, and one of the more curious Texans to wind up in Atalissa. He came from the small city of Canyon, in the Texas Panhandle, close to the haunting rocks and mesas of the Palo Duro Canyon, which had once inspired the artist Georgia O'Keeffe. His own artistic gift was in the stealing of cars — or, as he likes to put it, "borrowing a vehicle without permission."

Miles kept stealing one car in particular that happened to be owned by the city of Canyon's parks department. He'd take it out for occasional joyrides, he says, "but every time I brought it back, it had a full tank of gas."

The fifth time he "borrowed" the car, he was caught and presented before a judge who was also the driver of the young man's church bus. "The judge knew me since I was a little bitty shit," Miles recalls.

The delinquent was given a choice: "Fifteen years in prison, or fifteen years with TH." Which is why a string-bean teenager arrived at the Goldthwaite ranch one day in handcuffs, to be released to the custody of Henry's Turkey Service.

Miles, who did not have intellectual disability, lived for years in the schoolhouse as one of the "boys." He was an "equalizer," he says, bunking with the most vulnerable men to keep them safe from others who might take advantage. He eventually became someone to look up to: a "boy" who had made it. Johnson promoted him to full-time worker, free to live where he wanted, free to patronize the Corner Tap whenever he felt parched, free to marry whomever he wished, which he did, twice. With a foot in both worlds, a "boy" and yet a free man, he struggled with his balance. One minute he could be joking with his old bunkmates, and the next he could be screaming at them to work faster.

Randy Neubauer. Dru Neubauer. Danny Miles. These, then, were the three people with day-to-day responsibility for thirty-two men with intellectual disability, a responsibility that only increased as Johnson drank more and slipped deeper into the recesses of the bunkhouse. For his part, Randy Neubauer would later say that he tried to manage the bunkhouse as if it were the home of an extra-large family. Whipping up pancakes for the men on weekends, for example, and always making sure his office door was open, just in case anyone ever wanted to talk.

"They'd come in and watch TV in my office," Neubauer would say. "And it's just because they wanted companionship. Sometimes they felt alone . . ."

On this point, at least, Neubauer was right. There was an empty sameness to their days: the grind of the plant, the Friday-night beers, the monthly Saturday trips to the mall, the Sunday services, the return to the grind. Together, yet alone.

Gene Berg, Jeff Long, and a few spare others regularly used one of the bunkhouse telephones to speak with family members, but the rest of the men had no one to call — or, at least, no one to answer. Telephone numbers scribbled on paper and stored in wallets were generally no longer in service, but some of the men kept dialing the same numbers over and over and over throughout the years, unable or unwilling to accept the disconnection.

A few of the men, including Leonard Barefield, were denied access to a telephone on the grounds that they could not be understood even if they had someone to call, so profound were their speech difficulties. "Would you take a call from Leonard?" asks Kenneth Henry.

In their futile quest to reconnect with family, some men made a habit of checking in at the small post office, across from the Old University tavern. One postmaster, Regeana Arrowood, always had a stocked candy dish on the counter and a cache of token gifts tucked away — sample-size bottles of men's cologne, granola bars, toy flashlights — just in case someone was enduring a gift-free birthday. In thanks, an appreciative Willie Levi once presented her with a bouquet of flowers, picked from the schoolhouse garden.

Still, every so often, a package did arrived for someone. A handwritten Christmas note from an aging mother. A birthday gift from a faraway sister:

> Your watch is self-winding. Movement makes it run, so set it by pulling the winding-stem out, one time for the date and all the way for the time.
> Hope you enjoy your watch and candy.
> Love you

These notes and gifts were rare. In her dozen years as postmaster, Regeana Arrowood recalls answering yes only a handful of times to the earnest bunkhouse question: Any mail for me?

Ah, but the men had a plan, a retirement

plan, to comfort them on those nights when the reek from the bathroom seeped into bedrooms, when cockroaches nested in the guts of boom boxes, when rainwater dripped, dripped, dripped from the ceiling in the uneven marking of time until their last day of hanging, rehanging, and pulling crop.

Henry's Turkey Service had promised — TH himself had promised! — that when the turkeys just got too heavy to lift, those men without families in their lives would return in happy retirement to Texas. To Goldthwaite, in fact, where a corner of the Johnson ranch was being converted into a kind of retirement home, the construction costs covered in part by money deducted from the men's own earnings. In fact, every so often, a couple of the men in Atalissa — Frank Rodriguez and Keith Brown, usually — would be driven down to Goldthwaite to help with the labor.

"One day, we're all going back to Texas!" That's how Rodriguez remembers Johnson's promise.

It would be a haven, a sanctuary. "A place for the boys that didn't have families or families that wouldn't take them," is how Kenneth Henry describes it.

A home of their own.

Sometimes this was all the men could talk about. "Levi and one of the other ones, I can't remember who it was, were all excited about going home," Vada Baker, one of their friends in town, recalls. "They were going to get four-wheelers, they were going to live on a big farm, blah blah blah."

It was no blah blah blah to them. Imagine: three squares a day; fishing whenever you wanted; and if you didn't want to fish, or ride a four-wheeler, you could just do nothing. No silvery shackles swinging through your dreams, no one shouting, Hang 'em! Hang 'em!

You could just do — nothing. Nothing but sit there on the back porch, look out on the live oak and mesquite, and watch the Lone Star evening receive the setting sun.

# THIRTEEN

*The years melt into decades*

The Bunkhouse and the bossman declined together. Its windows boarded up and his body breaking down, the ceiling leaks and drinking, the twinned damage of general neglect to flesh and brick. One of his crew members refused to go on any more liquor runs for Johnson, saying the drink was killing him. The basement boiler stopped working, but instead of paying for repairs, the company bought space heaters, their many extension cords coiling like snakes in a fire inspector's nightmare.

Here Johnson was, the great and powerful TH, living like a shut-in a thousand miles from his home and family in Texas, drinking too much, hearing his headstrong assistant, Ardis Reyes, saying he needed to shave and shower. Yes, here he was, the National Association for Retarded Children's "Employer of the Year," 1968.

Unable to stem his own alcohol consumption, Johnson would rage instead against his occasional drinking companion, Keith Brown, who would get so drunk that Johnson sometimes had him locked in a room with a bucket until he sobered up. But the boss saved his fiercest anger for the nemesis that had hounded him for decades: the government.

In 2001, Johnson wrote a letter to his Texas congressman to complain that the US Department of Labor had been conducting on-site inspections and reviews on "more than a regular basis," including four time-consuming audits in two years. He noted that Henry's Turkey Service had received many awards and commendations over the years, and claimed that its work with the "mentally challenged" had saved the taxpayers more than $100 million. The company had followed every guideline set forth by every state and federal agency it had come in contact with, he wrote. "No discrepancies have ever been noted."

This was false. Four years earlier, the Department of Labor had determined that Henry's Turkey Service had failed to pay the men overtime for the labor they put in beyond the forty-hour workweek. But facts melted in the heat of Johnson's wrath. If the government harassment did not end, he warned, this life-affirming, tax-saving program "will cease to exist."

The congressman, Chet Edwards, followed up on his prominent constituent's complaint. Months later, he forwarded to Johnson a summary report from the Labor Department, along with his regrets "that the information could not be more favorable."

The government report laid out prior violations of the law by Henry's Turkey Service that allowed the payment of subminimum wages to employees with disabilities, as well as the company's persistent refusal to provide payroll records. At one point, it noted, Johnson had warned investigators they "would need to bring armed marshals in order to review the records."

The report also alluded to curious bookkeeping detected by the Labor Department's Office of Inspector General. Henry's Turkey Service was deducting $864 a month from each man's pay for lodging, meals, and other services; multiply that by forty, every month. It was paying $600 a month in rent for the schoolhouse, yet claiming yearly expenses of $67,200; the extra $60,000, it argued, went toward covering the costs of improvements it had made to the building more than twenty years earlier. And it listed

$100,000 in expenses for the construction of a retirement home — that sanctuary the men had been promised once the turkeys became too heavy to lift.

Despite Johnson's brash threat of violence, Henry's Turkey Service eventually provided the payroll records sought by labor investigators, only to be found in violation of the sub-minimum wage law, again. It paid the back wages, again, promised compliance, again, and broke that promise. Again.

Johnson saw these government inquiries as relentless attacks by bureaucrats who did not understand what he was trying to do. They simply did not appreciate that these boys would be warehoused in institutions if it weren't for him; that they had become like family. Sure, Keith annoyed him with his inability to hold his liquor, and Henry could be a drunken pain in the ass too, and Levi with his spoons, and Leonard with his mumbling, and, well, damn. He had known many of these boys since they were teenagers, practically. Raised them like his own. Damn bureaucrats.

Johnson must not have realized his good fortune. The truth was, the government bureaucrats he so loathed were still adhering to their long tradition of incuriosity about complaints regarding his operation.

In 1997, a Texas newspaper reporter inquired about allegations of financial exploitation and substandard living conditions at the Atalissa bunkhouse, prompting a Texas state official to contact Iowa's Department of Human Services. This, in turn, stirred up a comical frenzy in Iowa to avoid responsibility at all costs, as reflected in email exchanges that are case studies in the bureaucratic art of sidestepping:

The operation isn't a health facility, DHS has no purchase-of-service or other connection to the operation, and the local DHS offices has always maintained that the turkey farm employees are in an employer/employee relationship (not dependent adults). . . .

Gary said he had suggested to the woman that perhaps Div. of Voc. Rehab. in Dept. of Education may have some connection. . . .

I don't want us on the record with anybody as to the fact these folks are or are not dependent adults before we know what ground Gary has already covered and what his stand is at this time . . .

Also, I just talked with Gary and he and the county are concerned that with Texas doing whatever, Henry's Turkey farm may close, leaving these 40 "residents" in Muscatine County with Muscatine County holding the bag. Seems to us these folks are Texas responsibility. . . .

In the end, the officials at the Department of Human Services talked themselves into believing they had no jurisdiction to conduct so much as a "look-see," since they had not received any formal allegation of abuse concerning a dependent adult.

A few years later, Dennis Hepker, a long-time councilman and former mayor in Atalissa, drove up the hill to check on the chlorine levels in the town's water tower, which was planted at the southern corner of the schoolhouse property. As Hepker moved past the old, familiar building, he noticed its front door chained and padlocked. This not only symbolized how townspeople had not been invited inside for many years, it also represented the potential hazard of a blocked fire escape.

After receiving a mind-your-own-business response from Randy Neubauer, the on-site supervisor — "I've got nothing good to say about him," Hepker says — he let the matter marinate a bit before calling to share his concerns with the Department of Human Services office in Davenport.

"I told them about the door, and how I just had a feeling that things probably . . ." he says, pausing. "I just said I think you need to look into it, that's all. Just like if you saw a neighbor with a real skinny dog in their yard, you'd call and say, 'Maybe you oughta go check that dog out.' "

The government response stunned him.

"I was actually blown off," he recalls. "I was told that they were underfunded and understaffed, as all government agencies are, and did I have any evidence. And I said, 'Well, just the door being padlocked shut.' "

Hepker also complained to the local sheriff's office, though by the time a deputy came out, the padlock was gone. But the episode nagged at him, and still does, more than a decade later. He thinks that if he had indeed called about a skinny dog in someone's yard, the response would have been faster and more thorough.

Sitting on his porch, a few hundred yards from the schoolhouse, Hepker squints into the unfixed distance. "Maybe I should have been a more responsible citizen and looked into it," he says. "But I'd see those guys, and they were always clean, they always had nice clothes, and they always seemed — happy."

The complaints also came from within.

Ardis Reyes, the trusted aide who informed Johnson that she would no longer buy his alcohol, had worked at the schoolhouse for several years. A college graduate, she had been a teacher at a bilingual Christian preschool in West Liberty before going to work for Johnson, helping prepare the men's food, drive them to medical appointments, and cut their hair, always following his instructions to buzz-cut those who struggled with grooming. She also took them on trips — to Walmart, to Kentucky Fried Chicken, to the adult stores along Kirkwood Avenue in Iowa City.

Reyes felt for the men. She comforted Pete Graffagnino as best she could when he'd start talking again about wanting to be with his sister, Rose, in Texas. She did what she could to connect Willie Levi, Henry Wilkins, and others with their families, finding the last best addresses for their relatives and helping them write letters. If they had a telephone number scribbled down somewhere, she would help them place a phone call.

"None of the numbers ever worked," she says.

Reyes juggled many chores. She did some of Johnson's bookkeeping, cleaned his bedsheets, and shopped for Christmas presents for his wife and daughters. But she was no pushover. She did not drink and she did not use foul language. Johnson might feel free to cuss and yell at the men and at other crew members, but he didn't dare treat her that way. And when she saw any of the men being abused, physically or verbally, she never hesitated to report it straight away to Johnson — that day, for example, when a crew member shoved paper towels into a man's mouth to keep him from wailing.

Reyes liked Johnson most of the time, but she found herself in constant conflict with Randy and Dru Neubauer, the de facto supervisors who seemed to consider her a threat to their power. Then, one day, she abruptly left. Some say she was fired; she says that the cruelty and absurdity and sadness of the operation — more than thirty men with special needs, living in an old schoolhouse? — just hit her. Johnson said something that irked her, and she walked out.

Not long after, in June 2005, a call came into the complaint center at the Iowa

Department of Inspections and Appeals, the agency that inspects and licenses health-care facilities and health-care providers.

Complainant:
*Ardis Reyes*

Health Facility:
*Henry's Turkey Service*

What Are The Complainant's Expectations/ Desires:
*Close them down*

Summary of Complaint:
*Caller is a former employee and states there are 35 men that live there and work at the West Liberty Turkey Plant turkey farm (which is also owned by the same people) and as indentured servants from 4:00 a.m. to 2:00 p.m. The men are all mentally challenged and come from Texas. The men are paid for the work and the check goes to the corporation in Texas. The men are then given spending money, $5 every Tuesday and a total of $60 a month. They are charged $959 a month for room and board.*

The complainant, Reyes, went on to

describe the cockroaches in the food; the failure to provide medical attention to the men for ulcers, asthma, and other ailments; the wholesale neglect and constant abuse. Shoving paper towels in Tommy Johnson's mouth to keep him from talking. Forcing Henry Wilkins to eat jalapeño peppers. On top of all this, she reported, was the financial exploitation: *Last year, the Labor Department came in & made the farm pay the men for wages, but since they control all the money, they just took it out of one pocket & put it in another.*

The Department of Inspections and Appeals sent two investigators to the schoolhouse on three successive days. It then notified Johnson that the allegation of operating an unlicensed health-care facility had not been substantiated, on the grounds that his operation was not a residential health-care facility as defined by Iowa regulations.

Once again, Henry's Turkey Service had dodged censure and possible shutdown because its schoolhouse operation did not quite fit any description in Iowa's reams of definitions and regulations. If it was *not* a health-care facility, then other allegations were not of the moment.

The bunkhouse was a place unto itself.

■ ■ ■ ■

By early 2008, the fight was nearly out of Johnson. He had said good-bye to his boys and gone back to the Hill Country of Texas. Back to where he belonged. Where he had played high school football, become a proud Aggie, married the prettiest girl in Goldthwaite, fathered three daughters, and taken the chance of hiring a few young men from the Abilene State School.

Mister Christmas. Well finder. Employer of the year and thorn in the side of government. The man who'd give you money on the sly, and made sure you got to touch a woman now and then, but kept you subjugated your entire adult life. Angel and devil both in marked-up khakis, with that cash-choked billfold jutting from his shirt pocket. *Go get me some sardines, Levi. Here's a five, and keep the change. But don't tell anyone. Our little secret.*

Back in Goldthwaite, people hardly recognized the man, now all skin and bones where once a larger-than-life presence had been. "It shocked me to see him in that shape," says Elroy Poindexter, a longtime employee and a fiercely loyal friend, whose son Kevin also once worked for Johnson.

"Broke everybody's heart."

In those final days, Poindexter drove down to see his old pal TH, who was staying with a daughter in Burnet, where serenity is found in the wind's rustle of pecan trees and the shimmer of Lake LBJ. Several people were gathered around the sick man, but the two old friends managed to have a private moment. Elroy told TH that he'd always been like a father to him, and TH told Elroy that he'd been more than a good worker; he'd been a good friend.

*Well, I'm gonna get out of here and let you get some rest,* the visitor said.

*Okay, Elroy,* TH said, and closed his eyes.

■ ■ ■ ■

# FOURTEEN

■ ■ ■ ■

*Frank Rodriguez flashes his Henry's Turkey Service identification*

Atalissans will tell you right off: Those Henry's boys never complained. They'd mingle at the coffee hour after church, or browse at the minimart, or eat another community supper in the fire station, and some of them would prattle on and on about county fairs and NASCAR and Hawkeyes football. But they never whined. Never said boo about living in the same building and doing the same work at the same pay year after year, some of them since Ford was president.

Here it was, several years into the new millennium, and Willie Levi still joked with Vada Baker about sharing the same birthday in August. John Hatfield still patrolled the streets on his trike, collecting litter and embracing his status as an honorary city employee. Tommy House, the brooder, still showed up early at Zion Lutheran Church, waiting for the new pastor, Lynn Thiede, rain or shine. He'd escort her from her car to the office, help her slip into her pure-white alb and colorful stole — "and then he would hug me," she says.

Besides, you tend not to notice changes in those who are ever present. Flipping through old family photographs, you can't remember the father or brother sitting beside you ever looking the way he does in that picture. When did he lose his hair? And gain all that weight? Has it really been ten years? Twenty? Maybe a sort of cluelessness, born of the familiar, explains why everyone in town missed the telltale details. The limp from standing at the plant all day. The dam-aged nails from pulling crop. The fingers bent from the repetitive work. The rotting and missing teeth. The dried blood caked along the lips, caused by broken bridgework.

From the outside, at least, the schoolhouse looked as well maintained as ever, once you got past the turquoise paint job that clashed with all of Iowa. In summer, the tidy flower beds still sprouted, and at Christmastime, the light displays still glittered. The people of Atalissa naturally assumed that the manicured exterior reflected similar order within. What else did they have to go on, with the bunkhouse's open-door parties now a distant memory, and the No Trespassing signs as visible as those flower beds. "We never had any reason to doubt," says Dennis Hepker, the former mayor.

But why didn't the men complain? It is the same facile question that arises in cases of domestic violence, workplace harassment, and schoolyard bullying. The question comes from a position of doubt, at a safe distance: *Sure, these guys had — what's it called now? Right. So these guys had "intellectual disability." But how would that stop them from complaining if they were being mistreated?*

One answer could be that the bunkhouse boys believed they had nowhere else to go, so they thought it best to keep their mouths shut. Maybe they feared punishment if caught telling tales outside the schoolhouse. Given that most of them had little more than the setting of a state school to inform their worldview, maybe they figured this was as good as it got.

Or maybe, just maybe, they did not want to reveal themselves as vulnerable adults — grown up, but still "boys" — to the nice-smelling women they danced with and the rough-handed men they considered peers. Gene Berg, one of the few with a family involved in his life, never told his mother about the darker corners of the Atalissa bunkhouse. His reasoning is rooted in the western movies the men watched, in the clothes they wore, in that John Wayne poster once sizing them up in the dining room back in Goldthwaite:

"You take it like a man."

That's right, pilgrim. You take it like a man.

Because silver-steel shackles could not hang empty. Because balls of white feathers fluttered on waiting trucks. Because nobody else would put up with such a taxing job for so long. Because America needed its roast turkey, smoked turkey, and turkey bacon. Because there was money to be made. Because this was the best that could be done for some men with cognitive impairments and because, again, there was money to be made. Because this is the way they've lived most every day for more than thirty years. Just because.

It's three in the morning. Rise, if not shine, in that drafty schoolhouse on the hill. Get dressed. Cover the quilt over the stained and swayback mattress. Stop at the fetid bathroom with the open stalls, where everyone knows everyone else's business. Sleepwalk down the mazelike hall to long tables in the dining room for a quick breakfast prepared by one of their own, Pete Graffagnino. Pete has an allergy to the ammonia used at the turkey plant, so he spends his workday at the bunkhouse, peeling potatoes, shredding cabbage, putting meals together, including breakfast; he does his best with eggs and cereal. He is the meekest and kindest man in the house, often asking people to join him in prayer, the one they counted on to hand out Christmas cards: "To James F. *It's Christmas! May its special joy surround you!* Pete." He talks often of wanting to be with his sister in Texas.

In his domain, a sticky-floored kitchen, Graffagnino struggles to keep the cockroaches off the steam table and out of the food, and to sweep the shelves clean of mouse turds. He takes pride in always washing his hands after killing a roach and throwing it in the trash, just as you're supposed to do. One time he sat down to eat after feeding everyone else, only to find a roach adorning his mashed potatoes. A supervisor told him to just remove the bug and whatever it had touched, and eat the rest. But he could not, and he did not.

Impervious to fumigation, the roaches occasionally fall like black raindrops from the compromised ceiling in the dining room. The men have become accustomed to eating their meals with one protective hand over their plate.

"I always looked at my food before I ate it," Frank Rodriguez says.

The men who take medication — for asthma, or epilepsy — do so in come-and-get-it fashion. Their prescription pills rest in little indentations on an unkempt wooden board that is divided by names and a series of strings. The system relies mostly on honor, and one man's pill might very well roll into another man's row. Preston Pate and Robert Penner also have diabetes, but needles make Pate nervous, so Penner administers his friend's insulin as well as his own.

Their bunkhouse monastery may isolate the men from the everyday world, but it has not kept illness and death at bay. The men have an almost agricultural approach to life and death, a kind of she-got-cancer-and-she-died simplicity, as whenever they discuss the almost mythical death of their house-mate Alford Busby: *He got mad and he run away and he froze to death.* This matter-of-factness followed through when two other Henry's "boys," Bobo Johnson and Andy Sawyer, died.

"We had to take the bodies down to Texas, take them back to where they came from," Dru Neubauer once told the *Des Moines*

*Register.* "We pulled the seats out of the van and loaded them up, you know, in the coffin, and drove their bodies back down to Texas."

*Bobo Johnson: he got cancer and he died. Andy Sawyer: they took him to the hospital and he died. Put 'em in a van and brought 'em back to Texas.*

But you had to be nearly as sick as Bobo and Andy to avoid being on one of those same vans when they pulled away from the turquoise bunker before dawn, bound for the turkey plant. The men rarely received time off for illness, according to Gene Berg, who says he kept on pulling guts even as he struggled with the debilitating effects of chemotherapy treatment for throat cancer.

"Made me go to work when I was sick," he says. "I threw up at my house and I threw up at work."

Onto the plant property and into the white lab coats and hairnets and rubber boots. Back out onto the line. By now the men are no longer working the live dock, concentrating instead on hanging the dead birds on the infinite loop of shackles and eviscerating the carcasses as they sway past.

To feign compliance with federal regulations that allow for the payment of sub-minimum wages to people with disabilities,

Henry's Turkey Service keeps records that supposedly chart each man's production — although their supervisor, Randy Neubauer, would later say that he was instructed by his bosses to under-report the men's productivity — that is, the number of birds they moved up the line. Those records say, for example, that Gene Berg gutted 76 birds for every 125 birds gutted by a nondisabled colleague; that meant he earned $5.73 an hour, or 61 percent of the going rate of $9.40 an hour. Keith Brown, meanwhile, gutted 53 for every 125; James Fowler, 58; Robert Penner, 51. All nonsense, since the men receive the same take-home salary of $65 every month: $5 on some weeks, $10 or $15 on others.

The contract that Henry's Turkey Service has with the plant hinges on the number of birds gutted and sent down the line for processing — as much as $11,000 a week in revenue — which is why the chief supervisor, Neubauer, and his assistant, Danny Miles, patrol the line, urging the men to work faster.

But the men have given their adult lives to this brutal repetition. Many are well into their sixties, aching, weary. They work as fast as they can in the moist air to keep up with the pinkish blur of defeathered dead fowl whirring past them, and the suggestion that they sometimes dog it at work would rankle them for years to come.

"They wanted me to work faster," Henry Wilkins says. "I can't do that."

"I was doing the best I can," Jeff Long says. "Trying to do the best I can. But Randy got mad."

The system calls for Neubauer and Miles to jump into the line and spell anyone who needs to use the lavatory, but some of the men — at times denied a break, at times afraid to ask for one — occasionally relieve themselves in their pants. The evidence will be found by peers handling the bunkhouse laundry at night.

The system also calls for civility and respect in the workplace, but that too has broken down. Willie Levi says Neubauer shoved him hard against a wall because he wasn't doing a good enough job. Brady Watson says he saw Levi come out of a room with his mouth bloodied. Joe Morrell says he would sometimes stop to rest, only to have Neubauer kick him in the — well, he can't bring himself to say the word "ass." Several say that Miles repeatedly sprayed water from a hose into their rubber boots, a prank that seems to have led to serious fungal problems.

In the early summer of 2007, the plant's owner, West Liberty Foods, sent a letter to Henry's Turkey Service:

As you know, Henry's Turkey Service and West Liberty Foods are parties to a Turkey Service Agreement, pursuant to which your company provides services in our West Liberty, Iowa, processing plant. Under the agreement, Henry's is an independent contractor, and is responsible for managing its own employees. West Liberty Foods is not the employer of the Henry's workers, nor are we obligated or entitled to discipline the Henry's workers.

It has come to our attention that one of your supervisors, Randy Neubauer, has engaged in abusive behavior toward the Henry's workers in our plant. While Mr. Neubauer is not our employee, we cannot allow this type of behavior to continue in our facility. We have obtained written statements from several of our employees who have witnessed Mr. Neubauer abusively yelling at Henry's workers and physically punching them.

Please contact me at your earliest opportunity and let me know how you intend to remedy this situation. West Liberty Foods values its relationship with Henry's

Turkey Service, and we are hopeful that we can resolve this matter.

One of the incidents informing this letter occurred when Neubauer sent Johnny Kent, a small, obsessive man with a wide smile revealing few teeth, sprawling to the floor. Neubauer later said it was accidental; Kent was wearing oversize pants and he was just trying to adjust the man's belt. Kent disagrees: "He knocked me down."

West Liberty Foods chose to believe the accounts of its employees, and banned Neubauer from the plant. It is not hard to imagine the whispers among the plant's higher-ups: If he treats his guys this way in public, how does he treat them in private, behind those turquoise walls and boarded-up windows?

Henry's Turkey Service, meanwhile, responded to the damning allegation by doing nothing.

The bossman, T. H. Johnson, was quite ill by this point, so his partner, Kenneth Henry, handled the matter from Texas. Henry listened to Neubauer's version, but never talked to Johnny Kent because, he says, "on the phone you can't understand him at all." He decided in the end to keep everything in place, with Neubauer remaining responsible for the welfare of the very men he had been seen abusing in the workplace.

Sitting in his dim office down in Goldthwaite, recalling this turbulent period in the history of Henry's Turkey Service, Kenneth Henry suddenly asks: "Have you ever read the Book of Job?"

In late 2006, Henry was working with his wife and his younger brother, a carpenter, to repair the sagging carport beside the parsonage of the Proctor Baptist Church, near his hometown of Comanche. While they labored to shore up the structure, it collapsed on Henry's wife, causing severe injuries that led to the loss of her right leg, and on his brother, killing him.

In early 2007, his partner, TH, became too sick to remain in Atalissa, so Henry made a couple of weeklong trips to Iowa, staying in a nearby hotel rather than in the bunkhouse. "I didn't see all these problems in '07," he says. "Weren't there. The bunkhouse was the bunkhouse, and it isn't the fanciest place in the world, but it was surely livable. It was surely warm. The boys liked it."

In mid-2007, Neubauer was banned from the plant.

In late 2007, Henry had the first of five heart attacks over several months.

In early 2008, as TH lay dying in his daughter's home, Randy and Dru Neubauer came down from Iowa, met with the Johnson family in Burnet, and told everyone not to worry, they had Atalissa under control. The couple then traveled up to Proctor, Texas, where Henry was recuperating from his latest heart attack, to offer the same assurances.

Henry had no reason to doubt them, since the Neubauers had been working at the bunkhouse for more than a decade. And to Henry's mind, the couple's hands-on experience trumped the lack of any "official" qualification to care for people with special needs.

"I know some PhDs and a lot of attorneys that is dumb as wood," he says. "Education don't get you there. I never had any education. I graduated from high school. But we built all this.

"What I'm saying, then, is this. You go to college for four years and you get a degree. Does that make you smarter than someone who's been on the job for fifteen years? Doing the same exact thing?"

Except that Henry had received a warning, flashing red, in the decision by West

Liberty Foods to ban Randy Neubauer from the turkey plant for mistreating the "boys" of Henry's Turkey Service.

Here is the self-styled Job of Texas, then. Surrounded by the illness, injury, and death of those closest to him, struggling with his own heart ailments, being second-guessed by government officials, lawyers, and other book-educated know-it-alls, still insisting that he had done right by these boys, but that others — namely the Neubauers — had let them down.

"Three times they told me: Don't worry about it, we can do it, we can handle it," he says of the Neubauers. "Didn't happen."

Randy and Dru Neubauer have their own narrative, though, one that mostly blames Kenneth Henry for the bunkhouse's decline. In depositions and in court testimony, they portray themselves as the men's champions, constantly questioning the inequities in pay and the lack of Medicaid coverage for the men in Iowa. Constantly worrying, too. Through a friend at the county jail, they even had identification cards made for the men, just in case, God forbid, any of them ever wandered off and got lost.

The Neubauers say that after T. H. Johnson died, they received explicit orders from

Kenneth Henry to lower expenses. Cut back on the food bill, on the doctor and dental visits, on vacation money and the modest cash gifts at Christmas, on the repairs to the schoolhouse. It was *There's nothing wrong with them guys eating beans and hamburger.* No more Sunday steaks out on the grill. No more monthly outings to the modest buffet at Golden Corral; cheaper just to go to Pizza Ranch. No more TH, sober or not, sending a man out for some sardines and telling him to keep the change.

"TH seemed to care for the guys more personally," Randy Neubauer later said. "In my opinion of Kenneth, he was worried about the dollars, the dollar signs."

Many of the windows in the old schoolhouse had long been boarded up, for example, lending a hint of abandonment to the building's otherwise tidy exterior. A couple of windows had also rotted, letting in the wind and rain. What's more, the rancid-smelling bathrooms were in desperate need of repainting.

Neubauer claims he bought paint and a stack of plywood to make the necessary repairs, only to be instructed by Henry not to bother. In fact, the boss said, we'll have those supplies shipped down to Texas.

Along with the rain and the wind, something else was blowing through the cheap, compromised plywood. Coming up from Texas. Hot. Impatient. A change in attitude, saying this just ain't worth it anymore.

*Hang them birds! Hang 'em!*
After lunch and through the early afternoon, wearing lab coats freckled with the fresh blood of dead birds. Picking stray feathers from the carcasses. Hanging and rehanging them onto shackles. Reaching into birds to yank out those seed-filled crops, again and again and again, constricting hands and damaging fingernails.

"I lost that fingernail from cropping," Henry Wilkins says, holding up his big, bony hand. "Yeah, that'll make your fingers real sore."

What hurt more, though, he says, was getting yelled at even when he tried his best. "They bitched and made hell at us."

Driving back to the bunkhouse at the end of the workday, the vans sometimes stop at a local market in West Liberty so the men can dash in with their five dollars to buy a can of Copenhagen snuff, a Mountain Dew, a Honey Bun. But if the supervisors think you've been dogging it, they'll order you to stay in the van like a punished adolescent. *Go on, hurry it up, but Henry, you ain't going in. You neither, Levi. Maybe you'll work harder next time.*

The anger over the humiliation, the denial of a soda or a Slim Jim, would never abate. "They said I wasn't working hard enough," James Fowler, who pulled guts, recalls. "Damn lie. I *did* work hard enough."

The punishment continues at the bunkhouse. A man might be told to pull weeds. To stay in his room, with no television or radio. To forget about going to church on Sunday. To place both hands on a pole and stay that way until supper. To walk in circles in the gymnasium while carrying heavy objects — ten-pound weights, a bucket of rocks. "The doctor wanted them to do exercises," Neubauer later claimed.

It had nothing to do with doctor's orders. "They said I wasn't doing a good job," Levi says. "So — get your black butt and get them weights."

Keith Brown recalls spending a long, long time holding weights. The reason: "Didn't do the job right."

Some of the men manage to dodge the bullying. Brady Watson knew that if somebody didn't do a job right, there'd be hell to pay, with screaming and yelling and cussing — so he just learned to stay out of the way. Frank Rodriguez believes the supervisors picked on the weaker men "because they couldn't fight back." Mocked them, slapped them upside the head, made them eat jalapeño peppers for laughs.

Tommy Johnson suffered more than most. A gut puller at the plant, short, stout, wearing a look of never-ending woe, he rarely cleaned his room, often picked through the trash, and was forever in the crosshairs of his bosses, usually for not working hard enough. He became known as the man who kept getting kicked in the nuts. No wonder he wandered.

"I would walk," he says, illustrating with two fingers stepping along a tabletop.

But because he often had no money, Tommy Johnson's late-night walks sometimes led him into the bedrooms of other men in search of tobacco to soothe his craving. He needed to find a substitute, even if it meant shredding someone else's cigarettes and tucking a wad of loose tobacco into his cheek.

"Kept running off" is how Tommy House remembers him. "He did not want to vacuum or wash his bed down so he run off . . . we had to go look for him . . . he was down the road . . . Randy fought him bad . . . Tommy afraid . . . did not open his mouth . . . then to the bed."

Someone decided to teach Tommy Johnson a lesson. On at least one occasion, he was handcuffed overnight to his bed, the cuffs so tight he bled and howled. Randy Neubauer was coy about the matter later, denying that he had handcuffed Johnson but acknowledging that someone had. Another man, considered the strongest in the bunkhouse, says that he was ordered by Neubauer to do it, and that if he didn't obey, the supervisor would have "chewed out my tail, and then what?"

The image of Tommy Johnson sprawled on his bed in his coveralls, handcuffed and wailing, still haunts the man. He does not like talking about it, other than to say, "I don't go for that anymore."

Years later, several of the bunkhouse men would sit around a nursing home table and talk over one another as they recalled the singular abuse that Tommy Johnson endured, some trying to be polite, others just coming out and saying it.

Kicked in the balls.

Kicked in the nuts.

Kicked down there.

Tommy Johnson would sit among them, listening, his gums and few teeth the color of dark honey after decades of his beloved dip and chew. When asked if he had been kicked in the nuts, he would say yes, that it happened while he was pulling weeds in punishment before dinner. When asked whether he had been handcuffed to his bed, he would look to his brothers, as if searching for approval to tell his own wretched story.

After a pause, the chubby man with woeful eyes would give the slightest, saddest, most reluctant nod.

The men suffer one another's abuse collectively, as if they are all Tommy Johnson being handcuffed, or Henry Wilkins being forced to eat jalapeño peppers, or Raymond Vaughn carrying weights while walking in circles, or Jeff Long, denied the use of his own television because he didn't feel like working one day.

And every now and then, someone rises in defiance, as when Billy Penner stood up for Willie Levi after his friend was ordered once again to grab the pole and not move. Levi gets emotional in the retelling: "He say: 'You leave him alone.' He say: 'I'm going to deck you one.' "

The men are on their own. Unable or unwilling to tell others what it was like to see cockroaches nesting in their televisions and clock radios. To be assigned dehumanizing numbers that made sorting all the laundered socks and underwear that much easier (They remember their numbers still: Brady Watson was 2; Frank Rodriguez was 83; Keith Brown was 175.) To hear another man's repetitive tic as he tries to understand why he didn't get his five dollars that week, or why he wasn't allowed out of the van, or why he'd been called a dumb ass.

"I was doing the best I can," Jeff Long says again and again. "I was doing the best I can."

Pete Graffagnino tries to keep the bugs out of the food. Robert Penner gives Preston Pate his insulin shots. Frank Rodriguez and Brady Watson do the laundry, cleaning away the evidence that a few of their brothers have had an especially bad day; sometimes the clothes just have to be thrown in the trash. And on the rare occasions when the outside world is reminded again of how they are living, through a newspaper report or a tip from a former employee, the actions taken — if any — never interrupt the repetition of their everyday existence.

Even their supervisor Randy Neubauer knows that many of them are ready for a "change of scenery," as he would later put it. He knows, too, of the retirement home being built in Goldthwaite for them. "They

309

would go to this facility there on the ranch and they would still all be together," he would say, adding: "It was kind of like a brotherhood."

Supper. Television. Lights out early, boys, 'cause we're doing it all over again tomorrow.

The rain and snowmelt drips into pans and buckets placed around the gym, the bathroom, the garage, the kitchen, a bedroom or two. Plinking and plopping, the elements beat their relentless rhythm against the ancient schoolhouse structure, testing, knocking. Something has to give.

# FIFTEEN

*A Christmas farewell at the Atalissa community center, 2008*

The birds have gotten too heavy, boys. Forty pounds, fifty when it rains. Most of you are pretty much at retirement age anyway. Billy Penner here is sixty-four, and his little brother'll be sixty come August. Pete and Levi, you're both sixty-two. Henry, you're sixty-four, but Lord knows you don't act it. And where's David Crouch? You're sixty-eight, for crying out loud!

It's time, boys. It's time.

After a lifetime of assembly-line drudgery, the thirty-two men still living at the bunkhouse were told they were being retired. Removed from the turkey-plant machinery like old sprockets with teeth worn to the nubs, and with as much say in the matter. Done.

For more than three decades, nothing could stop the Henry's Turkey Service grind, which still earned the company a half-million dollars in revenue a year. Not

313

the early warnings of an Iowa social worker. Not the repeated violations leveled by labor investigators. Not the heads-up given by a local official about a padlocked door. Not the banishment of a bunkhouse supervisor from the turkey plant for abuse. Not the death by hypothermia of one of the "boys," swallowed into the frigid dark of an Iowa winter's morning.

But one of the company's founders, T. H. Johnson, was dead, and the other, Kenneth Henry, was struggling with family tragedy and a troubled heart down in Texas. The two men had always insisted on handling things their own way and in their own time, and now that time had come. In late 2008, Henry's Turkey Service arranged for a gradual separation from the West Liberty turkey plant, with some of the men retiring by the end of the year, and the others following them out the door by the middle of March.

"Several of the boys were getting older, and needed to go to a different place," Henry recalls. "They certainly didn't need to be working. Time to be through."

The news that the Henry's boys were leaving Atalissa tore through town like fire in a cornfield. It was delivered with the bundles of mail at the post office, dealt with the jacks

314

and queens over games of euchre at the Old University bar, bagged with the modest purchases at the Atalissa Mini-Mart.

Heart-struck, some civic-minded women who called themselves the ABCs — for the Atalissa Betterment Committee — turned their Christmas gathering that year into a farewell party for the first round of men to be leaving. Once again the firehouse became the Atalissa community center, the trucks pulled from their bays and replaced by long tables adorned with white tablecloths and pots of bloodred chrysanthemums. Beside the glass-encased display of mementoes from the town's long-closed high school, an artificial Christmas tree came alive with an electrified dazzle. Songs were sung and speeches made in honor of the men, some of whom wore their "Cadillac" clothes — their very best. Frank Rodriguez in his black leather vest. Billy Penner in a daring western shirt of psychedelic red and blue.

But hints of "Auld Lang Syne" infused the night's Christmas wassailing. The ABCs had, in their small way, taken care of the men over the years, giving them quilts and presents, cookies and pies. Now they were saying good-bye, and it was hard, just hard, says Lorna Pahl, who had gotten to know the men while delivering a weekly circular

315

in town. "One of the boys came up and asked me why I was crying."

Whatever sadness the men felt was tempered by their giddiness over a long-standing promise, one they prattled on about even as townspeople handed them gifts. The promise of that retirement home waiting for them at the ranch in Goldthwaite. They had helped pay for it with their turkey-plant toil. Rodriguez and others had spent time down there working on it. They could not wait.

But who could blame the men for talking a bit too much about their supposed Goldthwaite paradise? Difficult childhoods, traumatic family separations, formative years spent in a state institution, entire adulthoods spent in a schoolhouse, feelings numbed by the repetition of evisceration, the sameness of the years, a county fair, a clown outfit, a Honey Bun. Now here was their promised land: a place where men with no families could be their own family — fishing, hiking, taking in all of Texas with a cold beverage in their stiff hands.

A Christmas fantasy.

T. H. Johnson and Kenneth Henry had never finished the construction of that retirement dorm at the Goldthwaite ranch. Even today, years later, construction materials clutter the floors, as if the work had stopped in a hammer's midswing. Henry says his failing health and Johnson's death had trumped their grand paternal plans.

"We didn't get there," he says.

Neither did the boys.

Eleven men comprised the first group to leave. They said merry Christmas and good-bye to their bunkhouse brothers and that was that. They were parceled out like a fresh litter of mutts, in many cases never to see one another again.

A lucky few moved in with family members, including Johnny McDaniels, a quiet, elfin man of fifty-six who says he had been routinely kicked in the butt and yelled at for incompetence. After twenty-seven years of working for Henry's Turkey Service, he arrived at his mother's house with some worn clothes, a box of broken electronics, and a few other pieces of junk, his most valuable possession a pair of new tennis shoes, available for purchase at Walmart for less than forty dollars.

A couple of men landed at a one-story group home in Goldthwaite, including sixty-eight-year-old David Crouch, a hard worker with glasses, wispy white hair, and large, roughened hands. He arrived in a foul mood, cursing and limping, but it turned out he was wearing shoes two sizes too large to accommodate long toenails that had curled under to dig into the pads of his feet. Noticing that he also could not hear, the group home's operator, Frieda Johnson — a former school-teacher and T. H. Johnson's sister-in-law — took him to have his ears examined, fully expecting a prescription for hearing aids. Instead, the doctor removed two dime-size chunks of wax.

Ears cleaned and toenails cut, Crouch could hear clearly and walk pain-free. His mood brightened.

The remaining half dozen men wound up in a nursing home in Midland, in west Texas. They included Johnny Kent, who had been knocked down at the plant; Tommy House, who used to hug Pastor Lynn before church services on Sundays; big Leonard Barefield, whose speech impediment made his words difficult to decode; and kicked-in-the-balls Tommy Johnson, who arrived with his proudest possession, an electric fan, along with bladder and prostate problems and grotesquely swollen testicles.

Randy Neubauer later claimed to have immediate regrets after driving several of them from Iowa to the nursing home in Texas. "The day that I dropped them off down there, I wanted to load them back up and bring them back," he would say. "And I just felt that was not a place for them."

Such regret might have been rooted in Neubauer's desire to keep the schoolhouse operation going; it had been a family, of sorts, and a livelihood for him and his wife. But Kenneth Henry rejected their proposal to take over the program, and dispatched Warren and Segreta Davis, two former employees from Oklahoma now in their seventies, to help oversee the shutdown. Much to the displeasure of the Neubauers, the Davises settled into what had been T. H. Johnson's old room with their three pets, Trixie, Stinky, and Chatter. A dog, a skunk, and a raccoon.

"They just showed up and said, 'We're here to close the bunkhouse down,' " Dru Neubauer later said.

Even with their unusual menagerie, the Davises fit right in. They knew and liked the men, having previously worked at both the schoolhouse in Atalissa and the ranch in Goldthwaite. Some of the men remembered Warren Davis as the supervisor who, many years earlier, had pulled them from the turkey plant's assembly line when he determined that their nondisabled colleagues had been mistreating them. But whatever cherished memories the Davises might have had of the bunkhouse evaporated the moment they stepped inside. The space heaters, the hole in the kitchen ceiling, the roaches — oh Lord, the roaches. The taciturn Davis says he'd seen cleaner pigpens; his wife says she almost died from the stench.

Twenty-one of the Henry's "boys" continued to live in the growing squalor and quiet of the Atalissa schoolhouse. Every morning, they trundled off to the plant to eviscerate turkeys with their customary precision, leaving Pete Graffagnino behind to clean up and prepare food. By now, the evisceration supervisor for the West Liberty Foods plant was Dave Meincke, whom the men had befriended and mentored when he first joined the assembly line as a gawky kid out of high school, some thirty years earlier. Now, as he later said in an affidavit, he watched with admiration as they went about their final days with their typical professionalism:

I can say without reservation that these disabled workers not only worked hard, but could be relied upon to get the job done every day. I observed them working side-by-side with or across the line with a level of experience and ability that demonstrated their strong work ethic and years of skills development required to meet our company's production goals. They were always ready to go to work at 5:00 am, Monday thru Friday. . . .

In all the time that I worked with the Henry's workers, who were called "the boys" by Henry's supervisors, I found that the disabled workers performed their jobs with as good a rate of productivity, or better, compared to any of the other workers on the line. In fact, when we realized that the Henry's operation was closing down, we replaced the Henry's workers with full-time WLF employees. The disabled men even took pride in showing some of the newer employees how to perform the jobs they had been doing.

Hardworking men with intellectual impairments, training their nondisabled successors before heading off to a well-deserved retirement in their home state of Texas. This, then, was the parting impression that Henry's Turkey Service nearly bequeathed to Iowa. A heartwarming tale from the American workplace. A Midwestern triumph.

But another dime had been dropped.

True, a small fortune in dimes had fallen through coin slots over the decades, only to generate the bureaucratic equivalent of a recorded message to please hold. Hold your tip, your suspicion, your fury.

This last dime, though, found purchase.

Sherri Brown, of Fayetteville, Arkansas, did her best to keep in touch with her brother, Keith Brown, up there in Atalissa. He was a handful, but he was her kin, and the two of them shared a special bond of disability. His was intellectual, while she had EEC syndrome, the genetic disorder that had left her with her clawlike hands and feet. She liked to say that she and Keith were the family defects.

For many years, Keith's primary familial contact had been their father. The old man would visit him a couple of times a year, and he often took Keith for a week of camping beside a lake just outside Texarkana. But their father had died in the late 1990s, followed soon after by their older brother, losses that pretty much left Sherri responsible for Keith — no easy task. On one visit home he disappeared for ten days on a drunken tear. Another time, she paid for an airport escort to meet him when he landed in Minneapolis and take him to his connecting flight to Des Moines. He was lost for half a day.

Sherri called the bunkhouse at least twice a month to check on Keith, and she and Dru Neubauer would have long, gossipy conversations. *You need to talk to Keith,* Neubauer would say. *He's misbehaving.* Which was certainly conceivable, considering his drinking. But the last time that Keith came home for a vacation, he begged his sister not to send him back to Atalissa.

*I'll earn my keep, I'll mow the yard, please, please, please.*

If only she had listened, she says now. But then, maybe no one would ever know . . .

One day in early 2009, Dru Neubauer called Sherri Brown with the life-changing news that Henry's Turkey Service was shutting down, followed by a pitch: We know it might be hard for you to take care of Keith, so why don't you make us the payee for his Social Security benefits to cover his expenses, and then he can stay up here with us, along with some of the other boys?

Much of what Brown was hearing did not sound right. She had worked both in the roiling scrum of Arkansas politics and in the challenging mission of disability advocacy, and she prided herself on her gut instinct. She needed more information about Keith's options.

The company was apparently sending some of the men to a nursing home in Texas, but her brother was only fifty-seven; he didn't need that. Yet she had no insight into his financial resources. How much money had Keith saved after thirty-five years of working for Henry's Turkey Service?

She telephoned T. H. Johnson's widow, Jane Ann Johnson, the company's book-keeper in Goldthwaite, to find out.

The answer: $87.96.

Sherri Brown nearly blacked out.

*He's been there his whole life! How could he only have eighty-eight dollars after thirty-five years of hard labor?*

The bookkeeper had no answer, which only raised more questions. Why are some of the men suddenly being sent to a nursing home? What happened to that plan for a retirement home on the Goldthwaite ranch? If Keith has only eighty-eight dollars, does this mean that all the other men also have almost nothing in savings?

Brown needed to calm herself to think. She asked her husband, her sister, and other relatives what they thought she should do — even though, in the end, she already knew: the authorities in Iowa needed to be notified.

She remembers calling just about every Iowa agency save its national guard. The Office of the Attorney General. The Department of Inspections and Appeals. Various divisions within the Department of Human Services, each passing the buck, fobbing her off to the next office like some customer-service annoyance. Finally, she connected with someone willing to set aside the original script and level with this distraught citizen:

*I'm going to tell you something, and I'll deny I ever said it. There's an investigative reporter at the* Des Moines Register. *If there's anybody who can figure it out, It's Clark Kauffman.*

Tips come into a newsroom with junk-mail regularity. Some are passed on to a reporter like leftover hors d'oeuvres by an editor just back from a gaseous black-tie event. Some arrive in an envelope with the telltale return address of a correctional facility. Some appear on a laptop screen, the subject heading of the email in all caps to underscore the urgency. And some come by telephone. You see an unfamiliar number flash on the office phone. You debate whether to pick up, because you don't have time to waste on someone's personal vendetta against the Department of Motor Vehicles; but you pick up. At the very least, your job is to listen. You must listen.

Clark Kauffman knew and honored this journalistic code, even though he did not study journalism in college. He never went to college.

He was twenty-four years old, selling plumbing supplies at a True Value hardware store in his Iowa hometown of Bettendorf, when a childhood friend called with a proposition: *You know how you always wanted to work in newspapers? Well, I'm running two weeklies here in central Illinois all by myself, and I need help. You can sleep on my couch. What do you —*

Yes, Kauffman said.

He sold ads and operated the platemaking machine for the two Illinois weeklies, while seizing every chance to write an occasional news story. After two years, he moved back home to become a reporter for a weekly paper called the *Bettendorf News,* where he scooped the local daily newspaper, the *Quad-City Times,* with such regularity that the owner of both papers switched him to the daily's staff. Kauffman's beat was education, but he spent nights and free time on his own in-depth projects. Before long, he was the newspaper's one-man investigative unit.

In 2000, Kauffman moved up to Iowa's premier newspaper, the *Des Moines Register,* where he continued his deliberate approach to investigation, generating reams of Freedom of Information requests, making late-night phone calls to convince bureaucrats — sometimes gently, sometimes not — to discuss those public matters they would prefer to keep private. In 2005, he was honored as one of three finalists for the Pulitzer Prize for Investigative Reporting, following his explosive revelations about the "glaring injustice" in the handling of traffic tickets by Iowa officials.

Burly, light haired, and with a soft way of speaking that belied his bulldog nature, Kauffman had become a force in Iowa, someone whose calls and emails were ignored by officials at their peril. Some saw him as a champion, others as one big pain in the ass. As a reporter covering the Department of Human Services, he used his beat to give voice to the unseen and unheard.

When the telephone rang at Kauffman's document-blanketed desk that Tuesday night, February 3, 2009, most of the other reporters were already gone from the storied newspaper building on Locust Street, leaving the copy and layout editors to close that day's editions. Kauffman was engaged in one of his favorite pastimes — poring over 990s, the IRS tax forms filed by nonprofit organizations — while a framed photograph of his long-dead dog, Barney, sat nearby. Another reporter once questioned why anyone would keep a picture of a dead dog on his desk, but Kauffman knew such a question deserved no answer. He and his wife, Janice, missed Barney, and he found comfort in having a picture of the faithful stray beside him. Some 990s, Barney happy in life, and now the phone was ringing. Kauffman always picks up.

As Sherri Brown's words tumbled from the receiver, Kauffman struggled to keep up, jotting hurried words on Post-it notes, thinking as he wrote that the caller must be mistaken. She was describing a large, singular operation — Dozens of men with intellectual disability? Working at a turkey plant and living in a schoolhouse? — that was nowhere on his radar, even though he covered human services for the state's dominant newspaper.

He told the caller he'd get back to her and, intrigued, wandered over to a rumpled editor with a white mustache: Randy Evans, the *Register*'s longtime repository of knowledge and guardian of standards. When a reporter once told him she had made a tiny, little mistake, he responded: "There's no such thing as tiny, little mistakes. Just tiny, little reporters."

Every newspaper has, or needs, a Randy Evans.

*Ever hear of someplace called Henry's Turkey Service? Out near West Liberty? Supposedly uses guys with intellectual disability to work in a turkey plant?*

Evans paused a few seconds before summoning to memory a couple of stories written nearly thirty years earlier, in 1979, by two damned good reporters, Margaret Engel and Mike McGraw, that laid out the screwed-up operation. Kauffman never forgot what Evans said next:

*I thought they shut that place down.*

Kauffman's next stop was the far end of the newsroom, to the rows of file cabinets containing the day-by-day story of Iowa in the twentieth century, in the form of newspaper articles carefully clipped and cataloged. The newspaper's morgue. Soon he found a manila envelope marked "Henry's Turkey Service," inside of which were a few news articles the color of mustard and dating to the Carter era. One bore the headline "Retarded Texans Labor in Iowa Turkey Plant."

There came the twinned burn of embarrassment and rage. Embarrassment, because he had not heard of this case before, and he felt he should have. Rage, because of what the caller, Sherri Brown, had told him: *Yeah, they're still operating.*

Kauffman walked back to his desk and immediately called his tipster. *Just to let you know,* he said. *This is what I'm working on from now on.*

In the cold and snowless morning, Kauffman drove the 140 miles east to this place called Atalissa, where the turquoise building on the hill struck him as out of context with its winter-brown surroundings. The lurid color, the gothic feel, the mazelike extension at its back. More than that, he felt disbelief. On a main road in this town is a building with boarded-up windows and a front entrance in evident disrepair — yet everyone living around here knows it is home to dozens of vulnerable men. The exterior is *telegraphing* trouble within! Something is seriously wrong here.

His knock at a locked door went unanswered. He decided to head for the interview he had set up the night before with one of the operation's supervisors, Dru Neubauer, at the prefab house she and her husband were renting in West Liberty. Driving down from the hill, he noticed two Dumpsters planted along the north side of the schoolhouse.

Neubauer, slight, anxious, was motivated to talk, since the livelihood she and her husband had counted on for the last dozen years was about to vanish. She acknowledged that conditions in the bunkhouse were not the best — "The building gets cold, and it is drafty like you wouldn't believe" — and that the men were not always receiving the proper medical attention. But she blamed all this on her bosses down in Texas, who refused to provide enough money to run the operation properly.

She also contended that everything would be fine if she and her husband, Randy, were allowed by the men's families to continue running the bunkhouse. The Neubauers considered the boys to be like kin, she said. A couple had died in her arms, and she and her husband had driven their bodies back to Texas, after removing seats from the van to make room for their coffins.

"I don't know if I have any tears left," the woman said. "They call me Mom. I think of them as my boys."

She went on: "These guys have grown up

together. They're brothers. I don't want to see them scattered."

Kauffman had no reason to doubt the woman's sincerity. She clearly knew the men's individual habits and medications, and seemed fond of them. She also seemed to corroborate everything he had heard the night before from his tipster, Sherri Brown. But two or three questions in, he concluded that his chatty host was ill equipped to supervise a facility occupied by nearly two dozen men with special needs — a facility that also seemed to be operating without proper licensing or regulation.

Neubauer said she wasn't comfortable allowing Kauffman into the bunkhouse, but, sure, he was more than welcome to root around in those two Dumpsters on the side of the building. Who knows? That couple sent down by her Texas bosses to shut the operation down, Warren and Segreta Davis, had been throwing out all sorts of things.

Before day's end, Kauffman would be making telephone calls to Iowa government officials that would sound the alarm of something horribly amiss in a place called Atalissa, and putting everyone on notice that the *Register* was on it.

By the next night, a tired Iowa social worker named Natalie Neel-McGlaughlin would hear her cell phone ring as she tried to put her children to bed in a Muscatine home overlooking the Mississippi's forbidding flow. She would pick up, listen, struggle to comprehend, and ask that the message be repeated:

*Men with physical and mental challenges, living in an old schoolhouse, eviscerating turkeys for very little money, for decades.*

And by the weekend, Kauffman would publish the first of his many stories about the bunkhouse in Atalissa, forcing the state of Iowa to examine its laws, its procedures, its very perception of people with developmental disabilities. Fending off doubtful editors — *Do we really need another story about these guys?* — he continued to produce an impressive body of work that focused on the plights of the powerless, while always, always, answering a ringing telephone.

But at first there was just Clark Kauffman in a suit jacket and tie, standing inside a Dumpster beside an old schoolhouse, and feeling only sorrow as he imagined the stories behind these freshly discarded items. Suitcases packed with clothing. Urine-stained bedding. VHS tapes of movies from the 1980s. Cassettes of country-western music. And stuffed animals. Lots and lots of stuffed animals. The kind a kid might win at a county fair.

# Sixteen

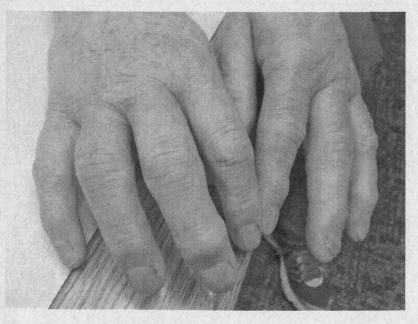

*The hands of Gene Berg*

Change came like a slap to the back of the head, a kick in the ass, a right-hard punch to the balls.

For so long, life in the bunkhouse had maintained a sleep-walking sameness, a year-in, year-out drudgery created by a company so out of touch with the new century that it saw no need for computers. Why buy computers when pens and type-writers work just fine? Why change any-thing? If it ain't broke . . .

But a round of disbelieving telephone calls in February 2009 had upended the decades-old system of Henry's Turkey Service in less than a week. An infuriated sister keeps dial-ing until she reaches someone who listens. An investigative reporter makes his own calls, motivated by remnants of stagnated lives found in a Dumpster. A state social worker receives a confusing late-night call, and now she is standing in a remote schoolhouse filled with unkempt men in crisis, many of them unnerved by the sudden attention to their rote lives.

Some, though, feigned casual amusement. In the midst of the disruption, Jeff Long and Brady Watson strolled down to the Atalissa Mini-Mart for their usual Friday-afternoon Cokes and chips. When they returned, they noticed an increase in the number of official-looking cars parked on the schoolhouse lawn. The Lone Wolf, also known as Jeff, turned to his best friend, the Texas Wolf, also known as Brady, and said:

*Well look-ee here.*

By late that evening, the visitors — including the social worker Natalie Neel-McGlaughlin — were still processing what they were hearing, seeing, and even smelling. They met big and handsome Gene Berg, who was difficult to understand, in part because his teeth had been pulled for a set of dentures yet to arrive. He told them he liked to work; if you don't work, you don't get paid. He proudly explained that he was responsible for all sorts of chores, including shoveling snow and burning trash, and that in his free time he tooled around on his John Deere Gator. He said he had lived at the bunkhouse for about a year, when the truth was actually closer to thirty.

They met spindly, drawn Keith Brown, whose sister had alerted the authorities and the press. With his bosses, Randy and Dru Neubauer, at his side, Brown said little, which investigators attributed to being self-conscious about his speech impediment — although he would later explain, quite clearly, that he feared retribution if he said anything damning in front of his supervisors.

They met Levi, who played the spoons, and the Penners, who said they hadn't seen any family members in six months — which was Penner code for since forever — and Frank Rodriguez, who had little to say except when it came to bragging about his daughter, whom he had not seen since she was a toddler. She was now in college, he said.

So many stories — so many *epics*! — had accumulated in this decrepit house. The social workers and investigators knew by night's end that they would be back in the morning with reinforcements. But just in case, they cobbled together a safety plan: they would have social workers walking the dusky halls every three hours, like security guards.

Pete Graffagnino, the cook, later told investigators that the Neubauers had gathered the men in the bunkhouse dining room that night for a private conference. The brochures about basic rights that had been handed out were ripped up, he confided, and everyone was ordered to keep their mouths shut — to keep everything in-house.

The Neubauers later denied saying such things.

Investigators returned Saturday morning like curious laity imposing on the cloistered world of twenty-one monks. Dru Neubauer provided a more in-depth tour to a small group of visitors that included Neel-McGlaughlin, who was disoriented by the labyrinthine complex. With pen and paper, she recorded the breaches in the duct-taped ceilings; the mouse droppings on kitchen shelves; the moldy mattress propped against a hallway wall; the cockroaches. And not just the sight but the *sound* of them.

Noticing the broken boiler, the space heaters scattered about, the curls of piggybacked extension cords, the investigators began asking about fire safety and other basic protocols, which seemed to agitate their defensive tour guide. State fire inspectors were alerted, and soon on their way.

The building was already crime scene crowded with an improbable collection of characters worthy of Agatha Christie: traumatized men with intellectual disability, astounded social workers, determined state investigators, grim FBI agents, the nervous husband-and-wife hosts, some officials from Muscatine County, a disability-rights representative from Iowa Protection and Advocacy Services — and three well-dressed women just up from Texas: T. H. Johnson's widow, Jane Ann, and two of their three adult daughters.

Saying they had made a sudden trip to Iowa to help the boys prepare for their return to Texas, the Johnson women tried to lend perspective to all these strangers coming in for the closing chapters of the Henry's Turkey Service saga. They had known these boys since forever, and, yes, it was clear they needed to retire. But you have to remember, things here ran smoothly for many years. When TH was alive, the men went bowling and camping, took trips to amusement parks, and enjoyed a vacation every year. Remember, too, that many of these boys might talk about relatives they keep in touch with, but it was all in their minds. Their families had moved on long ago. *We* were their families. When you put it all together, one of the Johnson daughters said, the arrangement here in Atalissa was "good for us and good for the boys."

The Johnson women even cited a booklet written long ago about Henry's Turkey Service. But given the surrounding squalor and the somber nature of the unfolding inquiries, its title had the ring of some dark, inappropriate joke: "The Magic of Simplicity."

Early that afternoon, a thin and fit woman named Denise Gonzales bought some convenience-store coffee and set off in her state-issue car, driving southeast from Davenport along a road that hugged the curves of the Mississippi River. A marathon runner, she had already done a quick six miles in the morning to help chase away the stress of her job as a regional supervisor for the Iowa Department of Human Services. But her mind was still racing, still trying to visualize what her alarmed colleagues had described.

Gonzales was forty-nine, with probing blue eyes, angular features, and more than twenty-five years of experience in social work. As a young mother, she had worked nights and weekends with teenage runaways, a job that led to a life-defining realization: This is where I belong. She'd earned a master's in social work, done tours both in Iowa and her native Illinois, and seen enough to say she had seen it all. But this — how could this be?

Gonzales had spent most of the last twenty-four hours on the telephone, co-ordinating with other government agencies and listening to the shocked accounts of peers whom she admired and trusted. But something told her she had to see this old schoolhouse for herself. What she was hearing sounded almost anti-American, too gothic to be believed. She had to go.

Finding the front entrance inaccessible, Gonzales slipped through a side door and into the gymnasium, where a disco ball hung over the room, three-foot panels painted like playing cards leaned against the garishly colored walls, and a barber chair sat in a corner, tumbleweeds of hair gathered around it. The place reminded her of a seedy frat house.

A few of the men soon emerged, extending bent, filthy hands in welcome, just as they had for Gonzales's colleague Natalie Neel-McGlaughlin the day before. One man apologized for the dried blood on his hands, saying he couldn't get it off, as though the turkey plant, the bunkhouse, all of it, had become a part of him.

Gonzales received every hand offered to her. She needed to convey calm, warmth, and the unmistakable message that she would protect these people. When she asked whether their constricted, almost forked, hands ached, the men gave the cause rather than the effect. *From pullin' crop,* they said, which made no sense to her. She also noticed that some of the men looked unhealthily thin.

*You the boss lady?* they asked, flashing grins of gap-toothed decay. *You in charge of us now?*

Yes.

They led her on a proud tour of their bedrooms and belongings. Frank Rodriguez's room was immaculate, as always, reflecting his artistic sensibility and the attention he paid to eliminating roaches. His leather vest and other clothes hung from wooden hooks on the yellow-painted cinderblock wall, just below a Jack Daniel's mirror. Another wall featured a crucifix and a large illustration of dogs playing poker.

But propped in the hallway, just outside his door, was that mildewy mattress, in contradiction. Many of the other bedrooms, though fitted out with televisions and stereos, nauseated Gonzales; she would never shake the sight of a pair of jeans too stiff with bloodstains even to be folded. Here and there were personal touches: ribbons saying "Parade Participant — Atalissa Days 1994"; sepia-toned photos of Carl Wayne Jones posing as a gunslinger; a shot of a smiling Paul Hayek with the inscription "Someone Special." But then she'd come across another upsetting sight, such as the peeling paint of red, yellow, and blue in the malodorous bathrooms, that tested her resolve not to betray panic or revulsion. She needed to reassure these people that all would be well, even if she had no idea how to back it up.

Meanwhile, her colleagues were doing the same, getting to know the men, listening to their stories, easing their anxieties amid the tumult. Neel-McGlaughlin, for example, sensed that a black man with a scrawny white beard and a noticeable limp — the one called Levi — was upset. They sat down for a talk.

He showed her his knee, which was swollen and hot to the touch. Slipped at the turkey plant, he said, but his bunkhouse supervisors told him he was faking the pain; he should just shut up and get back to work. Since then, he'd been applying Bengay to the knee, hoping to make it feel better.

Shocked, Neel-McGlaughlin ordered Dru Neubauer to take Levi to a doctor immediately. The supervisor tried to argue that

345

no doctor would have visiting hours on a Saturday, but the social worker persisted. *There's an urgent-care center in Muscatine,* she said. *Take him now.*

A couple of hours later, Neubauer and Levi returned with a definitive explanation for what had caused Levi such agony over the last two weeks. His kneecap was broken.

Night pressed down on Atalissa. With time running out for a command decision on the bunkhouse "situation," the SWAT team of county, state, and federal officials convened in the grim kitchen to discuss their options, cockroaches scuttling around them.

The Muscatine County attorney had said publicly that the bunkhouse conditions in his backyard posed no immediate threat to its residents. But here were two state fire investigators, fresh from an inspection with devastating findings. Heating system not up to code. Fire doors not up to code. Combustible materials in the hallway. Burned-out exit lights. Padlocked exit doors. Deactivated fire alarms. Piggybacked extension cords. Mere plywood separating bedrooms from the storage of gasoline and vehicles in the garage. No escape plan in place, and no drills ever conducted. All in all, a fire here would almost certainly result in death.

Later, one of the veteran inspectors on site that day would describe the building's lack of fire safety as "probably the worst I had ever seen."

The inspectors declared the building unsafe for habitation, and ordered an immediate evacuation. With that, all eyes turned toward Denise Gonzales.

It wasn't going to be the FBI or the Iowa Bureau of Criminal Investigation that would find shelter for these men overnight, and it sure as hell wasn't going to be Muscatine County. That task *had* to fall to the Department of Human Services, as much for karmic reasons as for practical ones. Gonzales was unaware of the full history of Henry's Turkey Service, and could hardly be blamed for thirty-five years of her DHS predecessors ignoring warnings, dismissing tips, talking themselves out of responsibility, and all but abetting this exploitative arrangement. Still, all eyes were on her, asking:

What are *you* going to do?

Gonzalez felt panic welling in her chest. *Holy crap,* she thought. *I just gave birth to twenty-one men.*

But her trepidation quickly yielded to confidence. *Holy crap,* she thought. *Now I can take charge.*

Gonzales became the Patton of the bunkhouse. She ordered subordinates to find a motel in Muscatine with thirteen rooms, arrange for food, book medical appointments, and enlist a psychologist in case any of the men became distressed. She issued a general request for off-duty social workers to come to Muscatine. She anticipated, strategized, saw into the next two or three days — but then what? All she knew was: I need to protect these guys.

Late that night, Gonzales gathered the twenty-one exhausted and confused men into the dining room for some thrilling news. *Guess what,* she announced. *Pack an overnight bag, 'cause we're going on vacation. We're going on vacation.*

Amid the shuffle and excitement, social workers helped everyone pack a few belongings, making sure that filthy clothes and bug-infested gadgets remained behind. A few men were understandably agitated. Any change in routine caused anxiety, and now, close to bedtime, they were being told they'd be sleeping elsewhere. The rest, though, embraced the sense of adventure and escape.

"I was pleased to death to get out of that bunkhouse," Henry Wilkins remembers.

As they had so many thousands of times

before, Wilkins and Levi and all the other men filed into the two company vans. The vehicles grumbled down the schoolhouse's gravel drive and slipped through a community in late-night repose. The few scattered lights of Atalissa vanished in their wake, replaced before long by the yellow-and-red neon of the Super 8 motel.

On vacation.

The men slept between crisp clean sheets and floral-patterned bedcovers, and padded to odor-free bathrooms on soft, blue carpeting. In the morning they found a continental breakfast laid out for them in the lobby, with hot waffles prepared by their new friends, including the new boss lady herself, Gonzales, who noticed some men with teeth so decayed that chewing even a soft waffle was a struggle.

They watched television, enjoyed a church lunch, went shopping, and had their photographs taken, partly to commemorate the "vacation," partly to document their physical condition. Over the next couple of days, they were taken to an urgent-care center to be examined, one by one.

There was Henry Wilkins, sixty-four, the gangly, jug-eared mischief maker whom everyone called "Dewey the Drunk," whose hearing aid had broken years ago when someone hit him in the head, and was never replaced. He was found to be malnourished — just as he had been during his last physical examination seven years earlier.

And John Hatfield, sixty-two, the ballet dancer and honorary Atalissa city employee, the trike-riding street cleaner, with arthritis so severe he could not make a fist. Records indicated that he had been diagnosed with hand pain and possible arthritis a quarter century earlier. But he said that whenever he complained of his aches he was told to get back to pulling crop.

And Raymond Vaughn, fifty-eight, abandoned as a boy by a father figure who left him in a courthouse, promising he'd be right back. Decades of repetitive plant work had constricted Vaughn's hand, causing acute pain that wasn't worth complaining about, since no one would listen. He hadn't seen a doctor since 2002.

Jeff Long, fifty, the Lone Wolf, with dried blood around his lips and cuts inside his mouth, caused by the jutting wires left behind by dental work that had fallen out.

Keith Brown, fifty-seven, and James Fowler, sixty-three, both with advanced fungal infections rampant in their feet and spreading up their legs. Paul Hayek, fifty-nine, with severe dental problems and fluid in his lungs. Preston Pate, fifty-nine and Robert Penner, sixty, the two diabetics; Penner would administer Pate's insulin, but the doctors determined that he could not meet his own diabetic needs, much less those of his friend. . . .

Living as a collective for so long had all but robbed the men of their individual identities. The Henry's boys seemed like one entity, sharing the same job, the same house, the same food, and even the same pains: fungal infections, dental needs, repetitive-stress injuries. Lost men, losing themselves.

Denise Gonzales recognized the chance to draw the men out of this collective clutch by providing them with individualized care and attention. Not Henry and Raymond and Preston, but just Henry. Just Raymond. Just Preston. Not the unit of "the Penner brothers," but Billy. Robert.

She developed a system in which each man was paired with a new friend all his own: a social worker who would find out who he was, where he came from, what his needs were, what he wanted everyone to know. These were standard dependent-adult assessments, but Gonzales came up with a catchy name for this crisis requirement:

"Stand by Your Man."

The social workers asked gentle, basic questions. Most of the men did not know how to tell time, or how much they had in savings, or even the address of the bunk-house. Most also acknowledged being alone in the world; "Just me and my brother," said Robert Penner, who would be considered one of the luckier ones. Carl Wayne Jones, sixty-two, soon to be diagnosed with an adjustment disorder, said he had a younger brother, Leon. The two used to be together in the Abilene State School, and then at Goldthwaite, until Henry's Turkey Service split them up: Carl Wayne to Atalissa, Leon to the Louis Rich plant in Newberry, South Carolina, more than nine hundred miles away. They hadn't seen each other in who knew how long.

Truly: Who knew how long? In answering a question about when he first came to Atalissa, Preston Pate spoke for all when he said, simply:

"A long time ago."

Gonzales also transformed the motel's kitchenette into her office and command center, complete with a communal toaster, a microwave, and, thank the Lord, a coffee machine. Opening her laptop and spreading documents on a round little table, she ad-

dressed assorted urgencies while simultane-
ously keeping a logbook of people leaving
or returning.

She had to get these men on Medicaid;
four income-maintenance caseworkers soon
arrived to process the paperwork needed for
eligibility. She had to obtain court orders
for protective custody and a legal guardian;
legal was working on that. She had to feign
welcome to Randy and Dru Neubauer, who
were in the motel; best to keep friends close
and . . . Most of all, she had to come up
with a plan for what came next; the men
could not take up permanent residence in a
Super 8.

As much as possible, Gonzales tried to
anticipate and resolve the men's immediate
problems. Some needed Orajel to ease
mouth pains. Some needed nail clippers and
athlete's foot spray. One needed a medicated
cream to clear the turkey blood embedded
in his hands.

The men had become accustomed over
the decades to receiving a five-dollar allowance on Tuesdays (deducted from their
pay), and now several were unnerved by the
fear of not receiving it. That five dollars
mattered. It represented tangible compensation for their hard work, and it offered a
fleeting moment of choice. Five dollars of

choice. Gonzales withdrew money from an ATM and handed each man his five-dollar allowance. She would do whatever she could to alleviate their stress. These men were in crisis. Five dollars times twenty-one equaled a small price.

At the same time, she also recognized the toll the upsetting assignment was taking on her colleagues, and she tried to comfort them, if only by listening. The social workers took turns all but collapsing into a chair in her kitchenette office and relaying breathless reports, often with the same wide-eyed prelude: You're not going to believe this.

*You're not going to believe this, but my guy can't remember whether he has any brothers or sisters.*

*My guy refuses to sleep in the dark, so I have to go out and get a night-light.*

*My guy? Oh my God. His feet! It hurts for him just to walk! I had to cut his toenails. And you're not going to believe this, but . . .*

In the sterile bedrooms of a Super 8, tucked between an Applebee's and an Arby's, the social workers cut the men's toenails. They drew out faint recollections of boyhoods spent in dreamlike laces called Orange and Sulphur Bluff; of adolescences in state institutions; of becoming unmoored from parents whose looks and smells and

354

voices could no longer be summoned for comfort. They sidestepped the occasional come-ons, as when one man asked a social worker he'd just met if she would have his babies. They listened to stories of being hit, yelled at, forced to stay in the van; of trying to do their best and being told that their best wasn't enough. *Hang them birds. Hang 'em.*

Then a break from memories for some food or a card game — anything but turkey talk. Gene Berg needed to go to Walmart, where he bought string cheese, Honey Buns, a twelve-pack of Pepsi, and aftershave lotion. He needed to check in with the Neubauers across the hall about the belongings he left behind in Atalissa. When would he get his John Deere Gator back? And his ostrich boots? And he needed to speak to his mother in Kansas. Berg had always prided himself on taking things like a man, but now, speaking by telephone to his mom about this sudden and uncertain change in his life, he became tearful.

Standing by their men by sitting beside them, often holding their hands, the social workers assured their fragile charges that all would be well. But every once in a while, they briefly excused themselves. They just needed a private moment, maybe a good cry in a bathroom stall, or a cigarette in the motel parking lot while staring out at the highway 61 flow. Then back to it.

These instant relationships between the men and their caseworkers lasted days but contained lifetimes, as when a young social worker named Jennifer Blake got acquainted with a man who had a slush-gray beard, a broken kneecap, and a couple of spoons tucked in his socks. Willie Levi.

After introducing herself to Levi late that Sunday morning, Blake began to draw him out. He shared his story, or part of his story, with nonlinear raggedness, naming relatives he wasn't sure were dead or alive, listing all the places where he had chased turkey for Mr. T. H. Johnson. At sixty-two, he was unaware of the year, unable to manage his money, launder his clothes, or cook his food — though he could make a sandwich — and in need of prompts to use soap. He confessed to getting depressed sometimes, and to screaming sometimes at night. Sometimes he tried to hurt himself, clawing at his own skin. Sometimes, Blake thought, he lives in that space between fantasy and reality.

Blake listened to Levi sing and play the spoons. She drove him and a few others to a free lunch at the First Presbyterian Church. She stood by as he underwent a physical that revealed, among other ailments, a fungal infection in both feet. She drove him to Walgreen's to buy grooming supplies and a photo album. She took photographs as he ate dinner with the other men at a local restaurant, where the boisterous gathering included toasts to the social workers and even to the Neubauers.

She accompanied him to a doctor's appointment in Iowa City, where a doctor determined that his broken kneecap required surgery. At night, she made sure that he showered and brushed his teeth, and in the morning, that he ate breakfast and took his medication. When she went home one night, she washed his clothes and the clothes of his roommate.

Blake drove Levi to Walmart so that he could buy a James Brown CD with his five-dollar allowance. She had the pictures developed, and placed them in his new photo album. She helped him leave a telephone message for pastor Lynn Thiede at the Zion Lutheran Church, and shared the pastor's return message that Atalissa missed him and the other men very much. She listened to his new CD, and, yes, to his spoons-and-comb musical performance in the motel lobby — and also to his confession. *Jennifer, I don't never, ever, want to work*

357

*again with turkeys.*

For the record, Kenneth Henry, the co-owner of Henry's Turkey Service, would come to believe that this Stand by Your Man program, including the brief vacation at the Super 8, was the source of most of the misunderstanding about what went on at the Atalissa bunkhouse.

"If you've got the mind of a thirteen-year-old, a fourteen-year-old, let's say," Henry explains, "and here a girl comes, and she don't have to be attractive to the boys. They don't understand pretty girls; they're girls, period. And all of a sudden that girl will let you put your arm around her and talk to her and she'll sit and talk to you. And if she says you need to say this, you think they wouldn't say it?"

Early Tuesday afternoon, two yellow school buses pulled in front of the motel's yellow-and-red marquee. On the side of each bus appeared a phrase that could be read as a declaration: "Exceptional Persons Incorporated." This was the name of the nonprofit organization — a community-based, Medicaid-funded operation for people with intellectual disability — that Gonzales had chosen to assist the men in their journey to a new life. It was based in the midsize Iowa city of Waterloo, 120 miles to the northwest.

Just as she had in the bunkhouse a few nights earlier, Gonzales gathered the men and laid out the plan. It is time to leave the motel. You are going to a new place — Waterloo! — with some very nice people. These people will help you find safe and clean places to live, and doctors and dentists to take care of your hands, your feet, your teeth. Waterloo has all sorts of things to do and ways to get around, and best of all: You choose. You get to choose what you want to do. I think you're going to be very happy.

Her audience of twenty-one men had twenty-one reactions. One man kept running down the motel's carpeted halls, shouting, *Yippee! Yippee!* Another asked, *Can I be retired?* Still another said, *I want to work in a grocery store. Can I work in a grocery store?* But more than a few reacted as anyone might to the wholesale upheaval of the only lives they had known. *Where am I going? What am I going to do there? What about my belongings? How will my family know where to find me? What's going to happen to me?*

The presence of Randy and Dru Neubauer triggered a variety of feelings. The couple had given the men Valentine's Day cards, a gesture that a few felt compelled to reciprocate, and some of the men hugged them. But others had no interest in hugs. Levi recalls a weeping Dru telling him that he was part of their family. "I'm my mother's family," he says he told her. "I'm not your family."

"Dru the one that cried," Levi says. " 'I miss my boys, I miss my boys, I want them back.' I say, 'Sorry, you ain't getting *me* back. I'm going to Waterloo.' "

Jeff Long says his farewell was even more succinct. Simply: "See ya."

The Iowa social workers and some staff members of Exceptional Persons did their best to make the journey as carefree as possible. When Levi walked out of the motel, for example, he carried a drink and a snack, the phone number of his new friend Jennifer, a Valentine's Day card, and a small care package that included a photo album of his Super 8 vacation in Muscatine.

Holding plastic Walmart bags and waving good-bye, Levi and the other men filed on board, stepping over the rectangular sign saying WATCH YOUR STEP and settling into one of the ten rows of brown upholstered seats. Soon the school buses were lumbering along I–380, bound north for Waterloo.

Some passengers leaned their heads

against the windows, staring into the Iowa blur. Others clapped hands and sang familiar songs. What a friend we have in Jesus. Give me that old-time religion. Amazing grace.

■ ■ ■ ■

# Seventeen

■ ■ ■ ■

*A new home*

The largest five cities in Iowa are Des Moines, Cedar Rapids, Davenport, Sioux City, and Iowa City. Then comes Waterloo.

The Cedar River, the railroad, economic booms and busts, the 1934 shootout that killed a lantern-jawed Dillinger gang member named Tommy Carroll, the loss of the five Sullivan brothers from Adams Street in the sinking of the USS *Juneau* — you should see the 1944 movie based on the event, *The Fighting Sullivans* — the brief residency of the serial killer John Wayne Gacy, an agricultural recession leading to a diversified economy, John Deere, the Crossroads Center mall and the Grout Museum of History and Science, the flood of 2008, the hottest winters, the coldest summers, and the most violent, beautiful storms: Waterloo.

But for twenty-one men from Atalissa arriving by rumbling school bus, the sixth-largest city in Iowa might as well have been enveloped in the emerald haze of Oz. Atalissa encompassed less than two-tenths of a square mile; Waterloo covered more than sixty-three square miles. Atalissa had three hundred people; Waterloo, sixty-eight thousand. Atalissa had a minimart and two taverns; Waterloo, a Walmart Supercenter, dozens of restaurants, more than fifty parks, reliable public transportation, and, come springtime, breathtaking fields of bluebells.

The buses pulled into the parking lot of an old drugstore that now housed the Deery Center, a place for adults with intellectual disability to relax and do volunteer work. As the men emerged from the school buses like students on their first day of school, small bags sagging with spare possessions, the Exceptional Persons managers waiting to greet them took quiet note of their poor physical appearance and the subtle signs of adjustment disorder and post-traumatic stress. Some men rejoiced in being liberated from bunkhouse servitude, yippee. Others closed themselves off in a kind of protective curl, wondering where they were going and what would be happening to them, fretfully asking if their Atalissa supervisors would be able to find them. Could those bosses round them up, return them to the bunkhouse, and make them pay for the folly of ever having left?

*Don't worry, Carl Wayne. You're not going back to the bunkhouse. We promise. And no, Preston. Randy and Dru won't find you here. Neither will Danny Miles. Please trust us. . . .*

But trust had been left at the state school gates. Left again in Goldthwaite. Left again and again and again in Atalissa. Maybe these buses were like the trucks that carried crated turkeys to their slaughter for all those years. Maybe these people I've never seen before are like Levi coaxing the birds out of their crates. *Okay, okay, Tom, quieten down.*

*Okay, Preston. Okay, Carl Wayne. Okay, Keith and Raymond and Henry and, yes, Levi. Okay. Quieten down.*

The person responsible for regaining their trust was Susan Seehase, the dark-haired, no-nonsense services director for Exceptional Persons. She had begun her real training in social work more than a decade earlier, as a supervisor filling in overnight at a group home that housed five people with disability. She had just earned degrees in political science and psychology from Luther College in Decorah, Iowa, but she did not know how to cook. After two straight nights of take-out pizza, the residents helped her find her way around a kitchen and among people with disabilities.

Now, at thirty-seven, Seehase was married to a grain farmer in a small town about forty miles north of Waterloo, raising four children and overseeing the services provided to more than five hundred people. Her professional demeanor was one of pleasant steeliness, her welcoming smile masking an implacable resolve to champion the rights of self-determination for people with disability. But neither she nor anyone else at Exceptional Persons had ever handled anything quite this daunting, a case of international notice and statewide mortification: twenty-one scared and defenseless men, bused in from someplace else and carrying so much more than just those small bags gripped in their aching hands.

Seehase blocked out the external noise, the avalanche of donated clothing, the monetary gifts for the "Henry's boys" from special collections at churches throughout northeast Iowa. She needed to focus.

*Listen to the men,* she told herself. *Anticipate. Meet them where they are. Win their trust.*

*One step at a time.*

That afternoon, Seehase and her colleagues led everyone into the Deery Center, where each man was directed to a staff member who would help him fill out paperwork at a table set aside specifically for him. Sloppy joes and baked beans and potato chips were served, although Keith Brown fretted about covering up the bowls of chips, for fear that something might fall into them. A karaoke machine was set up for diversion; among those taking a turn at the microphone was John Hatfield, who surprised the staff by handing over several hundred dollars in savings that he had spirited out of the bunkhouse.

Later that evening, the men were given rooms in an apartment and a couple of group homes until more permanent housing was secured. Many of them slept by themselves for the first time in decades. A few had nightmares. Social workers stayed close by.

As the days and weeks passed, the employees at Exceptional Persons worked down their complicated checklist. They arranged the Texas return of Lone Wolf and Texas Wolf — Jeff Long and Brady Watson — whose fathers soon placed them in group homes. They drove Levi to a hospital in Iowa City, where a staff member stayed by his side for two nights while he recovered from surgery for his shattered kneecap. They searched for relatives, often in vain, the contact information kept in wallets so old that the ink had blurred away.

They presented local doctors, dentists, and podiatrists with some of the more challenging cases of their medical careers, while also arranging for the men to undergo mental-health evaluations. Some required no return visits. Others entered intensive treatment for post-traumatic stress that would last for years.

They set up interviews with criminal investigators and state social workers, hoping to drill down on thirty-five years of what had happened to whom. These interviews summoned a chorus of memories about shoves and bugs, kicks and water leaks, get your ass outta bed it's time to work, go to your room you didn't work hard enough, your best ain't good enough — though the specificity of time was often difficult to discern.

As employees of a nonprofit social service organization, the staff at Exceptional Persons did not collect large salaries; far from it. Still, many were so moved by what they were hearing and seeing that they used their own money to buy the men items more personal than hand-me-down donations. Sweatshirts bearing the logos of NASCAR favorites. Sports apparel celebrating the purple and gold of the University of Northern Iowa. And bedsheets: high-quality bedsheets that at the end of another anxious day, offered linen cocoons of unfamiliar softness.

Still, the many possessions left behind in the Atalissa bunkhouse rubbed away at the men's sense of self. Gene Berg obsessed over his John Deere Gator, Frank Rodriguez his cherished red toolbox. Others wanted their televisions, radios, videocassettes, the money tucked away in secret hiding places. Oh, and those blankets that an Atalissa woman had spent a year quilting as Christmas presents for each of the men.

"I left my popcorn popper there, and my, my, my Detroit Lions jacket there," Levi says. Billy and Robert Penner try to outdo each other in describing personal items still in the bunkhouse:

A crowbar. A hammer.

A brand-new shirt. A brand-new TV.

My records. My bald eagle picture.

Both say they left behind Henry's Turkey Service windbreakers. Robert's was gray; Billy's was blue.

The worth of these possessions extended beyond monetary or even sentimental value.

Similar to the five-dollar "allowance" expected every Tuesday, the items represented validation of the men as consumers whose money was as good as anybody's at the Walmart in Muscatine, or the Sam's Club in Davenport. A clock radio. A Marty Stuart CD. A popcorn popper.

Staff members from Exceptional Persons sat with each man to record a wish list of what he really, truly wanted retrieved. But this would not be a simple matter of parking a truck outside the bunkhouse and loading it up; Seehase had no interest in transporting Atalissa cockroaches and filth to Waterloo. The lists themselves, long on televisions, radios, and other replaceable items, but short on photo albums, letters, or family keepsakes, told the story of institutional abandonment.

A week after the men were sprung from Atalissa, a team of would-be movers returned to the bunkhouse, including Seehase and big, quiet Frank Rodriguez, who had been chosen by the other men because they trusted him, so much so that he knew where they hid their money, if they had any.

The yellow moving truck pulled up to the eerie schoolhouse, inhabited now only by the caretakers, Warren and Segreta Davis, and their dog, skunk, and raccoon. The Davises were on a salvage mission of their own, sorting through and discarding the remains of several dozen lifetimes, but keeping one memento for themselves: a gray granite plaque they found embedded beside the weeping willow, bearing the name of the runaway who had frozen to death in a farmer's field. They pried the plaque from the ground to replant in their garden in Oklahoma.

Good old Alford Busby.

The warnings of colleagues had not sufficiently prepared Seehase for her first visit to the bunkhouse. As she entered through the side doors, eyes adjusting to the dimness, the odd jumble of primary colors on the walls made her think of a circus, but then came that smell — a foul blend of urine and feces and body odor and mustiness, she recalls, "all mixed with chewing tobacco." Coupled with this smell was the sight of touching remnants of the lives lived in this fetid place. Gene Berg's room, for example, featured a wall calendar on which he had meticulously X-ed out every passing day — the Xs as identical as the days — right up to the seventh of February, when the schoolhouse's longtime inhabitants went on "vacation," never to return.

Several of the Stand by Your Man social

workers, who by now had become extended members of the men's families, joined Seehase, Rodriguez, and a few staffers from Exceptional Persons in a room-by-room search for prized possessions, flicking away the occasional bug and sidestepping the occasional mouse. They found little to take back to Waterloo. The handmade quilts would not survive laundering. Most of the clothes, including Levi's Detroit Lions jacket, were worn and soiled beyond salvation. Roaches clotted nearly all the appliances.

They drove back to Waterloo with a single television and some boxes packed with VHS tapes, record albums, and a few other salvageable items. Seehase had the moving van and its contents "bombed" with pesticides, and then inspected by an extermination specialist.

His recommendation: bomb it two more times.

As caretakers in waterloo guarded the men's privacy and tended to wounds visible and not, the rest of Iowa roiled, the fire of its outrage and disbelief refueled nearly every morning by yet another Clark Kauffman revelation in the *Des Moines Register*. The Hawkeye State considered itself progressive on most social issues, and its senior legislator, United States Senator Tom Harkin, had long been one of the country's most ardent advocates for disability rights. He had coauthored the Americans with Disabilities Act, for God's sake!

"Doesn't this shock the conscience of everyone?" Harkin asked. "I mean, this is pretty close to slavery."

Adherence to a predictable script followed. Legislative hearings were held, task forces appointed, internal investigations launched, fingers pointed.

Soon, state legislators were gathering under the twenty-three-carat gold-leaf dome of the majestic state capitol in Des Moines to discuss the squalor in distant Atalissa. At hastily scheduled hearings on government oversight, they listened to Department of Human Services officials defend their agency, and to the former Atalissa mayor Dennis Hepker, wearing a blue sweatshirt for the formal occasion, recall how Human Services had ignored his report years earlier of the bunkhouse's padlocked front door.

These hearings provided a forum for legislators to express shock and demand reform, of course, but also to trot out their own small-town credentials, and to compliment Human Services for the effective response to the crisis by its committed social workers. But Wayne Ford, a legislator from Des Moines by way of inner-city Washington, D.C., dispensed with niceties in conveying his disgust for it all — the specious notion of "happy boys," the almost willful small-town blindness, the lax oversight.

"There's blood on everybody's hands," he said, his voice deep and damning.

While Iowa raged and wept over the plight of the men from the bunkhouse, the victims themselves seemed to exist only in the abstract. Seeking to satisfy the intense interest from the Iowa media, Human Services arranged for "availabilities" with some of the men in Waterloo. But two days before the scheduled event, state officials abruptly canceled the interviews on the insistence of social workers, who privately wondered about the inability of their superiors to grasp the breadth of the damage done.

"We appreciate your understanding in allowing distance for these men to adjust to their new lives," a Human Services news release said. "Please recognize that while they are progressing, they are still fragile — more fragile than had been thought when they first arrived in Waterloo. . . ."

Days later, the Department of Human

Services released three-dozen recently discovered pages from its conflicted past. Here were those back-and-forth memos from 1997, when agency officials used dialogue worthy of Joseph Heller to talk themselves out of investigating Henry's Turkey Service. Even more disturbing was a single memo dating to December 1974: that cri de coeur pounded out late one Muscatine night by a young social worker named Ed George, listing as if in a formal indictment his many concerns about this Texas company new to Iowa.

*Not since the days of slavery have we had an example of the antithesis of normalization as Henry's has provided. Their list of violations of this principle is endless. . . . Once the resident becomes an employee of Henry's Turkey Service, he for all practical purposes loses most basic human rights. . . . The idea of implementing any program like this in Iowa is obscene. . . .*

His words haunted the state.

The governor of Iowa, Chet Culver, issued a statement reaffirming his resolve to determine how Atalissa was able to happen and ensure it never happened again. "Under several different administrations, concerns were raised about the situation in Atalissa," he said. "And while it's hard to second-guess what did or did not take place in the past, one thing is clear: every level of government bureaucracy has failed these men since 1974."

All around, shame and regret. The state, for failing to heed repeated warnings. The *Des Moines Register,* for not following up on its own exposés of Henry's Turkey Service in 1979. Disability-rights advocates, for assuming the matter had long since been addressed. Atalissa, for . . .

A small farm town, known best as a name on an interstate exit, suddenly found its unhurried dozen streets cluttered with reporters on deadline. Into the Corner Tap they went, and the Old University, and the Atalissa Mini-Mart, and the post office, raising notepads and microphones along with eyebrows, and asking the same judgmental question: *How could you not know?*

Hearing the implication of complicity in the questions and comments of reporters and politicians — *After all, the town owned the schoolhouse!* — the people of Atalissa rose to defend their community's name. They recalled how the men had integral roles in the Atalissa Days parade. How if you danced with one you danced with all. How the men chipped in when the Cedar

River overflowed its banks. How they gathered to pray in the minimart after it had been burglarized. How they never, ever complained.

Karen Rock, who lived two houses away from the schoolhouse, spoke for all of Atalissa in her letter to the *Muscatine Journal.* She described the men as accepted members of the community, known to holler hello to neighbors on their strolls through town, and she recalled the beautiful, diverting facade of the school grounds: the Christmas displays, the spring flowers, even a tribute to the heroes of 9/11.

"Is it sad? Yes. Was it wrong for it to have gotten to this level? Yes. Did we all let them down? Yes. But could anyone only seeing the outside have known? No."

And one more thing: "If anyone thought the boys were in danger or mistreated, it would have been an uprising never seen before. These boys were part of our community; they were my neighbors (and good ones)."

The people of Atalissa complained that the media failed to understand the deep affection integral to the town's complicated relationship with the Henry's men. Even so, the negative coverage pricked its collective conscience. "I'm sure some of us — a lot of us, maybe — had second thoughts," Hepker, the former mayor, says, his tone weighted with regret. "That we should have looked into it a little deeper."

Intensifying the hurt and remorse was the abruptness of it all. The boys were there when Atalissa went to sleep on a Saturday night, and gone when it awakened on Sunday morning. Lynn Thiede, the pastor at Zion Lutheran Church, who had become accustomed to hearing their Lord's Prayer hum, and to having big Tommy House help her into her robes before every service, wept over the absence. "Like someone swooping in and taking your children for reasons you don't know," she says.

Requests by townspeople to visit or telephone their old neighbors, now living in Waterloo, were denied. People who considered themselves caring friends — who had bought the men presents, knitted them clothes, danced with them — could not understand what they had done wrong. These wounded feelings would never heal.

But the men's new guardians, in full protective mode, were imposing a psychological uncoupling from all things Atalissa. They were still trying to separate the good actors from the bad: Would it be helpful or hurtful to have the old bunkhouse supervisors stop by with a bouquet of flowers or a twelve-pack of beer? "In all honesty," Susan Seehase says, "we were trying to give them a break from that life."

Besides, Seehase had no interest in the Atalissa psychodrama. Rather than worry about the hurt feelings of a few townspeople a hundred miles away, she had to create permanent housing and a support system for nineteen helpless men who needed to be, who deserved to be, integrated into everyday society, each in his own way.

Take Frank Rodriguez. One pleasant clear day in April, he went for a walk through the natural refuge of George Wyth Memorial State Park with his girlfriend, Helen, the mother of his daughter, whom he had not seen in twenty-one years.

Frank wore his black leather vest, a blue short-sleeve shirt of Native American design, and a USA baseball cap; she wore a light-blue hooded sweatshirt and a red top. He gave Helen a small bouquet of white flowers; she showed him photographs of their daughter, grown now, and making her own way.

They found a booth at Carlos O'Kelly's, a Mexican American chain restaurant in Cedar Falls. They hugged, shared some salsa and chips, caught up. Before long,

Frank and Helen were living together in a small apartment in Waterloo, and Frank was working full-time at Sam's Club. Free of state schools, turkeys, Atalissa, social workers, support staff, all of it. On his own.

The newfound independence of Frank Rodriguez became a model of the possible, just as his room in the Atalissa bunkhouse had once been the model of orderliness. But he was the exception. The rest of the men needed help in addressing certain matters, beyond learning to hit the target when urinating, or to spit tobacco juice into a cup and not onto the floor. Because most had never had a meaningful relationship with a woman, they had to be taught when a kiss was appropriate, for example, and when a handshake, a hug, or even a simple smile should do. Most had never cooked or gone grocery shopping, except to buy a Honey Bun or Slim Jim at the minimart. In steering them toward healthful choices in the supermarket aisles, the social workers learned of the men's bottomless desire for ice cream and complete rejection of any turkey product.

"The men were very clear," Seehase says. "That whole poultry thing, they took leave of."

■ ■ ■ ■

Where do you want to live? And who do you want to live with?

Most people answer these questions at some point in their lives. Yet the nineteen Henry's men, now in their fifties and sixties, had never been asked. This was not about whether they wanted vanilla or chocolate ice cream, or whether they wanted to watch a NASCAR race or *Wheel of Fortune.* This was about a concept foreign to them: self-determination.

Social Security benefits and money earned from jobs would pay the rent, while Medicaid would pay for the on-site presence of Exceptional Persons employees in the homes. But first: *Where, and with whom?* With some guidance, the men — who, after thirty years, intimately knew one another's habits and faults — divided themselves into compatible sets of three and four. Then they went house hunting.

Once they narrowed their options to houses with easy access to a bus line and a good supermarket, the prospective renters turned out to be quite selective. Gene Berg, James Fowler, and Kenny Jackson, for example, insisted on a house with a game room that could accommodate a pool table. The Penner brothers, Henry Wilkins, and John Orange insisted on a backyard large enough for an elaborate vegetable garden. Everyone wanted a spacious garage with a workbench for his tools. Some of the groups visited five or six houses before settling on one, often checking out the garage before the kitchen or living room.

In body and mind, the men were far removed from Atalissa — where, on a clear and bracing April morning, a jowly auctioneer named Chuck Herrold sang out his rat-a-tat-tat scat of commerce to a crowd of hundreds. Over the years he had auctioned off livestock and antiques, farm machinery and farmland, in allegiance to his motto: "No Sale Too Big or Too Small."

Now, sitting at the open window of a trailer parked outside the bunkhouse, Herrold solicited "do I hear" bids for an odd assembly of items laid out on the once manicured property. A meat slicer. A coffeemaker. A couple of stoves. Some metal mixing bowls. A few stand-alone lockers that once contained the spare possessions of some men you might remember, longtime Atalissa residents who had recently moved north.

These men had found homes in Waterloo, and were joining the rest of us here in the twenty-first century. A split-level house on a quiet street. A house of red brick on a cul-de-sac. A ranch house on a busy avenue, where one of its new residents kept entering and exiting his room, as if testing the door. He paused at one point to ask whether he could have privacy whenever he wanted.

Yes, he was told. Smiling, he reentered his room, and closed the door.

■ ■ ■ ■

# EIGHTEEN

■ ■ ■ ■

*Robert Canino at the deserted bunkhouse in Atalissa*

Nearly every weekday morning in Dallas, a man with a briefcase, his baggy eyes suggesting a workaholic nature, walks past the Texas School Book Depository building, just as he's been doing for years. Past the plaque commemorating the event, with its word "allegedly" underlined by the scratches of conspiracy-theorist vandals. Past the X in the middle of Elm Street, marking where the motorcade was interrupted. Past the same speed-talking street hawker who's always urging him to buy a commemorative assassination newspaper, that sixth-floor window right there, it's all in this here newspaper, five dollars . . .

*Really,* the man with the briefcase has said, time and again. *You don't know me by now?*

His failure to leave much of an impression amuses more than annoys Robert Canino. His persona as just another middle-aged guy with a spray of gray in his curly black hair, a guy who could afford to lose ten or fifteen pounds, has served him well as a lawyer. It invites underestimation.

Canino continues down South Houston Street until he disappears into an off-white federal building known as the Terminal Annex. Built in the late 1930s as a grand downtown post office, the building was converted long ago into spillover office space for various military and federal agencies. Now an art deco lobby greets Canino each morning with sun-starred reliefs in the ceiling and two arresting murals on the walls. In classic Works Progress Administration tradition, both paintings by the artist Peter Hurd celebrate an idealized America. In one, *Pioneer Homebuilders,* a barefoot girl carries buckets of water past men swinging axes and hammers as they build a log cabin, all against a backdrop of big-sky possibility.

He takes the sleek elevator to the third floor, to the Dallas district offices of the federal Equal Employment Opportunity Commission — the EEOC — where he has worked for a quarter century. In the lobby, fifteen maroon-cloth chairs await those who feel they have been discriminated against in the workplace: fired, harassed, underpaid, or in some other way abused by employers because of race, gender, religion, age, or disability. Robert Canino has been the advocate and counselor for thousands of these people.

Finally, there's Canino's office, with the framed photograph of his wife, Loretta, and his two children, Brianne and Braden. The iconic photograph of the flag raising at Ground Zero. The Four Freedoms, by Norman Rockwell. Three law books and an ornate wooden cross on a shelf behind his desk, symbols of his profession and faith, intertwined. And, framed by his window, a site of American loss.

Canino was here in this office, on a mild but overcast February day, when a curious case from Iowa landed on his desk. Earlier that week, a colleague had come across an article in the *Houston Chronicle* with the headline "Mentally Disabled Workers Found in Squalor." Janet Elizondo, then the deputy director of the EEOC Dallas office, was so intrigued, or so incensed, that she reached out to the *Chronicle* reporter to gather more information. She then directed one of her investigators to contact the whistleblower, Sherri Brown, an Arkansas woman whose brother was among the men allegedly exploited in Iowa by this Texas company, Hill

Country Farms — or, as it was better known, Henry's Turkey Service.

The investigator, Tammy Johnson, called Brown, who was very emotional about what had happened to her brother, Keith. Very passionate about wanting something done. And very, very glad that the EEOC was looking into the matter.

Before long, Brown had provided the information to complete a formal complaint, known as a Form 5 Charge document, on behalf of her brother. It read:

I began my employment working on meat processing lines in approx. 1979, which continued until February 10, 2009. Throughout the term of my employment, Respondents subjected other employees with disabilities and me to a hostile work environment, physical abuse and other forms of harassment, denied us fair terms and conditions of employment, and failed to pay wages and other compensation commensurate with the work we performed, all in discrimination against us because of our disabilities.

I believe that a class of individuals and I have been discriminated against in violation of the Americans with Disabilities Act of 1990, as amended.

Soon informed that the case was his, Robert Canino hustled to catch up. He read a draft of the complaint and pored over the many shocking news reports coming out of Iowa. Inhumane living conditions. Confinement, isolation, and excessive control exercised over compliant and vulnerable workers. Modern-day slavery. Only allegations at this point, mere words on a page. Still.

Forty-six years earlier, from a window two floors above Canino's, a postmaster named Harry D. Holmes watched the motorcade through his binoculars. He saw the president's car come to a near stop; saw the first lady reach toward the backseat; thought the president and his wife were dodging something that had been thrown.

The president would leave behind a wife, two children, both parents, and six siblings, including a younger sister named Rosemary, who lived at Saint Coletta School for Exceptional Children in Jefferson, Wisconsin, her home since she had been incapacitated by a lobotomy that was meant to calm her violent mood swings as a young woman. Her intellectual disability had inspired her brother to champion broad legislation that would improve the lives of all Americans with such impairments.

Now, looking out of the window facing

Dealey Plaza, Canino felt similarly inspired. He sensed a deep connection between this Iowa matter and another human-trafficking case he had handled years earlier, one that now seemed divinely intended to prepare him for the challenge spread out in documents and news accounts before him. Might sound silly to say aloud, but he felt chosen.

Robert Canino remembers the day. He was home after classes at Duncanville High School in the Dallas suburbs, and the mail had come. His determined Mexican American mother, Edna, had applied to the law school at Southern Methodist University after having earned a bachelor's degree in political science in midlife. In her hand was the answer, its formality conveyed by the fine paper stock and impressive law school letterhead.

She read the words, settled into the living room couch, and cried. Rejected. To her mind, unfairly so.

Her husband, Roberto, a Puerto Rican who had become a civil rights activist on the mainland, was now working at the Equal Employment Opportunity Commission, providing lawyers with technical analysis and writing on the nation's new laws against discrimination. She was a middle-aged

Hispanic woman, deeply immersed in local politics, who knew about discrimination — and statistics. She would fight.

In a meeting that she willed the law school's administrators into granting, she laid out her case. She had As and Bs in college and had endured many hardships over the years. Oh, and by the way, the school appeared to have few, if any, middle-aged Hispanic women among its students.

So Edna Canino won herself a place in Southern Methodist University, Dedman School of Law, and graduated in 1978, the same month that her son Robert completed high school. Along the way, she had taught him about hitting walls, and going through them.

Canino chose to attend Bethany Nazarene College, in Oklahoma, following the path of a few friends he had made in high school and church. Naturally outgoing, with a big Afro and a goofy smile, he thrived in the morally conservative, evangelical Christian environment of the school, now known as Southern Nazarene University. By his junior year, though, he had failed to make a meaningful connection with any of the young women on campus. Until, that is, he joined a group of people throwing a Frisbee around the quad, and met Loretta Rutledge, a smart and attractive freshman from Tulsa, who seemed to get his humor.

For their first date, he somehow turned his lack of finances into a sweetly wacky theme. Treating Loretta to an evening picnic at Bethany Park, he laid out a bag of flour, instead of flowers. A gentle piece of sheet music, instead of a boom box. Some carbonated grape juice, instead of the wine they never would have drunk anyway.

*Interesting,* an amused Loretta thought. She was in for at least one more date.

After a pleasant second-date dinner — potato skins and two sweet teas, all he could afford — they took an evening stroll along Lake Hefner, hand in hand, until Robert abruptly stopped. *This is it,* Loretta thought. *He's going to kiss me.* Instead, he screamed, ripped his shirt open, and began beating his chest.

*Interesting,* Loretta thought again. *He has some, um, animal magnetism.*

A bee had found its way into the he-man's shirt.

Robert: "Very embarrassing."

Loretta: "Very funny."

Very nice.

They continued to date while seeking postgraduate degrees at the University of Oklahoma, hers in architecture, his in law. As a recent graduate with an interest in pursuing justice, possibly through broadcast journalism, Canino had begun working as a clerk for District Judge William R. Saied in Oklahoma City, whom he considered a mentor. For what it was worth, the judge told his eager young aide that he might not be suited for a career in law. *You'd get too attached to the people you'd represent,* Saied said. *This inability to separate might prove too hard on you.*

Still, Canino felt a calling, one underscored by the painting in the judge's chambers of a robed Jesus knocking at a wooden door ("Behold, I stand at the door, and knock."). The young clerk dedicated himself to law, and to being worthy of Loretta, though this latter pursuit seemed to be taking him some time.

By the fall of 1984, they had been dating for four years, and here they were, eating Thanksgiving dinner with Loretta's family in Tulsa, when Robert began agitating to visit the Gilcrease, a well-known local museum. Now! Even though it's Thanksgiving Day, and even though Robert is famously uninterested in museums. Now!

A puzzled Loretta relented, and her family indulged their demanding guest by going on a post-turkey visit to take in a collection of American art on a day that celebrates America. Loretta moved slowly through the exhibits, admiring the work of Remington and the Lakota, of Homer and Cassatt. When she reached the last room, though, Loretta noticed a painting by a friend of theirs named Melanie, resting on an easel. It depicted a man and a woman walking arm in arm down an autumn-gold country road toward a white-steepled church in the distance. On a dark log in the bottom-left corner was written: "Will you marry me?"

Loretta looked up, confused, as Robert pulled out a plastic-rose paintbrush from one pocket and a thimble-size container of white paint from another.

Imagine the meticulous planning that went into this marriage proposal. The pestering of Melanie to paint the scene according to his sketch. The improbability of convincing a family to visit an art museum on Thanksgiving Day. The smuggling of a container of paint past the museum's security guards and in near proximity of irreplaceable art. The audacity.

Loretta accepted the rose and, with family watching and security coming down the hall, painted her yes on the canvas.

■ ■ ■ ■

Canino worked for a year with an Oklahoma City law firm that specialized in insurance defense and medical malpractice, but he felt unfulfilled. He wanted to be a white hat pursuing justice, even if it meant a significant reduction in earnings and no promise of a partnership payoff. He joined the Equal Employment Opportunity Commission, paid his dues, and impressed his superiors: trial attorney in its Miami office; supervisory trial attorney in its Dallas office; special assistant in Washington; regional attorney in Dallas; a go-to person for championing society's most vulnerable.

He was lauded in particular for convincing both the EEOC *and* the federal courts that cases of human trafficking, normally relegated to spotty criminal prosecution, fell well within the agency's civil mandate. He argued that if litigated as violations of the basic rights protected under civil employment laws, these disturbing cases could liberate thousands of lives and realize millions in penalties. And he backed it up with *Chellen and EEOC v. John Pickle Company.*

The Pickle company had recruited dozens of young men from East India — steelworkers, electrical engineers, and a cook — to work at its plant in Tulsa, where it manufactured equipment for the oil industry. But once these employees arrived, at great personal cost, the company pulled a bait and switch. It confiscated their identification and immigration documents and paid them between two and three dollars an hour, while their non-Indian colleagues were paid about fourteen dollars an hour for doing the same kind of work. (The cook was paid one dollar an hour for his eighteen-hour shifts.) The company rationed their food, subjected them to ethnic slurs, tapped their phones, and housed them in a warehouse "dormitory" behind barbed wire, while watchful foremen and an armed guard prevented their escape into a country that, they were told, blamed them for 9/11.

With the help of area churches, the men eventually did manage to flee, and their story reached the EEOC's Dallas office. Canino spent the next three years preparing for trial, sorting through records in a hot, unventilated facility in Tulsa, interviewing Indian plaintiffs — most of whom could not speak English — outside a motel in muggy Louisiana, and taking the testy depositions of company officials.

In May 2006, his hard work paid off. An

outraged federal judge ordered the John Pickle Company to pay $1.32 million to the fifty-two men for its unlawful and egregious treatment of them.

As Robert Canino read the accounts from Atalissa, he could hear another knock at the door. He had done this before. He was the one to do it again.

In early April, Canino flew to West Texas to visit a few of the Henry's men who had been sent to a Midland nursing home after the first round of departures from the bunkhouse. The one-story facility, Terrace West, was like any other average nursing home. The staff in scrubs, the halls a traffic jam of wheelchairs and walkers, the air an olfactory swirl of institutional cooking and cleaning products. When death, illness, and mismanagement thwarted the plans of Henry's Turkey Service to build a retirement home for the men on the Johnson ranch in Goldthwaite, co-owner Kenneth Henry reached out to David Johnson, who worked as an administrator for the nursing home's parent company.

Though he and his uncle TH had never been close, the younger Johnson had grown up with these men, trading jokes and baseball cards, sharing chores and Sunday barbecues. Feeling a strong connection to them still, he agreed to help.

Among those living in the nursing home were Tommy Johnson, chubby as ever, who had been handcuffed to his bed in Atalissa, and who was now wearing the good-old-boy uniform of suspenders and beat-up, sweat-stained cap; big Leonard Barefield, the "Bear," still unintelligible to all but the most attuned ears, who spent his days working on a flower bed; and little Johnny Kent, once knocked down in the plant by Randy Neubauer, now wearing a maroon Dewar's cap, flashing a two-tooth smile, and keeping himself busy by cleaning all the dining room tables. Here, too, was a glowering Clarence Dunning, a product of the Lufkin State School who started working turkey when he was twenty years old. He was nearly sixty now, his hair and mustache white, his adulthood lost to a distant turkey plant, his mind smoldering from the teasing he endured for moving too slow because of bad feet, and from being called names, especially "nigger." While others flitted about — one man, Doyle Trantham, kept asking for business cards to add to his collection — Dunning wanted to talk only business.

Seeking privacy from the other nursing-home residents, Robert Canino led the men out onto the patio, where he soon began to grasp the complexity of his task. His clients seemed hesitant to speak, as if still fearing repercussions. When they did talk, their sense of time's passage was off by years, if not by decades.

Gradually, though, they opened up about the abuse and exploitation, while one man buzzed nervously around the patio table, chattering about documents he had seen, money he was owed, money *everyone* was owed, and you gotta look at that. When another man told the story of Tommy Johnson getting kicked in the balls, Johnson flinched and covered his crotch with his hands. Dunning kept telling him, *You gotta talk for yourself, Tommy.* But Dunning was also hesitant to trust these visitors, so often had his trust been broken before. What words he did share were revealing. When Canino asked whether he had family, his answer lingered.

*I got no family,* Dunning said. *I have a sister, but I don't have no family.*

Three weeks later, Canino and Tammy Johnson, the veteran EEOC investigator who had helped Sherri Brown file the complaint against Henry's Turkey Service, flew to Des Moines, with no doubt about where they would go first: Atalissa. They wanted to see, they needed to see, the hilltop bunkhouse that held such gravitational pull in this case.

The building had recently been cleaned out to an auctioneer's song of going, going, gone. Now it was vacant and shuttered, enveloped in that loud kind of quiet.

After circling the property, Canino climbed an external stairwell to the second floor, looking for an open door, a cracked window — anything that might grant a glimpse inside. Tammy Johnson, though, was unnerved by the no-trespassing signs and all-around spookiness. She just about tiptoed up to the building, car keys in hand, ready to bolt at the slightest movement. "Very creepy," she recalls. "A place I wouldn't put my worst enemy in."

Unable to find entry, Canino and Johnson proceeded to Waterloo, to meet many of the Henry's men in a side room of a local church. For the investigators, these people by now were like central characters from a disturbing novel come alive. The spoon-playing guy with the broken kneecap: Willie Levi. The earnest guy with a girlfriend and daughter somewhere: Frank Rodriguez. The brothers: Billy and Robert Penner. One man was having such a bad day that it was decided he should skip this discussion. Too upsetting.

Canino introduced himself as a federal lawyer and provided a basic outline of his purpose, ever careful not to slip into legal babble-speak. He explained that a complaint had been filed against the men's former employer, Henry's Turkey Service, and that he was interested in hearing their stories. The men eagerly obliged, some talking over others as the rest nodded in assent. Stories of being kicked, called names, denied pay, forced to carry weights, ordered to sit in the van, denied permission to go to church. Of wanting a Detroit Lions jacket returned. Of working turkey until it hurt.

They were asked how long these abuses had gone on.

A month. A year. A dog's age. Forever.

One man, apparently frustrated by a speech impediment that thwarted his ability to be understood, became so agitated by the discussion that he kept popping up from his chair to take a cool-down walk around the room, only to pop up again at the mention of yet another transgression. Canino later learned his name: Keith Brown, complainant of record.

Another, slight and with oversize glasses, identified himself as the bunkhouse cook and asked to speak to Canino in private because he didn't want to talk about his business in front of everybody. Off to the side, he confided that Henry's Turkey Service *owed me money, and the person who's supposed to help me in the kitchen, the lady Dru, never does, always going outside for a smoke instead, and Robert Penner was giving insulin shots to another man for diabetes and he really shouldn't be doing this, but I don't want to get him in trouble, and I want to go home, to Houston, I have a sister there, her name is Rose.* This was Pete Graffagnino, and he so wanted to go home.

Listening, observing, Canino realized the considerable courtroom challenges he would be facing. In the *Pickle* case, the Indian plaintiffs spoke several different languages — difficult but, with the help of translators, surmountable. These men before him spoke English, but their common disability affected their command of linear progression. As frustrating to them, he imagined, as Keith Brown's speech impediment.

But then would come another remarkable insight into the degradation these men had suffered in the workplace. A few recalled how they were sometimes not allowed to take a bathroom break while working on the line at the turkey plant, and how some had no choice but to go in their pants. Canino asked how we know this to be true.

A man sitting beside him, whom he at first mistook for a staff member, spoke up. *I did the laundry,* Frank Rodriguez said. *I had to clean those pants.*

On the flight back to Dallas that she shared with Canino, Tammy Johnson reflected on what she had seen and heard, all through her personal prism as a black woman, the mother of two college students, and an EEOC investigator for nearly twenty years. If truth be known, she had not been particularly moved when she first recorded the complaint by Keith Brown's sister, Sherri, two months earlier. At that point, only words.

But now the travails of these men, so wounded and yet still so generous, had become flesh-and-blood real. She was even carrying a plastic keychain lanyard, a handmade gift from Billy Penner.

Nothing but modern-day slavery, is what she thought.

# NINETEEN

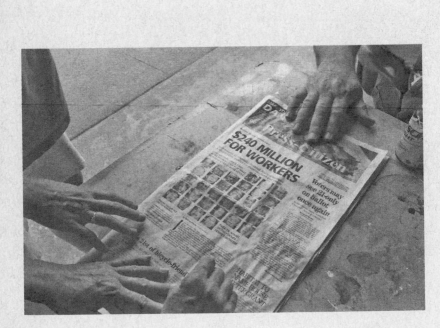

*Vindication*

A potential juror whose religious beliefs would not allow him to sit in judgment of others had been disqualified. Another juror with chronic back pain was told he could stand and stretch at any time. The court reporter was wonderful in all ways, lawyers were informed, save for one problem that should not be misinterpreted during testimony: she has an eye condition that occasionally causes her to weep.

In a sleek federal courtroom in Davenport, where the blond wood and recessed lighting would soon stand in contrast to descriptions of squalor and neglect, the civil case of *Equal Employment Opportunity Commission vs. Hill Country Farms, Inc., d/b/a Henry's Turkey Service* was about to begin. Finally.

More than four years had passed since the men had been rescued from their fetid surroundings in Atalissa, and so much had happened since. The country had reelected

411

President Obama, Iowa had chosen a new governor, a team of Navy SEALS had killed Osama bin Laden in Pakistan. Yes, so much had happened, and so much had not. All those demands for accountability, once resounding so furiously in the startling case of Henry's Turkey Service, now echoed hollow through the corridors of the state capitol.

Just ask John McCalley, then the director of the state's Department of Elder Affairs. Shortly after the schoolhouse rescue, he had been deputized by Governor Culver to lead a multiagency task force with the mandate to ensure that another Atalissa never occurred again, and this task force took to its mission. At a bill-signing ceremony less than three months later, Atalissa was invoked so often — conjuring images of eviscerated turkeys, damaged hands, and cockroach infestations — that all the Henry's men seemed present in spirit. McCalley watched with pride as the governor used a beautifully crafted corncob pen in signing into law a few of the task force's early recommendations. The pen had been made by McCalley's brother, Mark, who has Down syndrome and who was on his way that very moment to his job at a Walmart.

McCalley realized that these new laws,

412

including a requirement that unlicensed group homes register with the state, were only modest steps toward greater protection for the disabled. But he assured reporters that the task force was continuing to review the Atalissa case, and would likely make other legislative recommendations in the months to come — to no avail, it would turn out. More concerned with the struggling economy than with an unsettling scandal that grew older by the day, the state of Iowa moved on.

"There was an opportunity to advance the ball, but we failed to do it as a state, collectively," a frustrated McCalley says. "Persons with disability are still out of sight, out of mind, in this society."

Even with all the exposure of its inner workings, Henry's Turkey Service remained a charmed entity, still able to sidestep true accountability. It showed no intention of paying nearly $3 million in fines and back pay exacted by state and federal labor agencies for various wage violations. And those expecting criminal prosecution would only come to share McCalley's disappointment.

Law enforcement officials chose not to prosecute, seeing insurmountable challenges to proving criminality beyond a reasonable doubt. The attorney general's

413

office reported that it could not prove the company's two surviving owners, Kenneth Henry and Jane Ann Johnson, "had actual knowledge of the deteriorating conditions" in the bunkhouse. It also concluded that an inconsistency in the men's recollections — about perpetrators, time frames, and circumstances — would thwart successful prosecution of charges alleging physical and mental abuse.

The unwillingness to prosecute appalled disability-rights advocates and other observers. What about the criminal referral made by the state Department of Inspections and Appeals to the attorney general, officially accusing Henry's of operating an unlicensed care facility for dependent adults? What about the allegations of financial exploitation? Of dependent-adult abuse through the denial of medical care? Of the worst fire-safety violations ever seen by state inspectors?

Muscatine County sheriff David White seemed particularly incurious about the case. "The staff at Henry's were very caring people that took good care of the men," he later explained. "They were regularly taken out for community events throughout the area (such as church suppers, fire department breakfasts, county fairs) as well as regular shopping trips. These men took great pride in their work and were always happy whenever I had contact with them. They had about every game, game table, yard games etc. to play in their off-hours both indoor and outdoor. I don't believe there is any one of my staff that felt that these individuals were in any way abused or mistreated."

The last hope for justice for the men from the bunkhouse rested with this EEOC case about to unfold. More specifically, it rested with the agency's lawyer, Robert Canino. And he knew it.

Canino had spent nearly four years assembling the case, interviewing social workers, experts in intellectual disability, and, of course, the victims themselves. Once, while listening to their recollections during a group interview in Waterloo, he became so disturbed by the heartbreaking accounts — and so clearly troubled by the challenges he'd have in proving them — that lanky Henry Wilkins stepped forward to encourage the lawyer. One of the gut pullers, Wilkins was now in his late sixties, afflicted with emphysema, problems keeping his balance, and a keen loneliness from having no family in his life. He leaned in to put a large hand on the lawyer's shoulder.

*Don't worry about all that courtroom stuff, Robert,* he said. *We've got your back.*

This fluttered moment took on larger meaning for Canino. It gave him strength to think that these defenseless but resilient men had *his* back, as he delved deeper into their segregated, nearly forgotten world.

Each night, as he walked past the Texas School Book Depository building, he carried more and more documents home. The kitchen table served for a while as his home office, the television offering distraction, the decorative signs on the wall providing perspective.

One said: "Trust in the Lord."

Another: "Remember, as far as everyone knows, we are a nice normal family."

When the records threatened to take over the entire kitchen, he commandeered the formal dining room and redecorated it in a style that might be called Legal Obsession. The glass-top table, the chairs, and the white carpet were soon covered with reams of Henry's Turkey Service payroll records, social worker assessments, and decades of stultifying regulations and laws. His wife, Loretta, and their two teenage children served as Canino's support staff, motivated as much as anything by a concern for his well-being. He was gaining weight, losing his sense of humor, absenting himself from church and baseball-coaching duties — a sleep-deprived bundle of stress, trying to understand "pulling crop," and "rehanging," and "intellectual disability," and "section 14 (c) of the FLSA."

Canino's family noticed bruising on his forehead, as if the immensity of the material he had to digest and the acute responsibility he felt had seriously overtaxed his brain. The bruises turned out to be caused by his habit of rubbing his forehead in worried thought.

Loretta and young Braden slapped evidence stickers on documents and used a calculator to tally the money owed to each man for the hours he worked. Brianne, home from college, searched the Internet for potential witnesses. They did anything they could to ease the workload of a perfectionist who, as his mentor once said, took cases too personally. Now here he was, representing thirty-two defenseless men who most likely could not testify in their own behalf. Thirty-two individual stories he had to know intimately, in order to be able to say, instantly and with authority: *This* is the man who was handcuffed to his bed; *this* is the man who had an untreated

417

broken kneecap; *this* is the man who was knocked to the turkey-plant floor. *These* are the men.

Canino had become, in a way, the thirty-third man.

Three weeks before trial, Canino all but sequestered himself. He needed to meet with witnesses and plot out a legal strategy, but mostly he needed to be alone. He filled a government-issue Dodge Grand Caravan with boxes of documents and a couple of suitcases, and drove seven hundred miles to Iowa to open his portable law office. He spent nearly two weeks in motels in Des Moines and Waterloo before moving into the Hotel Blackhawk, a century-old institution beside the federal courthouse in Davenport, the city known as "Iowa's Front Porch."

Once the gem of Davenport, a place where dignitaries stayed and first-class big bands played, the eleven-story Hotel Blackhawk had fallen from grandeur in recent decades, enduring half hearted renovations, foreclosure proceedings, and a steady slide toward fleabag status. A stolen Lincoln Continental spent eight years under a tarp in the parking garage before being discovered in 1984. A meth-lab fire in 2006 destroyed an entire floor. But a more dedicated renovation in 2009 had restored the building's Italian Renaissance luster, making it once again a preferred Davenport destination. The amenities included an indoor pool, a spa, a fitness center, even a bowling alley — none of them to be enjoyed by the preoccupied guest staying at a discounted government rate in room 512.

Determined to maximize his nineteen-hour workdays, Canino turned his suite into a pretrial bunker. He bought cases of Diet Dr Pepper, filled the refrigerator with cheeses and cold cuts, and stuffed the room's dresser drawers with crackers, cereal, chips, cans of tuna fish, and packages of ramen noodles. To break the silence of isolation, the dumbfounding dialogue of television programs he had never seen before — *Pawn Stars, Storage Wars, Duck Dynasty* — droned on, commingling the contrived situations of reality TV with the actual dramas and horrors detailed in the court documents spread before him.

By this point, he had already won a $1.3 million judgment against Henry's Turkey Service for two years of back wages, after successfully arguing that, under the Americans with Disabilities Act, each of the thirty-two men should have been paid the same market rate as their nondisabled colleagues doing similar work. In their final weeks of employment, Canino noted, some of the men had even trained their successors.

Certain damning stipulations had been made at this trial; namely, that for more than thirty years, Henry's Turkey Service applied the same wage calculations, resulting in a cash payment of sixty-five dollars a month for each man no matter how many hours he worked; that the company used the men's earnings and Social Security benefits to "reimburse" itself for their board, lodging, and other costs; and that it had continued these unfair practices even after being cited by the Department of Labor.

With these violations a matter of record, Canino planned to zero in on the emotional harm caused by the verbal and physical abuse, substandard living conditions, denial of proper medical care, and restrictions of basic freedoms. What civil rights law calls "loss of enjoyment of life."

Nearly forty years of discrimination suffered by the plaintiffs, and nearly four years of preparation by their lawyer, came down to this courtroom moment. And it did not begin well for Canino.

He had only recently tried wearing a

contact lens in his right eye to ease the strain of all the required reading, but had not yet learned how to insert the lens properly. Before coming to the courtroom, Canino had hurriedly tried to force the tiny piece of plastic into place, and now his eye was bloodshot and his sight blurry. What's more, he felt dizzy, a little faint, even light-headed.

*What have you been drinking?* his parale-gal, Barbara Fuller, asked.

*Diet Dr Pepper. By the case.*

*You're dehydrated,* she told him. *Start drinking water. Fast.*

The lawyer gulped down glass after glass of water, emptying the carafe on the counsel table. Swapped that irritating contact lens for a pair of Dollar Store reading glasses. Collected himself. And set about to tell the story of the men of Atalissa.

In preparing for trial, Canino weighed whether to call any of his clients to the stand. He feared brutal or tricky cross-examinations, and worried that the pressure of testifying might affect their continuing recovery. After a process of elimination, Canino chose Gene Berg to be the men's representative, and helped him pick out his Sunday best, including a sharp western-style shirt, for his court appearance.

But at the last moment, Canino pulled back. Berg was already beginning to exhibit signs of stress, especially after being informed that his old boss, Kenneth Henry, would be present during his testimony. The lawyer thanked the disappointed Berg for his support and courage, and promised him a steak dinner — *after we win* — so that he could wear that special outfit after all.

It would be left to others to speak for the men.

Denise Gonzales, the former supervisor for the Iowa Department of Human Services and the architect of the Stand by Your Man policy after the rescue, described her first impression of the conditions in the bunkhouse: "It was — filthy doesn't describe it. The bugs, the mice, the smells, the garbage, the paint coming off the walls, the debris, the smell, the bugs and mouse droppings in the kitchen, the rats. It was horrific."

Natalie Neel-McGlaughlin, the Iowa social worker and first responder to the bunkhouse, recalled the stories of abuse the men had shared, and provided commentary for the bunkhouse photographs she had taken, now flashing on a courtroom screen: "This is one of the men's living quarters as well, where the ceiling was caving in, and the men had attempted to fix the ceiling, or the leaks coming down, with duct tape . . ."

Neel-McGlaughlin's friend and colleague Kim Cronkleton laid out the men's medical conditions at the time of their rescue: the dental wires digging into the gums of Jeff Long, the weight and hearing loss of Henry Wilkins, the painful swelling in the hands of Raymond Vaughn, "due to the repetitive motion of working at the turkey plant for all those years and having to pull crop. . . ."

Kyle Gorsh, then an assistant supervisor for the Iowa Fire Prevention Bureau, and a veteran of as many as three thousand inspections, used photographs to illustrate his findings after an emergency tour of the bunkhouse: "The level of fire safety is probably the worst I had ever seen, and we had to take action that evening in a way that I had never had to do, which we had to evacuate the building. So it sticks out, definitely."

Susan Seehase, the services director at Exceptional Persons, remembered her staff's struggle to cut through the plaintiffs' trauma and establish trust: "Several of the men were very concerned that Dru and Randy would be coming to get them. They were very concerned that their number and their addresses would be given to them and that —

you know, they really didn't trust us at that point that they were safe."

And Randy Neubauer, the former supervisor, admitted that he had slapped and kicked a couple of his charges — although, he said, one incident was a joke and the other an accident. He also blamed the decline in bunkhouse conditions on the persistent refusal of Kenneth Henry to pay for repairs.

The words of each witness were like paint strokes to an Iowa landscape unimaginable to Iowa itself. But no one framed the landscape better than Canino's expert witness, Dr. Sue Gant, a nationally recognized authority in developmental disabilities whose extensive curriculum vitae required twenty-three pages. Among her many touchstone assignments over the decades had been to help residents of the notorious Willowbrook Developmental Center in Staten Island find housing and acceptance in their communities. But she could not be dismissed as some out-of-stater passing judgment on Iowa. Sue Gant was a farm girl from Hawarden, in the northwestern corner of the Hawkeye State.

Gant had met with all the men still living in Iowa, and spoken by Skype to those in Texas and elsewhere. Based on those interviews, and on all the depositions, case reports, and individual assessments she had examined, it was clear to her that Henry's Turkey Service had violated the basic human rights of these men.

"They were hidden away for decades," Gant testified. "They were isolated. They were relegated to hazardous living conditions. They were subjected to abuse and neglect. They sustained physical and psychological injuries, and they suffered irreparable harm due to a loss of a lifetime of opportunities."

Gant cited the consistency in the men's stories. She spoke of the care they took in sharing what they had seen, rather than what they had only heard. Jeff Long, for example, said he once saw Levi coming around the corner at the plant with a bloody nose and mouth, with Randy Neubauer following close behind — but had not seen Neubauer hit Levi. Keith Brown was clear to say he saw Neubauer go into Tommy Johnson's room, and then saw Johnson handcuffed to his bed, but did not see Neubauer put the cuffs on Johnson.

She explained intellectual disability to the jury in understandable terms ("the inability to learn in typical ways"), laid out the advances in disability rights over the last thirty years, and put the thirty-two plaintiffs in context — made them come alive. She recounted how L. C. Hall motioned with his hand to reenact a supervisor slapping his roommate, Preston Pate, in the face. How Carl Wayne Jones recalled being grabbed by the neck and called a dumb ass. How Jeff Long vividly described being pushed down some stairs.

The Texas company had segregated and dehumanized the men, forcing them to work at an arduous, stigmatizing job and casting them into structural poverty, Gant concluded. "The aggrieved workers could have enjoyed a good life. Instead, they lost decades of healthy life experiences."

Henry's Turkey Service presented a spiritless defense. At one point its Muscatine County lawyer, David Scieszinski, claimed to have no knowledge of a stipulation of facts — in which the company did not contest its exploitative pay practices — even though he had signed the document. ("If I signed a stipulation, I'll live with it," he said. "But I don't recall it, Your Honor.") Meanwhile, the company's two principal representatives, Kenneth Henry and Randy Neubauer, spent a good portion of their testimony blaming each other for the bunkhouse's abusive culture and conditions.

Even Henry's descriptions of men he had known for decades came across at times as more condescending than affectionate. *No wonder Johnny McDaniels was emotional during his interview with Gant; he's always like that — it's part of his "affliction." . . . Keith Brown was an alcoholic who'd go into rooms of other boys and take their beer. . . . Gene is "a good boy." . . .*

The six-day trial provided an upsetting recitation of inhumane conditions and treatment, as well as a tense assemblage of characters in an Iowa passion play. Kenneth Henry clacking into the courtroom with his walker. Danny Miles, Neubauer's sidekick, in his cowboy hat and dramatic cowboy duster, looking like he just rode into Davenport with a herd of cattle. Keith Brown's sister, Sherri, the whistleblower, smoking cigarettes and trying without success to control her temper. During one break she followed Henry past the courtroom's heavy glass doors to the lobby and shouted, *Why did you do this to these guys?* She would never forget his response: *You ruined my life.*

Now it was nearly over. During closing arguments, the defense lawyer, Scieszinski, surmised that the jury will no doubt wonder, "Why didn't those boys come here and sit on the witness stand and tell us their

427

stories?" He urged the jurors to recognize that for more than thirty years, Henry's Turkey Service had provided "the direction, the love and care" these men needed.

But Canino described this same company and its supervisors as moral vandals. "They broke some people," he said, continuing: "Broken hearts, broken spirits, shattered dreams. And ultimately the broken lives of thirty-two intellectually disabled men who happened to be employees of Henry's Turkey Service."

The judge provided the jurors with a few final instructions, promised a prompt delivery of some delicatessen food, and released them to their deliberations. In their absence, Canino fretted:

Would the jurors understand the concept of "loss of enjoyment of life"? Would they question why none of the Henry's men had taken the stand? Had Gant, Seehase, Neel-McGlaughlin, and all the others effectively conveyed the un-Americanness of it all? The decades-long denial of basic human rights?

Late the next morning, the five women and three men in the jury returned to the blond-wooded courtroom with recessed lighting. Took their seats. Stared straight ahead. Then the senior judge, Charles R. Wolle, a tall, fit man with a get-to-the-point demeanor, announced the verdict:

The jury had ruled in favor of the thirty-two former employees of Henry's Turkey Service, awarding each of them $7.5 million for emotional harm and punitive damages.

A landmark $240 million judgment. Historic.

Canino dropped his head into his hands and wept so hard his shoulders shuddered. Struggling to recover, he wiped his face with a sleeve and made a point of looking up at the jury, so that its members could see his pride and appreciation for what they had done: the right thing.

His sobs came from exhaustion. From finally being unburdened of the weight of so many heartbreaking stories contained in those crates of documents he had carried for four years. Unburdened, too, of the dinners of ramen noodles and Diet Dr Pepper, the bruises on his forehead, the missed church functions and baseball games — the suspension of his own life.

Canino's tears also came from the sudden realization that these men, long invisible, had at last become present among us. The astounding size of the award would only amplify the significance of their story, make it national news, expose people in power to some small sense of what it must have been like to be Willie Levi, or Pete Graffagnino, or Tommy Johnson.

And the tears sprung from sorrow. He knew the $240 million award, the one soon to be heralded in an EEOC news release as the largest in agency history, would not stand. The men would not be receiving $7.5 million each. That was an illusion, as unreal as the retirement home they had once been promised. In a few days, the judge would have no choice but to dramatically reduce the award, under a federal cap on damages for a business with fewer than 101 employees.

Even so, the gravity of the verdict seemed to rest on the hunched shoulders of Kenneth Henry as he made his way slowly out of the courthouse, stunned by what he saw as a miscarriage of justice. The jury seemed not to hear his testimony that he had suffered five heart attacks. Not to realize how these boys would tell you anything you wanted to hear if you were a pretty young woman, like some of these social workers, and you let a boy put his arm around you. Not to notice that the men's families could have collected them anytime they wanted, but didn't, for more than thirty years. Surely those families ought to feel a little guilty, maybe a whole lot guilty, about that. Asked by reporters about the damages awarded to the men, he said:

"Do you think I can write a check for that?"

Yes, Canino knew that the multimillion-dollar award would be reduced to a small fraction, just as he knew that Kenneth Henry and Jane Ann Johnson had already transferred their share of the company's assets to their children, which would make the collection of damages difficult, if not impossible. He knew, and it made his stomach ache — but he wouldn't acknowledge it publicly, at least not now. This was a moment of celebration. However ephemeral, the $240 million verdict awarded by the jury of eight reflected communal outrage. It sent a crystal-clear message of equal rights for all, and ensured that the name of this landmark case would become shorthand in courtrooms and halls of government for the segregation and exploitation of people with disabilities.

*Henry's Turkey Service.*

Several weeks after the trial, Canino returned to Iowa for a lawyer-client conference in Waterloo. Carrying a briefcase and wearing a tie, he walked into a small conference room at the Deery Center, the meeting place managed by Exceptional Persons. Waiting there were seven of his clients, all former employees of Henry's Turkey Service. Their colorful clothes reflected allegiance to two states: Carl Wayne Jones wearing a blue and white Dallas Cowboys cap, James Fowler a yellow and black Iowa Hawkeyes jacket, Willie Levi a burnt-orange Texas Longhorns lanyard.

Canino opened his arms to receive hug after hug as the men eagerly filled him in about their dishwashing jobs, camping plans, girlfriends who liked to slow dance. Henry Wilkins, once known as Dewey the Drunk, told his lawyer that he didn't drink alcohol anymore, except for one beer on his birthday. Paul Hayek showed off the scar on his wrist, following surgery to repair damage caused by decades of repetitive motion.

As they talked, each man called out his longtime job at the turkey plant, as if reciting in chorus a prose poem of assembly-line evisceration: *Hanging. Three-pointing. Rehanging. Pulled guts. Pulled crop. Cut the heart.*

Canino listened to every story. Then he began: "I know that some of you don't want to talk about Atalissa anymore."

Several shook their heads. "No way," said

Fowler, who had pulled guts for thirty years. "No part of that."

"I understand," the lawyer said.

Aware that his clients had only the most basic understanding of money, Canino spoke in a conversational tone that was calibrated and deliberate, not condescending. He explained that the $240 million judgment in the big court case had been reduced to $1.6 million. This would come out to about $50,000 each "for how they treated you." But remember, he added, the findings in an earlier, related case would add another $25,000 to $50,000 to the wages they were owed.

This meant between $75,000 and $100,000 for each of them, Canino said. But he was quick to add that collecting the money would be a considerable challenge, now that the owners of Henry's Turkey Service had taken steps to move or protect their assets.

"I can't promise you what I can get you," he said.

A quiet overtook the room, as the men tried to make sense of the words, the numbers, the money owed to them for work done and pain suffered. Money they might never see.

Then Henry Wilkins broke the silence by

echoing something he had said four years earlier, when Canino first embarked on this case. "I got your back on that," he said.

Canino smiled to the floor. "Well, that's why we won," he said, voice trembling. "People knew you had my back."

■ ■ ■ ■

# TWENTY

■ ■ ■ ■

*Demolition on an Atalissa hilltop*

The prehistoric jaws of a John Deere excavator takes its first bite, and then another and another, ravenous in its taste for turquoise. At times the jaws become a fist, delivering lazy punches with deceitful force. Other times it is a claw, swiping away hundreds of pounds of debris with an easy, thoughtless sweep. A smell you can almost see rises from the site, the commingled aromas of clay, desiccation, and abandoned belongings once held dear. Swarms of flies, irritated by any pause for reflection, bite the living.

The hilltop schoolhouse of Atalissa had loomed over the Iowa flatness for more than a century, ever since its construction became, as the *Muscatine Journal* proclaimed, "the feature of any story of the year 1911 in this prosperous Muscatine county town. . . ."

437

The building is of hollow tile construction, the interior being finished in rough-cast stucco placed over the tile. . . . On the lower floor are two large rooms and hall-way with the stairway leading to the upper floor. On the upper floor is the large as-sembly hall, a class room, a library room, teachers room, while the front of the as-sembly room is a rostrum or stage. . . . Thus the assembly hall may when it is desired be conveniently utilized for the purpose of entertainments or meetings. . . . A room 20 by 40 is apportioned off as a playroom for the use of the children at such times when the weather prevents their spending their recess periods out of doors. . . .

The newspaper's level of detail, normally reserved for a museum's grand opening or a cathedral's consecration, reflected an understanding that this eight-thousand-dollar structure was to be more than just a schoolhouse. It would be a theater as well, a sports arena, a dance hall, wedding hall, and assembly hall: the place for the community to be in secular communion.

Now, with the excavator's every swipe and bite, moments of the past escape into the Iowa summer of 2014 — moments so distant that few even constitute memories, for who alive would remember them? The indignant whispers of three teachers, Misses Vida Stick, Bessie Mosher, and Edith Watters, who absolutely refused to work for the superintendent, Miss Dora Massman, resulting in no school for a week in 1914. The polite handclaps at the close of the 1939 junior class production of *Oh! Susan!* and the admiring coos for the new stage drapes sewn by Mrs. Lynn Watters, Mrs. Ivan Wolf, and Miss Bertha King, with help from Mrs. Burl Johnson and Miss Marjorie King. The erupting cheers after Atalissa's Nevin Roberts swished a corner jump shot in sudden-death overtime against the Buffalo quintet in 1954; the guffaws during the "Sunbonnet Sally and Overall Jim" skit at the Fun Festival in 1948; the careful pronunciation of fifteen-year-old Clella Federlein as she opined on the subject of "Universal Peace" during the annual declamatory contest in 1932. The barn dances and firemen's balls, the wedding receptions and alumni socials, the commencement pomp and circumstance. . . .

For now the town of Atalissa has decided that the vacant schoolhouse has to come down. Yes, it is still structurally sound, and planted deep enough into the hilltop earth to have withstood the winds of a hundred Iowa winters. But in its abandonment and disrepair, the building has become a dangerous lure for children whose imagining eyes see horrors and specters behind its boarded windows. Thus the presence of a fifty-thousand-pound excavator and a track loader working to erase it from the landscape.

A truer reason, perhaps, is that the sight of the schoolhouse has become too damned painful, an incessant reminder of the Henry's "boys" who once lived inside. For thirty-five years, those boys — sorry, but that's what we called them, with affection, not condescension — had been a part of this community, dancing at the taverns, singing in the church, waving from the street. They were mostly charming and sometimes annoying, but always accepted as neighbors. Then we go to sleep one night and in the morning our boys are gone, all but smuggled out of town while we slept, leaving guilt and acrimony in their wake.

Atalissa. The very name of our town has become an Iowa shortcut for: "Am I my brother's keeper?"

So the schoolhouse had to go. Dennis Hepker, the former mayor who had attended parties there, when the men first moved to town in the 1970s, back when he was a bachelor living on Falstaff beer, had advocated for demolition, so disgusted was he by the stream of gawkers taking pictures, asking questions, keeping the pain fresh. Always calling it a bunkhouse. It was a *schoolhouse,* dammit.

"Out of sight, out of mind, maybe," Hepker says.

Maybe. But the schoolhouse wasn't the only reminder. *Everything* in Atalissa, it seems, summons memories of the Henry's boys, down to its very streets. Remember the small guy with the big glasses and tilted head who used to pedal a trike up and down, collecting litter? What was his name? He had this big goofy grin, looked sort of like one of the seven dwarves. Smiley, we called him.

John. John Hatfield.

The town eddies now around their absence. The Atalissa Mini-Mart, where the men bought their Honey Buns and Mountain Dews and beer, has closed, its silvery door and gas pumps ceding to the creep of rust. The annual Atalissa Days parade, once featuring clowns on floats that rumbled with antique tractors and fire trucks down Cherry Street, has ended. And the all-women Atalissa Betterment Committee, whose members devoted a good amount of time to visiting with the schoolhouse men, have long since called it a day.

A few of the former ABCs gather to reminisce about the dance-with-one-and-you-dance-with-them-all enjoyment of the boys, and the smell of turkey on them, reminding everyone that they did what no one else wanted to do, and the time the boys chipped in after the Cedar River flooded its banks in 2008, and . . .

The women sit around a dark-wooded dining room table, many of them now in their sixties, summoning another memory with each sip they take from soda cans tucked into neoprene holders.

"I miss 'em," Carol O'Neill says suddenly. The men always called her Cheryl. "I miss 'em walking by. It's lonely."

"It's empty. You know?" Vada Baker says in agreement. She learned the Texas two-step from the men, and now feels guilt about telltale signs missed or maybe ignored. She hopes God will forgive her.

"You'd expect to see, you know, groups of two of them walking down with their radio on," Baker says. "They're waving and hollering at ya, and whatever — and you don't see that anymore."

"It's almost like a ghost town," Gracie

Gritton says. She worked for years and years at the turkey plant.

Everyone nods, saying that's the phrase for it: ghost town.

"It most definitely is not the same, nor will it ever be," O'Neill says. "It just, ya know. It just died."

An unsettling quiet has also come to the Zion Lutheran Church. A couple of years ago, its yoked relationship with Our Redeemer Lutheran Church, in West Liberty, ended, after which Our Redeemer issued a new call to pastor Lynn Thiede, who had been serving both congregations. This meant that within a couple of years, the Atalissa church lost both a resident pastor *and* a core of worshippers who hummed the Lord's Prayer, played kings and shepherds in the Christmas pageant, and brought a tambourine vibrancy to each Sunday service.

"They were joy, they were fun, there was no darkness in them," Thiede says of the Henry's men. "It's when they left that the soul of that place left."

Now the marquee outside the church tells of the absence.

"WELCOME"
WORSHIP: 10:00

443

One of the Spilgers, the dominant clan that helped found Zion Lutheran more than a century ago, drifts through the empty church, recalling the men. His name is Dennis Spilger, and his beard matches his gray Chicago Bears T-shirt. Rooting about, he finds the tambourine that Levi used to play; the pencil-colored map of the United States that allowed the men to return to Texas, if only with pushpins; and two photo albums, one brown, another floral patterned. Soon he is peeling apart the cellophane pages.

"Preston, and Tommy, and Johnny, and Levi . . ." he says, pointing. "Here they are, like Jesus and Joseph and stuff. . . ."

Taking a seat in one of the pews, he speaks in echoes of when the church thrummed with worshippers. The boys usually sat in this pew. Dwight at the organ would give them the signal, and they'd come up and sing. And boy, did they love shaking everybody's hands when the congregation exchanged wishes of peace.

"We didn't know nothing about how they were treated up there," Spilger says. "It was none of our business. When that all came out, we were just devastated. And then they took 'em away."

He looks toward the altar and its portrait of Jesus holding a lamb. After the men disappeared, he says, the congregation's loss hovered somewhere between what is felt after a good-bye and after a death. The depth of it surprises him still, several years later, as the old die away and the young stay away, as another traveling minister passes through, as the assurance of church perpetuation, once sustaining, dissipates.

"Not to have that, them humming and playing their tambourine and stuff — it was like silence," he says. "We'd sing our songs and stuff, but it wasn't the same. You'd wonder where the tambourine — where the guy keeping the beat was."

The excavator spins to the roar of its own heavy-metal music, demolishing with purpose, separating salvageable aluminum from disposable wood, reusable brick from crap concrete. Then its junior companion, the track loader, dumps the piles into the holds of waiting trucks.

Everything has its place. The metal will be exchanged for money, although the building had been relieved of its copper piping even before demolition began. The concrete, including the chunks painted day-care colors of red and yellow and blue, will go to a local farmer looking for fill. The paint and other hazardous materials will be set aside. The weeping willow in the front yard, toppled by a recent violent storm, has been yanked from the ground and chopped for firewood. A local farmer has already taken the distinctive wagon-wheel gate.

The rest, though, will go to the dump, including the flecks of personal belongings jutting from the great mounds. A dartboard. A remote control. A coffee mug. A bicycle wheel. A record collection, ruined by rain. A mattress, spilling its guts.

Overseeing the demolition is a general contractor named Travis Parry, forty, a child of Atalissa who grew up around the previous owners of these items. He'd see them walking through town, dancing at the bars, keeping the minimart open. If you ask him, the bunkhouse operated pretty well for a while. "But they just didn't keep up with the times," he says. "That's just my opinion."

Sunglasses conceal his eyes, gray dust cakes his youthful face, and squadrons of agitated flies fail to earn even a wave of his hand. He says that people have been stopping by, asking for souvenirs, and he has obliged, granting them square chunks of turquoise.

A 1990 Oldsmobile Toronado, dents in its blue, lurches to a gravel-spitting halt in front of the schoolhouse. A tall man with a camouflage baseball cap accommodating his ponytail steps out. He wears blue jeans and a western-style shirt with a pack of Pall Malls in the pocket and the sleeves cut to reveal large biceps and one faded tattoo. He comes around and opens the door for his passenger, an oxygen tank on wheels, and connects its translucent tubes to his nose. He looks up toward where the schoolhouse had been, his thick eyeglasses magnifying the shock in his eyes.

Danny Miles.

As a teenage delinquent with a penchant for stealing cars, Miles had been remanded by a sympathetic judge to Henry's Turkey Service, rather than to a Texas prison — although he had a learning disability, and not an intellectual disability. Miles worked turkey and lived in the bunkhouse as one of the "boys" for many years, before being promoted as one of the minders of men he likes to call his brothers. But they do not remember him as fondly, saying that he became Randy Neubauer's unpleasant sidekick, a bully and prankster who had forgotten what it was like on the opposite side of the ability-disability divide.

Now he is a fifty-three-year-old married father with chronic obstructive pulmonary disease, and he is paying his mournful respects to the building that defined his adult life.

He rolls his tank of breath up the hill with a body language that all but dares someone to say he is trespassing. Parry, the dust-caked demo man, comes over, and Miles says, "I used to live here," and for a while nothing else is said.

Miles talks a little bit about the flower beds that used to line the driveway, then walks over to the trunk of the weeping willow and begins kicking at the ground with the toe of a boot.

"You find a memory plaque?" he asks.

"A what?" the demo man says.

"A memory plaque," Miles says again. "It was right here. About the size of a concrete block. Had the name Alford Busby."

"Haven't seen it."

Miles keeps digging at the upturned earth, searching for something long since removed — that granite tribute to a Henry's "boy" who ran away and paid the price.

Soon, Danny Miles would huff back down to his Toronado, tuck in his life-support passenger, and pull away. Soon, the last truck would haul away the final load, the chasm would be filled, and the property would be left in what the demolition contract called a "mowable state." But for now, the excavator continues to punch and bite and swipe, releasing moments of Atalissa history into the fly-specked air: graduations and Christmases; performances for parents and one private performance for a pastor; punishing gym classes and gymnasium punishments; bleats of joy, cries of pain.

The schoolhouse. The bunkhouse.

"What do they plan to do with it?" Danny Miles asks.

"Nothing," answers the demo man.

# TWENTY-ONE

*Billy and Robert Penner in their Waterloo kitchen*

Nightclubs in Iowa do not, as a rule, enjoy much business in the early evenings of late March, but car after car is prowling the lot of Lofty's Lounge, hunting for parking spaces under a fish-belly sky. Planted between a pharmacy and a closed diner promising to reopen soon, the cavernous club has paneled walls and the hint of old cigarette smoke, and the two Christmas wreaths over its front entrance are either three months too late or nine months too early.

Lofty's is *the* gathering place here in Evansdale, a Waterloo suburb cradled by a looping curve in the Cedar River. It is where Thanksgiving Eve reunions begin and charity motorcycle rides end, and where, on Wednesday evenings like this one, clients from Exceptional Persons Incorporated and other local service providers enjoy a karaoke night just for them. The passengers alighting from cars head inside with purpose, some requiring a friendly arm to steady themselves, others breaking into a run, including a young man with Down syndrome who beats a companion in a race to the front door.

A polished-gray Chevy Malibu circles the lot before finding an available space on the fringe. Its driver is Sam Smith, twenty-four, a tall, clean-cut, and purposeful man who is working his way through Upper Iowa University in Fayette. He cleans hospital rooms in the morning, attends classes in the afternoon, and spends his Wednesday evenings with the four residents of a tan raised-ranch house in Waterloo. Three are with him now: Carl Wayne Jones, who plans to sing "I Walk the Line"; Raymond Vaughn, who will summon his inner Elvis for "Jailhouse Rock"; and Willie Levi, who refuses to reveal what he will sing.

A surprise, he says.

Jones emerges from the front passenger seat wearing his customary uniform of a blue and white Dallas Cowboys cap and a matching sweatshirt. He spent his adolescence at the Abilene State School with his brother, Leon — "washing dishes," he says — and then the two of them joined Henry's Turkey Service, where, he likes to say, the charismatic co-owner, T. H. Johnson, "raised me." He spent most of his adult life in the bunkhouse in Atalissa, while Leon spent most of his in a bunkhouse beside a turkey plant in South Carolina. They have a sister somewhere in Texas.

For decades, Jones worked in "three-pointing" — grabbing the tail of the freshly dead turkey with one hand, the neck with the other, and placing the head in the "V" of the shackle as the carcass moved through evisceration. Old photographs of Jones at leisure show him with a cowboy hat, a thin dark mustache, and a big smile flashing troubled teeth, looking like a suave villain from one of the old television westerns he loves. He is sixty-six now, gaunt, moving with head down as if in melancholic thought.

Like many of the other men, Jones arrived from Atalissa with a catalog of physical and emotional damage. Adjustment disorder. Arthritic hands. An unsteady gait. Chronic back problems, probably from standing along an assembly line for nearly forty years. A fungal infection in his hands and toes. Hepatitis B. Incontinence. He had three teeth pulled, underwent emergency surgery for a perforated ulcer, and was diagnosed with dementia, which explains his moments of confusion and poor memory. Even so, some things he has not forgotten. The time one of the crew chiefs grabbed him by the neck and called him "dumb ass." The time he had his television taken away for no good reason. And the money, all that money, still owed him for the work he did. He earned the pay but not the abuse, he says. "I did a good job."

True, life is better now. Jones has his own room, where he keeps a CB radio within reach of his bed, and an autographed photograph of Deputy Cletus Hogg from *The Dukes of Hazzard* on his dresser. He has a girlfriend named Gail. He has people encouraging him to eat, monitoring his physical and mental health, nudging him gently into this world beyond the bunkhouse. A few months ago, he even talked to his brother, Leon, for the first time in no one knows how long.

And on Wednesdays he sings karaoke, usually a Johnny Cash classic with the steady *boom-chicka-boom* beat. Like a freight train that's carrying you away, or maybe coming right at you.

Even after the men's rescue and all that followed — including the stunning court victory that became national news — a sense of incompleteness continued to nag at two of the Iowa social workers involved in the case, Natalie Neel-McGlaughlin and Kim Cronkleton. They worried that other so-called Henry's boys were still out there somewhere, living in anonymous exploitation. Records that the two women had come across during their investigation in 2009 indicated that someone was collecting the Social Security benefits of a Leon Jones, living on Louis Rich Road in Newberry, South Carolina.

The detail had haunted the two social workers, in part because Carl Wayne Jones had often talked of a brother. Someone has to go to Newberry, South Carolina, they kept saying. Someone has to go.

In the small, tidy city of Newberry, along Louis Rich Road, there sits a colossal gray-concrete meatpacking plant operated by Kraft Foods, the owner of the Rich brand. A short dirt road across from the plant leads to a shabby bunkhouse in a half circle of tired mobile homes, including one with its door open in abandonment, not welcome.

A hesitant knock on the screen door.

"Hi," says Leon Jones, offering a thick hand that seems too large for his body.

He is tall and thin, with a full head of graying hair and a thick mustache to match. He wears a long-sleeve black shirt tucked into jeans pulled high on his torso. He extends an invitation into the building's shadows.

Jones walks through the dusk along a worn carpet, past furniture that looks discarded, past a small rec room with an old television, and into the sprawling dormitory-like room he shares with other workers. Most of the men come and go, it seems, in a hot-bed arrangement; he is the constant.

His own narrow bed, neatly made, is tucked into a corner to the immediate right, near a window covered by a bedsheet tacked to the wood paneling. He has a bottle of mouthwash and a can of foot powder arranged beside a clock radio on the tiny nightstand, and a baseball cap hanging on the wall above a fire extinguisher. His bed sits about six feet from a young man sprawled on a Barcalounger and watching a Spanish-language television program at high volume.

Jones has about twenty-five square feet of space to himself. Nodding to his nightstand, he says, "I got a radio and everything."

He also has a locker at the center of the room, near a few beds partially concealed by red and blue blankets slung across dangling wires. In that locker he keeps two pairs of cowboy boots, a winter coat, a few shirts, some pants, and a plastic envelope containing yellowed cards and letters, the latest one dating from 1992. He also has a few snapshots. Here are Leon and Carl Wayne standing with their mother, so long ago that everyone's hair is dark. And here are Leon and Henry Wilkins: Leon with his arms folded in faux confidence, Henry with an expression suggesting plans for some more childlike devilry.

At sixty-five, Leon Jones is the last of the Henry's "boys" still working turkey. The very last one.

Three other men from Henry's are also living in this bunkhouse: Claude Wren, seventy-five, who left the Mexia State School in 1969; Johnny Hickman, seventy-one, who left Mexia in 1970; and Carlos Morris, sixty, who left the Austin State School in 1973. All but Jones have been retired. After decades of hanging live birds, he is now on modified duty, working the evening shift, disposing of the already dead turkeys that arrive by truck. The DOAs, they're called.

How can this be? How can one brother be retired and living in improved circumstances in Iowa, while the other continues to work turkey and live in neglect in South Carolina? In 2014?

Many years earlier, Henry's Turkey Service sold its Newberry operation — and, effectively, Leon Jones and a few other men — to a former Henry's employee named Paul Byrd. The Atalissa scandal may have spurred various state and federal investigations in Iowa and Texas, but those inquiries never followed the paper trail leading to South Carolina and to Leon Jones, who has a radio and everything.

Byrd, his boss, lives in Texas. But whenever he comes to Newberry to check on his business of supplying workers to the Kraft plant and other companies, he stays in a large, well-appointed apartment at one end of the bunkhouse, behind a locked door just a few steps from Jones's bed.

Reached by telephone in Texas, Byrd explains that the men's Social Security payments are deposited directly into an "association" account, from which the costs of their room and board are deducted. None of them has personal bank accounts, he says, because "I don't have birth certificates or anything on them to get ID." When it is pointed out that the men must have identification if they are receiving federal benefits, he says he bought the company as is in 1985, with no paperwork.

According to Byrd, Jones uses his eight-dollars-an-hour earnings and his Social Security benefits to pay for his bed and food, which comes out to about eight hundred dollars a month. He receives fifty dollars a week in spending money, with the rest kept locked away, in an envelope. About six thousand dollars — the life savings from forty years of hard labor.

Byrd says that Jones never goes on vacation because it's too hard to arrange. Instead, he goes to Walmart and a couple of other stores once a week, and spends his free time watching sports in that worn rec room. Byrd pauses at this point, as if hearing for the first time the sad neglect of it all.

"I know it's a long way from a perfect situation," he says.

After providing a visitor a tour of the Newberry bunkhouse, Leon Jones is asked what he'd like to say to his brother, Carl Wayne. His answer: "Say, 'How ya doing?' "

After learning of Leon's Jones's circumstances, Robert Canino, the EEOC lawyer, immediately booked a flight to South Carolina. His visit, along with a subsequent story in the *New York Times,* prompted county and state officials to remove Jones and the other Henry's men from the bunkhouse, find them proper housing and services, and

461

open several investigations.

While Canino was in Newberry, though, he drove Leon Jones to the public library for a surprise. An iPad's monitor flickered, and then, through Skype, there appeared on the screen the image of a man wearing a Dallas Cowboys cap: Carl Wayne, whom Leon had not seen since forever.

Carl Wayne explained that he lived in a house in Iowa with a couple of the Henry's men, and that he had a girlfriend. He sort of chided Leon for still living in a bunk-house, and passed on the news that their mother had died. A while ago.

The brothers caught up as best they could. They talked about favorite foods, about their Cowboys, and about maybe, just maybe, getting together sometime.

But since their Skyped conversation a few months earlier, Carl Wayne has consistently balked at the prospect of a reunion. In his mind, he equates Newberry and Atalissa and even his younger brother with working turkey. He thinks it resurrects the chance that he will have to go back to the plant, back to swinging shackles and dead turkeys.

No, he has said. Can't.

So the eyes of Carl Wayne Jones are drilling the ground as he walks with purpose toward karaoke night. His brother, Leon, remains as far away as ever. His body is wracked with arthritis. He is having difficulty remembering things, difficulty communicating what he wants to say. Each step seems uncertain. And now with head down, he half pitches toward the door, bumping into people as he makes his way to where music plays.

Walking close behind is Raymond Vaughn, sixty-three, just off his shift cleaning pots at Rudy's Tacos. He wears a camouflage baseball cap, a pair of glasses that magnify his eyes, and a billowing white beard that he is growing to Santa Claus length as a declaration of fraternal connection, newly found.

Until recently, Vaughn knew little about his past. He has no memory of his parents, though he has a faint recollection of being abandoned at a courthouse. He wound up at the Mexia State School, where he worked in the dining room during the day and helped the school band at night, packing and unpacking instruments. He loves telling the story of the band director inviting him to take over ("And I do like this," he says, moving his arms like a conductor's. "I would lead them when they playing they instruments.").

Sent to the ranch in Goldthwaite when he

was twenty-one, he has fond memories of fireworks, bowling, and feeding calves with bottles. He also learned the skill of catching turkey hens. "Grab them and hold them," he says. "Then them other guys popped them" — that is, artificially inseminated the hens.

Vaughn worked turkey for Henry's Turkey Service in Missouri, Illinois, and South Carolina, but spent most of his years living in the Atalissa bunkhouse and toiling at the plant in West Liberty. He liked some of the supervisors he had over the decades, but detested working for Randy Neubauer, in part because the compact between boss and employee kept changing. His understanding was, do a good day's work and all would be fine. Instead, sometimes he would do a good day's work and there would be no television, no going into town, no money.

"Every time when I tried to give him, do him a good job at Louis Rich," Vaughn says. "And when I get in, we had to go to the garage and hold the poles up. And when we did that, he came on and kicked us in the ass. And I didn't like it."

Standing in the garage, with both hands pressed against a pole. Walking around the gym carrying weights. Pulling weeds. Getting kicked in the ass. Outrage informs his every word. He says the working conditions were steamy and sticky and feathery, and sometimes he would have to step outside because his nose would begin to bleed. His bosses would get mad, which meant that when the van stopped for snacks at the market on the way home — he recites the boss's words from memory:

"Raymond, stay in the van. You can't go in."

After the men's rescue from Atalissa, Vaughn arrived in Waterloo as yet another medical mess from Henry's Turkey Service who had not seen a doctor in years; yet another man with wax plugging his ears, fungus creeping up his ankles, and toenails curving toward the pads of his feet. Pulling crop and hanging turkeys for thirty-five years had left the joints of his hands so swollen that he required medication and the draining of fluid from his left middle finger.

It took time, but Vaughn found his Waterloo rhythm. Working at Rudy's Tacos. Fishing at George Wyth Lake. Dancing on Monday evenings at a club called Spicoli's. Developing a relationship with a woman named Carol, with whom he was baptized at Nazareth Lutheran Church. "I got my own lawn mower," he says. "A John Deere."

Along the way, he received a tantalizing

and troubling gift. After the men's rescue from Atalissa, a caring, protective Muscatine County employee named Laura Lee Porter-Soukup was appointed as the group's legal guardian. In meeting with Vaughn, she shared the scant details in his Henry's Turkey Service file, including the names of his parents: Percy Vaughn and Margie Blair.

Percy Vaughn and Margie Blair.

Nearly sixty years old, and he was hearing the names of his parents for the first time. Instant, simultaneous connection and separation. His heavy burden of knowing nothing about who he was, or where he came from, was now replaced by the heavier burden of knowing a little.

Percy Vaughn and Margie Blair.

In the spring of 2013, Vaughn sent an email to the *New York Times* that began, "My name is Raymond Vaughn and I am one of the Atalissa boys." The note, written with someone's help, went on to explain what little Vaughn knew of his past:

I have not seen or spoken to any of my family in a very, very long time. . . . I don't recall what they look like and all I know is that I have two sisters, two brothers, and a mom and dad. The last time I heard from

466

my father was when I was living in Texas, before I was in Atalissa. He had sent me a letter in the mail telling me that he was a policeman and my mother did hair. I believe my father's name is Percy Vaughn and my mother's name is Margie Blair. These were the names my previous guardian, Laura, gave to me. She has now passed away. I don't have any other information to give to you, though I wish I did. . . . I would be extremely grateful if you would help me try to find my family. I have a lot of built up emotions about not being able to see or speak to my family in such a long time. Any kind of information will bring me closure. . . .

Back in the 1940s and 1950s, anyone curious about the availability of carnival acts knew to turn to *The Billboard* magazine, which recorded the weekly whereabouts of the acts in a section set in agate type. There, beside advertisements for burlesque acts ("DANCING GIRLS for Winter's Work, No Traveling, Frank Webber, wire Waco, Tex.") and sideshow attractions ("Hanky Panks — Wheels and All Types of Percentage Games") and essential equipment ("Parakeets 70 cents, babies, $1.00 minimum order, 40 birds"), are fleeting mentions of a traveling tattoo artist:

*October 21, 1950:* Happy Raye closed a successful season with his Side Show on Capell Bros Shows and is now booking indoor dates under veteran auspices. Other Capell personnel leaving were Tex Vaughn, tattoo artist, and wife, who joined the Hutchens Modern Museum on the Alamo Expedition Shows. . . .

*December 16, 1950:* Mae Joe Arnold reports from Harlingen, Tex., that the Mid-Winter Fair there gave the Mary Webb Side Show good business. Recent additions to the show include Slim Curtis, human skeleton, Marjorie Little, Punch and Judy, and Tex Vaughn, tattoo artist. . . .

*July 7, 1956:* David Chick, former carnival man, visited Leona Lee and George V. Ice, of the Penn Premier Shows, when that organization most recently played Columbus, O. During the show's Marion, O., stand, there was a birthday party for Miss Lee in the Side Show top. Among those attending were Colonel Jeffery, Chuck and Thelma Ward, George V. Ice, Frances Lopez, Vicky Lowell Wood, Eddie James, Tiny Tim, Marjory and Tex Vaughn, Tom Hatfield and Jerry Perez. . . .

Fast-forward to this millennium, and here is a Facebook page called "Railroaded," dedicated to a "lost family" looking to reunite. Its author, Michelle Hilman, has spent years chasing the loose strands of information about her extended family. Through court records found in Texas, Wisconsin, and upstate New York, she has knit together an intriguing but incomplete history:

Her grandmother, Margie Blair, was a housewife in upstate New York, married to an abusive farm laborer and boxer. The circus came to town, and Margie and her three children fled under night's veil with the troupe's tattoo artist, Tex Vaughn, who found work for Margie as a sideshow snake charmer. Drama followed, including a supposed marriage in Ohio; a fire in Kentucky that destroyed all their belongings, including the tattoo stand; children taken by the authorities in Wisconsin and scattered to institutions and foster families; and then more children, as Tex and Margie made their way south, to Houston. Among the children born and, presumably, given up: Raymond Larry Vaughn, on May 22, 1951.

Try as she might, Hilman could not track down her uncle Raymond. He was a name, not a person; the long-ago casualty of an itinerant dysfunctional family. "Well, waitin' for any answer from Raymond in TX," she wrote at one point.

Then Hilman received a call from someone who had seen her Facebook page and put two and two together: *Here's where your uncle Raymond can be found.*

On a late August evening in 2014, a telephone's ring broke the quiet of a raised-ranch house in Waterloo. One of the residents, Raymond Vaughn, was summoned to pick up the phone. It was for him.

The caller asked him a couple of personal questions, which he answered in his customary directness, wasting not a word. Then the caller said: *Well, Uncle Ray. This is your niece, Michelle.*

Vaughn began to sob. When he was able to talk again, he told her he had been waiting his entire life for this very call. *I was so lost,* he said.

He asked her to hold on for a second, and the line went quiet. After a while, someone else picked up the phone to explain.

*Raymond just needs a moment. He's pretty emotional.*

"I never seen them," Vaughn later explains. "I never seen them all of these years."

The uncle and his niece talked for a good hour, attempting to make up for lost time that was gone forever. They arranged to talk again. Taking his new, avuncular role seriously, Vaughn called her the next night, and the next, and the next, always giving the same sweet but confused greeting.

"All the time," Vaughn says. "I say, 'This is Uncle Ray, your son.' "

Two months later, an Exceptional Persons staff member drove Raymond about three hundred miles northeast for a family reunion at his niece's home, in Mosinee, Wisconsin. The car stopped outside a century-old house, its lawn transformed into a Hallowe'en wonderland of carved pumpkins and hay bales, eerie orange lights and a parking spot for the broomsticks of witches. A slim, barefoot woman in a tank top and jeans appeared on the front porch, her shoulder-length hair a calico mix of blond and red and brown.

*Uncle Ray, is that you?* Michelle Hilman called, though she knew the answer. The face of the man in the passenger seat. The resemblance. Unmistakable.

"And when I got out of that car," Vaughn recalls, "her start running down them steps and gave me a hug" — the first hug he had received from a family member in more than a half century.

That night, Vaughn met other family

471

members, including his brothers, Edward and Percy Jr., retired now from rough-and-tumble careers as carnival grunts, farmhands, and handymen. Percy's cumulous white beard mesmerized Raymond. Soon he would be growing out his own white beard, so that he could look, and be, just like his brother.

They gathered for dinner inside the big old house. In the months to come, there would be more family reunions, and more long-distance chats between Uncle Ray and his niece, always beginning with *It's Uncle Ray, your son.* She would explain to him that his parents split at some point; that his father, Tex Vaughn, died in Houston in 1971 and that his mother, Margie Blair — well, maybe she would leave that part a little vague. The trail for Margie Blair had gone cold somewhere around West Madison Street, in Chicago: Skid Row. So all that his niece would say is *We're still looking for Margie, Uncle Ray. Still looking.*

But on this first night of reunion, the stories of abandonment and separation, of carnival work and turkey-plant work, of state schools and orphanages — of "longing for a memory they don't have," as Hilman says — were left unsaid, as if stipulated. Instead, they ate fried walleye, coleslaw, and

472

scoops from a casserole called "funeral potatoes," and drank themselves some beer.

Last out of the Chevy Malibu is Willie Levi, who searches the backseat for something, finds it, and now is walking toward karaoke night with that found thing, a bongo. He wears a long gray winter coat in which, like Harpo Marx, he keeps unusual items, including spoons, a harmonica, and a small computer tablet bought at Walmart for forty-five dollars. On his head sits a green Baylor University baseball cap propped beneath a yellow University of Iowa baseball cap. His competing worlds, Texas and Iowa.

At the time of his rescue in 2009, Levi had a broken kneecap that required immediate surgery. His teeth had been neglected, his ears required hearing aids, and his feet were infected with fungus. He spoke of nightmares, of hurting himself, of wanting to go home to Orange to see his family.

He is immersed now in Waterloo days of leisure and gentle challenges. He has a girlfriend named Rose, and they go out once a week to Wendy's, or Burger King, or, for special occasions, a sports tavern in Cedar Falls called Pepper's Grill. They also meet on early Monday evenings to slow dance at a local nightclub, although his pulse races to James Brown. "I like it when he say, 'Get on the good foot,' " he says. " 'Get back.' 'Get up.' 'Stay on the scene.' "

He attends a local church, socializes during the daily hubbub at the Deery Center, run by Exceptional Persons, and shops every week for his own groceries. He tries to buy enough vegetables to balance out the hamburgers and hot dogs he eats, but it's not easy. No broccoli. Absolutely no broccoli. But ice cream? Keep it coming.

Still, his yearning to return to those two shotgun houses on Mill Street in Orange, Texas, has not abated. He says he wants to get in touch with his parents, either unaware of or ignoring the near certainty that both are long dead. He says he wants to get an email to his "lazy daddy," Ernest, who used to drink so much that only a thrown splash of water could rouse him for work. And his mom, Rosalie? Who used to make up the beds at the Jack Tar Orange House Hotel?

"She's kind of young, but she's older now," he says. "Still kicking the bucket."

Levi follows Carl Wayne Jones and Raymond Vaughn into Lofty's Lounge, with their escort, Sam Smith, close behind. Dozens of customers mill about the tables and along the bar, many sipping soft drinks

474

and eating cheeseburgers, as a succession of singers perform on a dim stage offset by the silvery shards of light falling from a disco ball above. The organizer, a large man with a shaved head and a black T-shirt who goes by the nickname Flipper, is working his way through the crowd, collecting the three-dollar admission fee for this weekly special event, which he established more than a decade ago after sensing the need. As Flipper walks, a nearsighted young man named Julian holds tight to one of his hands, keeping it close to his face as he rubs circles of fascination and discovery in the open palm.

"A texture thing," Flipper explains.

A stringy-haired young man in a green cap and long green winter coat is tracking the order of performances. A woman sings a halting version of "Let It Go," from *Frozen,* the animated Disney movie. A man chooses "Boot Scootin' Boogie," the country-western song by Brooks and Dunn, but remains quiet as the words — *get down, turn around, go to town, boot scootin' boogie* — scrawl up the karaoke machine's monitor. A Stevie Wonder song leads to the "Battle Hymn of the Republic," which leads to a remix of "On the Road Again" and "Who Let the Dogs Out?"

While waiting for their turns to sing, Jones

and Vaughn order food at the bar counter, a cheeseburger for Jones and a pork tenderloin for Vaughn. They eat in silence while *Wheel of Fortune* spins on the television above the bar. A speech pathologist from Oregon is trying to solve the puzzle of:

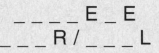

"Achieve your goal," she says triumphantly, as the men finish eating and pay their tabs with their own debit cards.

Carl Wayne Jones makes a preperformance visit to the men's room, and then his name is called. He takes the stage and stares into the glow of the black karaoke prompter on the floor, holding the microphone somewhere close to the Dallas Cowboys star stitched to his sweatshirt. The distinctive sound of Johnny Cash and the Tennessee Two begins to play, but Jones has somehow switched off the sound to the microphone. He sings of walking the line, but, as has been true most of his life, no one can hear him above the *boom-chicka-boom, boom-chicka-boom.*

When Raymond Vaughn hears his name called, he is in the midst of examining a palm-size toy truck with the same intensity that Julian has been examining Flipper's hand. He tucks the toy back into his pocket and strides to the stage.

As the opening notes of the Elvis classic begin to sound, he starts to move his thick body, ever so slightly, to the beat. His hips do not swivel, his lip offers no half curl. But he rocks to his own moment as he sings his customized version of "Jailhouse Rock," a version that features no warden throwing a party in the county jail, no prison band wailing. His is the purest "Jailhouse Rock" there is, a steady, sonorous repetition of those two words forty-two times, as if in celebration of a prison break.

*Jailhouse rock*
*Jailhouse rock*
*Jailhouse rock*
*Jailhouse rock*
*Jailhouse rock*

# TWENTY-TWO

*Gene Berg at home in Waterloo*

Carl Wayne Jones and Raymond Vaughn sing for the joy of it. For their solo moment in the spotlight. For the long-denied thrill of standing before others and claiming their own place in the chaotic chorus of everyday life. Channeling Johnny Cash and Elvis Presley, they sing the anthem of the individual.

They sing for all who cared for them, in Atalissa, in Waterloo, in Texas. The women who knitted and baked for them, the supervisors who took them on camping trips, the co-workers who invited them to family gatherings, the ministers who welcomed their Lord's Prayer hums, the social workers, investigators, and those who noticed. That government lawyer, Robert Canino, who at this moment was still trying to collect the money his clients had long been due.

And, several months later, Canino would

succeed, exposing a questionable plan by the principals of Henry's Turkey Service to redirect to their children several hundred thousand dollars that was owed to the men in unpaid court judgments. "An intentional scheme concocted solely to shield a substantial sum of money from the United States' collection efforts," a federal judge who blocked the arrangement would say.

This would mean about $25,000 for each man. Not all they were owed for their hard work and suffering, not by a long shot. Still, it was something.

But Jones and Vaughn sing most of all for their brothers, the dozens of men once known as "the Henry's boys," who passed through the turkey-plant bunkhouses in Iowa and Illinois, Missouri and South Carolina, killing and eviscerating turkeys for the country's cheap deli lunches and annual days of giving thanks.

Gene Berg is one of the brothers. He lives by himself in a cottage he rents in Waterloo, in quiet rejection of the Henry's Turkey Service assertion that none of these "boys" could get by on their own. He's up before dawn several days a week, eating a bowl of cereal, packing a bologna sandwich for lunch, pinning his name tag to his shirt — Clayton Berg, dishwasher, county sheriff's office — and catching the Route 2 bus. Soon he is rocking to the behemoth's gentle sway as it heaves and sighs through the city, just another working stiff, with a lunch bag in his lap and a whisper-white scar on his right wrist, marking where surgery repaired what pulling turkey guts had damaged.

Berg loves living alone. He has a red-felt pool table in the basement, some John Deere equipment in the garage, several prepared dinners in the freezer, and a spare room for when his mother, from Kansas, and his sister, from Texas, come to visit. He keeps in regular contact with Exceptional Persons — its staff is always on him to drink less Cherry Coke — but he doesn't socialize much with the men he used to live with in the bunkhouse. Thirty-five years of being forced to live with the same people can suffocate a guy.

"It was time to move out," Berg says. "To do something different."

There is Frank Rodriguez, who now lives with Helen, the mother of his adult daughter, in a small apartment in Des Moines. On a wall of that apartment hangs a small plaque, honoring Frank as the employee of the year for a Sam's Club.

There are the Penner brothers, Billy and Robert, and Henry Wilkins, and John Orange, who live together in a spacious house on a busy Waterloo road. Late one morning, Billy Penner is found alone. His brother, Robert, is at his job as a custodian at a gym. Wilkins, with his emphysema and problems with balance, is at a doctor's appointment. And Orange, who now knows that his surname is *not* Owens, was socializing while working at the Deery Center. So it is just Billy Penner, retired, by himself, at home.

"I don't do nothing," boasts Penner, whose entire adulthood was dedicated to pulling guts and cutting hearts.

He sits at the kitchen table, sipping the coffee he has just made with the Black & Decker coffeemaker he bought for three dollars at Goodwill, staring out at the chilly gray of an early spring day. Too early in the season to cut the lawn with the new mower in the garage. Too early to plant the tomatoes and peppers in the backyard garden.

The house telephone rings, disturbing his moment of domestic nothingness. "Can't they leave me alone?" Billy Penner says as he rises to answer, acting the cranky retiree.

Jones and Vaughn sing, too, for Keith Brown, who has left Iowa behind. Although Brown lives close to his sister Sherri, he lives independently, in an apartment complex in

Fayetteville, Arkansas. Every weekday morning at six, he takes a paratransit bus to Elizabeth Richardson Industries, which provides services for people with developmental disabilities. But Brown is the first client to join the staff as a full-time employee, his sister boasts, earning above minimum wage for helping the nonprofit organization meet piecemeal contracts for companies like Walmart.

"He operates a forklift," she says.

"A palette jack," Brown corrects her.

This does not mean his decades in the bunkhouse are well behind him. The times he was locked in his room. Forced to carry weights around the gym because he wasn't doing his turkeys right. Called "retard" — to which he would cry, *I am NOT retarded.* Nearly six feet tall, Brown weighed just 134 pounds when he was rescued, had badly infected feet, and required surgery for a hernia; he also needed medical treatment for depression and arthritis. Today, he still takes medication for posttraumatic stress syndrome, because, his sister says, "He's afraid they're 'gonna come find me.' "

Brown has a large desk in the center of his apartment's living room, facing a television kept at a high volume because he has lost some hearing. This is where he maintains detailed charts of his work shifts, paychecks, and bills, and where he stews about the money owed to him by Henry's Turkey Service.

"I want that money!" he says.

Still, he likes his life now. The refrigerator is filled with Dr Pepper and Gatorade — no beer — and he has a mixed-breed dog named Chi-Chi, rescued from a shelter, to keep him company. He points out all his appliances: the toaster, the fryer, the grill.

"I bought them all for myself," says Keith Brown, employee, not client. "This, this, this, this. . . ."

The men who made it back to Texas aren't forgotten, either.

In Midland, several remain effectively institutionalized, this time in a nursing home. With no family involved in their lives, they rarely leave the grounds for anything grander than a visit to a fast-food restaurant. But one of them, Tommy Johnson, delights now in being able to walk to a nearby 7-Eleven for tobacco snuff, Cheetos, and, if he has the money, Honey Buns.

In San Angelo, Tommy House and Clarence Dunning, both African American, live in group homes a notch or two above shabby, their days centered on whether it'll be Chinese takeout from Wok & Rice or Mexican takeout from Little Angel's. House used to sing in the church choir in Atalissa, while suffering abuse in the bunkhouse. Dunning, who has bad feet, was mocked and slapped for moving about too slowly. They remember the names they were called. Not just "retard." Also "nigger," and "bitch."

"I told 'em right back," Dunning says, smoldering. "I ain't no bitch."

Dunning refuses to return to Atalissa, even if only by gazing at old photographs, while House studies each image with burning intensity, as if he hopes to melt the freeze-frame moment and make the image come alive. "I know them," he says. "Gene Berg. Kenny Jackson. There's Billy Penner. . . ."

When it is time to leave, House, in suspenders and a Houston Astros cap, follows his visitors out of the group home and into the broiling Texas noon. At the last moment, he calls out a message:

"Tell all them people I said hi. Tell 'em — I said hi."

And in the suburbs of Dallas–Fort Worth, where two close friends, Brady Watson and Jeff Long — the Texas Wolf and the Lone Wolf — live separately in group homes twenty miles apart, though it may as well be two thousand, so rarely do they see each other. One day, though, they manage to meet for lunch. Watson, the dominant of the two, is wearing a red, white, and blue REBEL baseball cap, blue jeans, and a checkered shirt. He keeps his cell phone attached to his belt buckle, in a leather case that features the three crosses of Calvary. He recently left a job as a custodian, and will soon be checking out employment possibilities at a Walmart, a feed store, and a lumberyard. He has gained some extra weight since his rescue, but maintains his aura of ladies' man.

Long, wearing blue jeans and a light-blue golf shirt, has also added heft to his once-sinewy frame. The dental wire that used to cut his gums is gone, but so are his front teeth. He works at Foodland, collecting and stacking shopping carts in the parking lot. When he climbs into the backseat of a visitor's car, Watson says, "Jeff, put on your seat belt."

Talk returns, as it often does, to Atalissa, which means that Long gets upset, as he often does. "I was doing the best I can with the turkeys," he says.

On the ride home after lunch, the two friends continue their decades-long conversation, free of the seams that separate past and present. The sardines that the bossman, T. H. Johnson, ate. The men who wore diapers on the assembly line. The cockroaches. As the car passes a lake, Watson looks out at the distant sunbathers and says, "I'd like to see a couple of them girls in bikinis."

"Oh yeah," his friend agrees.

Back at his one-story group home, Watson gives Long a tour of his room, which has an Xbox, a large television, and, on a desk, a sketchbook containing more than a dozen colorful drawings. One depicts a monster truck adorned with a large "TW" — for his alter ego, Texas Wolf. Long, the Lone Wolf, likes it.

Another, more ominous drawing depicts a two-story house, its four windows and front door boarded up, the branches of the large tree beside it pointing down, as if in submission. A gray-black storm cloud unleashes a torrent of rain. A lightning bolt leaves a yellow tear in the dawn-blue sky.

"Is that the bunkhouse?" someone asks.

"Maybe," Watson replies.

Finally, here on a karaoke night stage, Carl Wayne Jones and Raymond Vaughn sing for the dead. For Bobo Johnson and Andy

Sawyer, whose bodies were returned to Texas in the back of a company van; for Doyle Trantham, who spent his last days in a nursing home, leaving behind a billfold crammed with his collection of business cards, bearing the telephone numbers of people he never called; for L. C. Hall, who did not like being called "nigger;" and for David Crouch, who was thought to be deaf until his ears were cleared of wax. Crouch and Hall are buried in a cemetery in Goldthwaite, in a mostly grass-free plot reserved for the unclaimed men of Henry's Turkey Service.

They sing, too, for Pete Graffagnino, the vulnerable little cook with big glasses who tried his best to keep roaches out of the food. Who led people in prayer before meals and after meals and during meals and whenever the spirit struck him. Who sent earnest Christmas cards to his bunkmates, knowing they would not receive any others. Who was the first to inform investigators that the bunkhouse abuse went far beyond financial. And who never stopped talking about his life's desire: to return to Texas and live close to his older sister, Rose.

Rose Barton sits now in her worn living room couch, an old photo album in her lap. She points out the alcoholic mother frozen in black-and-white, the long-suffering father, and the younger brother as a little boy — before he "went to a home for retarded kids." When word came of the bunkhouse being shut down, she had nightmares of her naive little Pete being victimized as a result of his natural friendliness. What was she to do? And then she thought: "If anybody can help me get Pete to Texas, it's Pastor Metz."

Pastor Metz. Yes. Pastor Erwin Metz, who has been Rose Barton's spiritual adviser and father figure since she was sixteen. His hair is white and his compact body stooped, but his bearing still announces rectitude and order, as do the red appointment books he keeps always at hand. A pastor's old habit.

Since the pastor and his wife were planning to visit family in Minnesota in the summer of 2009, they agreed to stop in Waterloo to meet Rose's beloved brother Pete. They came upon a small man still recovering from trauma, fresh from having been diagnosed with a hernia, poor eyesight, foot fungus, body rash, dental and gum problems, high blood pressure, and a heart condition. He had arthritis in his hands, spasms of incontinence, and the need to go home.

At the close of their visit, Graffagnino escorted the Metzes to their car and asked if the three of them could join in prayer. But before the pastor could collect his thoughts, Graffagnino was already beseeching God in the parking lot with such passion and humility that Metz and his wife wept for miles afterward.

In August 2010, Pete Graffagnino finally returned to Texas, to the unincorporated town of Cypress, not too far from Rose's home in Houston. He moved into a residence for people with developmental disabilities that was managed by the Bethesda Lutheran Home, whose former chaplain, Metz, had pulled a few strings. In a red-brick house with live oaks and a white swing on the front lawn, the former bunkhouse cook was soon leading his housemates in spontaneous prayer. He had his own bedroom, television, and cell phone.

"That was the biggest mistake," his sister says. "Giving him the cellular. He'd call every hour."

*Cookie, what are you doing?*

*Doing laundry, Pete.*

But sometimes her little brother's calls unnerved her.

*I'm happy now, Cookie. But I'm not going to be in Texas very long. I'm not going to be here very long.*

*What are you trying to say, Pete? Where do*

*you think you're going?*

*I can't explain it.*

Graffagnino's heart condition worsened, leading to several lengthy hospital stays, the last of which began on Good Friday of 2011. He died two days later, on Easter Sunday, at the age of sixty-four. His long-awaited return to Texas had lasted eight months.

"He just succumbed to the rigors of his life," Pastor Metz says. "He knew it, and he was ready."

Pete Graffagnino left little behind, materially speaking. A cheap camera his sister does not know how to operate. A two-dollar bill he once gave her, along with a note she keeps in her jewelry box; "To Rose — I love you — Pete Jr.," it says. And, after a lifetime of work in bunkhouses and turkey plants far from home, about two hundred dollars in savings. Nowhere near enough to bury him.

But once again, Pastor Metz was there for the Graffagninos. He explained the situation to an old congregant of his, the owner of a prominent funeral home, and was told not to worry, Pastor, everything will be taken care of.

The pastor is standing now in the shade of tall pines at the Klein Memorial Park in Tomball, studying a detailed map of the expansive grounds. He is trying to find the spot where, a couple of years earlier, Pete Graffagnino was laid to rest during a small graveside service, Pastor Erwin Metz presiding.

He knows the cemetery well. A son of his is buried a few rows away, and Metz and his wife expect that someday they will be buried here, too. But he cannot find Pete's grave site. There is no headstone. Too expensive.

The pastor searches the ground for a good twenty minutes, looking as if he has lost something of value among the fallen pinecones and plastic floral bouquets. Then: "This might be him here."

He stands still over a narrow space between two headstones that are planted a few yards from the whining rush of the living along highway 249.

Yep. This might be Pete. Right here.

# TWENTY-THREE

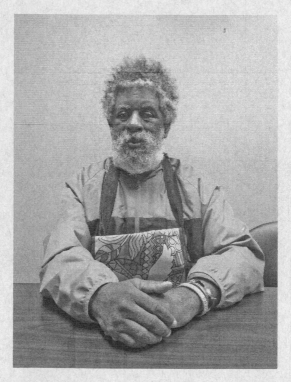

*Willie Levi*

Now it is Willie Levi's turn.

He takes his place on the karaoke stage, his wild white beard in cumulus glory, his Harpo-like coat bulging with hidden curios, his two baseball caps, the Iowa yellow over the Texas green, secure somehow on his head. The bongo by his side suggests that here stands Thoreau's different drummer. Levi, the mad prophet.

He holds the silver-headed microphone as if it were an afterthought, evoking a veteran lounge singer's casual cockiness. Performing in front of an audience has never fazed him, whether in church or at the county fair, and Lofty's Lounge is just the latest gig. Soon a few basic musical notes start to sound, revealing the song he had refused to share in advance, had wanted to be a surprise. Familiar words flow.

*Don't know much about history . . .*

Levi ignores the words crawling with

497

insistence up the karaoke prompter. He knows the lyrics as well as those to "Jesus Loves Me," and besides, he cannot read. Swaying like a human metronome, he joins Sam Cooke, the long-dead king of soul, in professing ignorance about biology, trigonometry, and the worth of a slide rule. Beside him stands his dark-haired girlfriend, Rose, who is wearing a teal hoodie that matches her sneakers. The two have already slow-danced and swapped kisses, and now they are rocking in synch to the music. She holds a microphone too, but leaves the singing to Levi and Sam.

*Maybe by being an A student, baby,*
*I can win your love for me . . .*

Lofty's Lounge is a busy place. Not everyone is listening. What Levi sees as he looks out from the stage is the scrum of America framed by a bar's wood-paneled walls. Billiard balls being clacked under a Bud Light lamp. Waitresses in black delivering burgers and fries. Cans of soda, Pepsi and Diet Pepsi, Mountain Dew and A&W Root Beer, cluttering the foldout tables. Men hunched to the contours of the bar counter, peering up at a television game show. NASCAR decals and Budweiser posters and Arrow Liqueur bar mats and University of Iowa Hawkeye T-shirts and clutches of people in private orbits, talking as a man serenades them from the stage.

*And I know that if you love me, too . . .*

But Willie Levi, formerly of Orange, Texas, pays no attention to the attention not paid to his plaintive request. He once sang turkey-call songs that summoned birds to their death. No more. With one arm draped around his girlfriend, he joins Sam Cooke in imagining the wonderful world that could be.

This, now, is the song Levi sings.

# THE 32 MEN

Douglas Barco (Snoopy): b. 1948; formerly of the Austin State School; living in a nursing home in north central Texas.

Leonard Barefield (Big Bear): b. 1945; formerly of the Mexia State School; living in a group home in Lubbock, Texas.

Clayton Berg (Gene): b. 1955; formerly of the Abilene State School; living in a two-bedroom home in Waterloo, Iowa.

James Keith Brown: b. 1951; formerly of the Denton and Mexia state schools; living in a one-resident apartment in Fayetteville, Arkansas.

David Crouch: b. 1940; formerly of the Lufkin State School; died in 2014 at the age of 73 while living in a group home in Goldthwaite, Texas.

Clarence Dunning: b. 1950; formerly of the Lufkin State School; living in a group home in San Angelo, Texas.

James Fowler: b. 1945; formerly of the Austin State School; living with housemates in a four-bedroom home in Waterloo, Iowa.

Pete Graffagnino Jr.: b. 1946; formerly of the Mexia State School; died in 2011 at the age of 64 while living in a group home in Cypress, Texas.

Leon Hall (L.C.): b. 1953; died in 2014 at the age of 60 while living in a nursing home in Midland, Texas.

John David Hatfield: b. 1946; formerly of the Mexia State School; living with housemates in a four-bedroom home in Waterloo, Iowa.

Paul Hayek: b. 1949; formerly of the Richmond State School; living in a group home in Waterloo, Iowa.

Tommy House (Moose): b. 1950; formerly of the Abilene State School; living in a group home in San Angelo, Texas.

Kenneth Jackson: b. 1952; living with housemates in a four-bedroom home in Waterloo, Iowa.

Tommy Johnson: b. 1952; living in a nursing home in Midland, Texas.

Carl Wayne Jones: b. 1947; formerly of the Abilene State School; living with housemates in a four-bedroom home in Waterloo, Iowa.

Johnny Kent: b. 1949; formerly of the

Lufkin State School; living in a nursing home in Midland, Texas.

Ronald Lashley (Cowboy): b. 1952; formerly of the Abilene State School; living with a relative in the Houston, Texas, area.

Willie Levi: b. 1946; formerly of the Mexia State School; living with housemates in a four-bedroom home in Waterloo, Iowa.

Jeffrey Long: b. 1959; living in a group home in Fort Worth, Texas.

Johnson McDaniel (Johnny): b. 1952; formerly of the Abilene State School; living with his family in the San Angelo, Texas, area.

Joe Morrell: b. 1943; formerly of the Mexia State School; living in a nursing home in Midland, Texas.

William Murray: b. 1948; formerly of the Mexia State School; living in an assisted-living facility in the Austin, Texas, area.

Robert O'Bier: b. 1947; formerly of the Austin State School; living in a group home in central Texas.

John Orange: b. 1960; living with housemates in a four-bedroom home in Waterloo, Iowa.

Preston Pate: b. 1949; formerly of the Lufkin State School; living with housemates in a four-bedroom home in Waterloo, Iowa.

Billy Penner: b. 1944; formerly of the Abilene State School; living with housemates in a four-bedroom home in Waterloo, Iowa.

Robert Penner: b. 1948; formerly of the Abilene State School; living with housemates in a four-bedroom home in Waterloo, Iowa.

Frank Rodriguez: b. 1950; formerly of the Austin State School; living with his life partner in an apartment in Des Moines, Iowa.

Doyle Trantham: b. 1930; formerly of the Mexia State School; died in 2011 at the age of 81 while living in a nursing home in Midland, Texas.

Raymond Vaughn: b. 1951; formerly of the Mexia State School; living with housemates in a four-bedroom home in Waterloo, Iowa.

Brady Watson: b. 1969; living in a group home in the Dallas, Texas, area.

Henry Dewey Wilkins: b. 1944; formerly of the Mexia State School; living with housemates in a four-bedroom home in Waterloo, Iowa.

# ACKNOWLEDGMENTS

I am so thankful to so many.

There are my many colleagues at the *Times,* who became invested in the stories of these men and then helped to produce a multimedia package that gave them full voice: my national editors, Sam Sifton and Alison Mitchell; my friend, Deputy Executive Editor Matt Purdy; Executive Editor Dean Baquet, who cares deeply about this subject; Meaghan Looram; Beth Flynn; Justine Simons; John Woo; Jacqueline Myint; John Schwartz; and Chuck Strum, who edited every word and was kind enough to read an early draft of this book. Most of all, I thank the videographer Kassie Bracken and the photographer Nicole Bengiveno, for teaching me about reporting, and for being so committed to telling the men's story with dignity.

So many people in Atalissa and West Liberty helped me along the way, including

Pastor John Beck, Dennis Hepker, Dave Meincke, Carol O'Neill, Sue Spies, Denny Spilger, Dan Waters, and, especially, Vada Baker.

So many in Iowa endured my many return visits, including Kim Cronkleton Fish, Ed George, Denise Gonzales, Natalie Neel-McGlaughlin, and, most of all, Susan Seehase, of Exceptional Persons, Inc., whose passionate commitment to the welfare of these men never flags. I am also considerably indebted to Clark Kauffman of the *Des Moines Register*. He was first to this story, and he never let up; his work in 2009, in particular, is a model of hard-nosed reporting that holds government accountable.

So many in Texas provided assistance and perspective, including Laura O'Pry and Randall Bryan at the Mexia State Supported Living Center; Steven Bridges, the editor of the *Goldthwaite Eagle;* and, in particular, Dave Johnson at the West Terrace Nursing and Rehabilitation Center, in Midland. And, of course, there is Robert Canino, who continues to champion the men's rights, both in and out of the courtroom.

Many others have helped. Barry Harbaugh provided early guidance and enthusiasm. Caleb W. Robinson, an employee at the federal Department of Labor in Washington, would not give up until he had located an obscure document. Douglas Platt at the Museum of disABILITY History in Buffalo shared many artifacts that reflected society's changing views of intellectual disability. Margaret Nygren, the executive director of the American Association on Intellectual and Developmental Disabilities, helped me to find the words. R. Michael Hulet, an associate professor of poultry science at Penn State University, walked me through the complex world of turkeys. Jaylon Fincannon, a disability-rights advocate and consultant, was generous with his deep knowledge of intellectual disability, as were Sue Gant, a nationally recognized expert based in Iowa, and Michael Wehmeyer, an author and professor of special education at the University of Kansas. Both Gant and Wehmeyer read an early manuscript and did their best to steer me from embarrassing myself. And, of course, there are the family members of the men, who shared their stories, including Sherri Brown, Wanda La-Grassa, Richard Long, Wesley Penner, and Howard Watson.

The dedicated team at HarperCollins helped me immensely: Milan Bozic developed the striking cover; designers Leah

Carlson-Stanisic and William Ruoto helped to evoke the mood; Stephanie Cooper and Kate D'Esmond put out the word; Nate Knaebel improved each successive draft; and Kate Lyons worked heroically into many long nights to ensure that the center held. Lastly, David Hirshey, my editor, understood the worth of this story from the start, and both encouraged and challenged me to tell it properly. Thank you.

I thank my long-time agents, Todd Shuster and Lane Zachary, for their wise counsel. And, as always, I deeply thank my wife, Mary Trinity, and my daughters, Nora and Grace, for just about everything.

Finally, I thank the men — not the boys, but the men — of the bun<u>kh</u>ouse. I have learned so much more from them than they might have learned from me. I have learned about grace.

# A NOTE ON THE SOURCES

Various government documents were used as resource materials for this book, some of them gathered and kindly shared by Clark Kauffman of the *Des Moines Register*. In addition to reports from the federal Department of Labor and several Iowa agencies, they also include many assessments by the Iowa Department of Human Services, as well as transcripts of the depositions and testimony taken as part of *Equal Employment Opportunity Commission vs. Hill Country Farms, Inc., d/b/a Henry's Turkey Service.* These depositions proved valuable in reflecting the viewpoints of Randy and Dru Neubauer, who declined to speak to me. Family members of T. H. Johnson also chose not to speak to me, although his oldest daughter, Mina Kay Martin, sent a note that read, in part:

"My dad was a great and generous man who gave his life to teaching and caring for the boys. He gave them a purpose in life. He taught them how to work. He taught them to do so many things that we take for granted. They were a part of our family and would still be today."

Two booklets provided some understanding of the operations of Henry's Turkey Service: *The Magic of Simplicity: Developing the Abilities of Developmentally Disabled Persons* (Goldthwaite, Texas: Hill Country Farms Inc., December 1980) and *Hill Country Farms: Program Description,* by Gary V. Sluyter (Goldthwaite, Texas, November 1, 1980).

In researching the social history of intellectual disability, I visited the Museum of disABILITY History in Buffalo, New York — absolutely worth the trip — and relied on many books and publications, including: *No Offense Intended: A Directory of Historical Disability Terms,* by Natalie Kirisits, Douglas Platt, and Thomas Stearns (Buffalo: People Ink Press, in association with the Museum of disABILITY History, 2013); *A Disability History of the United States,* by Kim E. Nielsen (Boston: Beacon Press, 2012); *Angel Unaware,* by Dale Evans Rogers (Los Angeles: Fleming H. Revell Company, 1953); *Good Blood, Bad Blood:*

*Science, Nature, and the Myth of the Kallikaks,* by J. David Smith and Michael L. Wehmeyer (Washington, DC: American Association on Intellectual and Developmental Disabilities, 2012); *Inventing the Feeble Mind: A History of Mental Retardation in the United States,* by James W. Trent Jr. (Berkeley and Los Angeles: University of California Press, 1994); *The Story of Intellectual Disability: An Evolution of Meaning, Understanding, and Public Perception,* by Michael L. Wehmeyer and contributors (Baltimore: Paul H. Brookes Publishing Co., 2013).

To understand anything about Texas, one must call upon the vast and impressive resource that is the Texas State Historical Association (tshaonline.org).

I am indebted to Mikel Jean Fisher Brightman for providing a copy of her 1971 report *An Historical Survey of the State of Texas' Efforts to Aid the Mentally Ill and the Mentally Retarded.* Other works I consulted include "Mental Illness and Mental Retardation: The History of State Care in Texas," in *Impact,* a publication by the Texas Department of Mental Health and Mental Retardation (July/August 1975); "A Ranch Where They Raise Spirits," in *Performance: The Story of the Handicapped,* a publication of the President's Committee on Employment of the Handicapped (March 1969); "When the 'Afrika Korps' Came to Texas," by Arnold P. Krammer, *The Southwestern Historical Quarterly,* Vol. 80, No. 3 (January 1977); "German POWs: Coming Soon to a Town Near You," by Ronald H. Bailey, Historynet.com (August 10, 2012); "History of Mexia State School," provided by the Mexia State School; "Closing Down La Grange," by Al Reinert, *Texas Monthly* (October 1973); "Fifty Years of Service," *Las Sabinas,* Vol. XXIII (1996); and *From German Prisoner of War to American Citizen: A Social History with 35 Interviews,* by Barbara Schmitter Heisler (Jefferson, North Carolina: McFarland & Company Inc., 2013).

I also relied on the archives of various Texas newspapers, including the *Mexia Daily News* (which has provided extensive coverage of the Mexia State School over the years); the *Abilene Reporter News;* the *Austin American-Statesman;* the *Brownwood Bulletin;* the *Comanche Chief;* the *Goldthwaite Eagle;* the *Haskell Free Press;* and the *San Saba News.* Of particular help were "Labor Contractor Sainted or Tainted," by Mark Nelson, in the *Fort Worth Star-Telegram*

(January 13, 1980), and the two prescient *Des Moines Register* articles from December 23, 1979, written by Margaret Engel and Mike McGraw, that are referred to at length in Chapter Nine.

For the history of Atalissa and Muscatine County, I consulted: *The Community of Atalissa, IA: A History of its City & Farms,* compiled by the Atalissa Betterment Community, December 1999; *History of Muscatine County, Iowa* (Chicago: Western Historical Company, 1879); *History of Muscatine County, Iowa,* Volume 1, Irving B. Richman, supervising editor (Chicago: S. J. Clarke Publishing Co., 1911); *The Adventure of a Pearl Button,* compliments of Pearl Button Industries Inc. (reprinted by the Pearl Button Museum, Muscatine, Iowa); *Life on the Mississippi,* by Mark Twain (Boston: James R. Osgood & Co., 1883); *Everything is True, Except the Parts I Made Up,* by F. P. Kopp (Bloomington, Indiana: Trafford Publishing, 2006); and *Waterloo: A Pictorial History,* by Margaret Corwin and Helen Hoy (Rock Island, Illinois: Quest Publishing Inc., 1983).

Other resources regarding Iowa included "Moving Ahead with West Liberty — Bicentennial Year 1976" and "Rolling into the

Future: West Liberty Iowa Sesquicentennial, 1938–1988"; "The Up and Down History of the Zipper," by Ninette Dean, *Unbound* (blog), Smithsonian Libraries (May 3, 2010); "Overview of Artificial Insemination in Poultry," in the Merck Veterinary Manual (merckvetmanual.com); and various articles in the *Muscatine Journal,* the *West Liberty Index,* the *Quad-City Times,* the *Des Moines Register,* the *Waterloo-Cedar Falls Courier,* and the *Cedar Rapids Gazette.* Other information came from CalvinEarl .com, RadioIowa.com, BraceroArchive.org, WLFoods.com, and MuscatineHistory.org.

Finally, in trying to at least start to understand the experiences of the men of the bunkhouse, I found the single-most instructive document to be the Final Expert Report submitted by Dr. Sue A. Gant on behalf of the plaintiffs in the case of *Equal Employment Opportunity Commission v. Hill Country Farms, Inc., d/b/a Henry's Turkey Service,* submitted March 20, 2013.

# ABOUT THE AUTHOR

**Dan Barry** is a reporter and columnist for the *New York Times.* In 1994 he was part of an investigative team at the *Providence Journal* that won the Pulitzer Prize for a series of articles on Rhode Island's justice system. He is the author of a memoir, a collection of his About New York columns, and *Bottom of the 33rd,* for which he won the 2012 PEN/ESPN Award for Literary Sports Writing. He lives with his wife and two daughters in Maplewood, New Jersey.